D1872160

Tolley's Tax Data 2013–14

Finance Act 2013 Edition

LexisNexis®

Members of the LexisNexis Group worldwide

United Kingdom	LexisNexis, a Division of Reed Elsevier (UK) Ltd, Lexis House, 30 Farringdon Street, London, EC4A 4HH, and London House, 20–22 East London Street, Edinburgh EH7 4BQ
Australia	LexisNexis Butterworths, Chatswood, New South Wales
Austria	LexisNexis Verlag ARD Orac GmbH & Co KG, Vienna
Benelux	LexisNexis Benelux, Amsterdam
Canada	LexisNexis Canada, Markham, Ontario
China	LexisNexis China, Beijing and Shanghai
France	LexisNexis SA, Paris
Germany	LexisNexis Deutschland GmbH, Munster
Hong Kong	LexisNexis Hong Kong, Hong Kong
India	LexisNexis India, New Delhi
Italy	Giuffrè Editore, Milan
Japan	LexisNexis Japan, Tokyo
Malaysia	Malayan Law Journal Sdn Bhd, Kuala Lumpur
New Zealand	LexisNexis NZ Ltd, Wellington
Poland	Wydawnictwo Prawnicze LexisNexis Sp, Warsaw
Singapore	LexisNexis Singapore, Singapore
South Africa	LexisNexis Butterworths, Durban
USA	LexisNexis, Dayton, Ohio

First published in 1981

© Reed Elsevier (UK) Ltd 2013

Published by LexisNexis
This is a Tolley title

All rights reserved. No part of this publication may be reproduced in any material form (including photocopying or storing it in any medium by electronic means and whether or not transiently or incidentally to some other use of this publication) without the written permission of the copyright owner except in accordance with the provisions of the Copyright, Designs and Patents Act 1988 or under the terms of a licence issued by the Copyright Licensing Agency Ltd, Saffron House, 6–10 Kirby Street, London, EC1N 8TS. Applications for the copyright owner's written permission to reproduce any part of this publication should be addressed to the publisher.

Warning: The doing of an unauthorised act in relation to a copyright work may result in both a civil claim for damages and criminal prosecution.

Crown Copyright material is reproduced with the permission of the Controller of HMSO and the Queen's Printer for Scotland. Parliamentary copyright material is reproduced with the permission of the Controller of Her Majesty's Stationery Office on behalf of Parliament. Any European material in this work which has been reproduced from EUR-lex, the official European Communities legislation website, is European Communities copyright.
A CIP Catalogue record for this book is available from the British Library.

ISBN for this volume: 9780754546634

Printed in Great Britain by Hobbs the Printers Ltd, Totton, Hampshire

Visit LexisNexis at www.lexisnexis.co.uk

About this book

Tolley's Tax Data is a compendium of essential factual information for the tax adviser, covering all the main UK taxes and related matters. This edition includes the provisions of the Finance Act 2013 together with further important information up to and including 17 July 2013.

Comparative figures for up to six years are included in many of the tables. Statutory references are also given.

Comments on this annual publication and suggestions for new material and improvements will always be welcome.

Abbreviations

ACT	Advance corporation tax
AIM	Alternative Investment Market
CAA	Capital Allowances Act
CGT	Capital gains tax
Conv	Convertible
CTA	Corporation Tax Act
Cum	Cumulative
EIS	Enterprise Investment Scheme
EU	European Union
ESC	Extra-statutory concession
FA	Finance Act
FB	Finance Bill
FII	Franked investment income
HMRC	Her Majesty's Revenue and Customs
ICTA	Income and Corporation Taxes Act
IHTA	Inheritance Tax Act
IR	Inland Revenue
IRPR	Inland Revenue Press Release
ITA	Income Tax Act
ITEPA	Income Tax (Earnings and Pensions) Act
ITTOIA	Income Tax (Trading and Other Income) Act
NI	Northern Ireland
NIC	National insurance contributions
Ord	Ordinary
PAYE	Pay as you earn
PET	Potentially exempt transfer
PSA	PAYE settlement agreement
Pt	Part
RPI	Retail price index
RTI	Real time information
s	Section
Sch	Schedule
SI	Statutory Instrument
SP	Statement of Practice
SR & O	Statutory Rules and Orders
Stk	Stock
TCGA	Taxation of Chargeable Gains Act
TMA	Taxes Management Act
UK	United Kingdom
VATA	Value Added Tax Act
WDV	Written down value

Adviser's favourite facts

This page is provided as an aide-memoire of the most commonly encountered facts and figures by advisers. It is not intended as a substitute for the full detailed facts and figures set out in the rest of the book as it excludes various details.

Income Tax

	2014/15	For full details see pages 57–67 2013/14	2012/13
Basic personal allowance	£10,000	£9,440	£8,105
Personal allowance fully withdrawn; taxable income	£120,000	£118,880	£116,210
Personal allowance plus basic rate band (a)	£41,865	£41,450	£42,475

(a) The personal allowance plus the basic rate band gives the threshold for higher rate tax for someone earning under £50,000 (the limit for the child benefit charge).

NIC (a)

	For full details see pages 83–87 2013/14	2012/13
Employees / self-employed; threshold above which contributions are payable	£7,755	£7,605
Rates:		
— Employees above the primary threshold	12%	12%
— Self-employed above the lower annual limit	9%	9%
Employees / self-employed; upper threshold	£41,450	£42,475
Employees / self-employed; rate above the upper threshold	2%	2%
Employers NIC threshold	£7,696	£7,488
Rate employers NIC	13.8%	13.8%
Class 2 NIC – per week	£2.70	£2.65

(a) The employee details above relate to those not contracted out.

Income tax rates individuals 2013/14

	Bands	For full details see pages 57–67 Rate	Dividend rate (a)	Effective rate on net dividend (b)
Basic rate (c)	£0 – £32,010	20%	10%	0%
Higher rate	£32,011 – £150,000	40%	32.5%	25.0%
Additional rate	Over £150,000	45%	37.5%	30.6%

(a) Dividends are taxed as the top slice of total income. The dividend rate is subject to relief for a non-refundable tax credit of 10%.

(b) This column represents the additional tax due on a net dividend wholly taxable within a band ignoring the high income child benefit charge (potentially can apply when income exceeds £50,000) and the withdrawal of the personal allowance when income exceeds £100,000.

(c) Ignoring starting rate.

Corporation tax

	Bands	For full details see pages 36–39 FY 2014 (a)	FY 2013	FY 2012
Small profits rate	£0 – £300,000	20%	20%	20%
Marginal rate	£300,001 – £1,500,000	21.25%	23.75%	25.0%
Marginal relief fraction		1/400	3/400	1/100
Full rate	Over £1,500,000	21%	23%	24%

(a) The small profits rate for FY 2014 has not yet been formally announced. The column for FY 2014 shows estimates of the relevant figures.

Adviser's favourite facts

VAT

For full details see pages 110–118

	From 1.4.13		
Registration threshold, taxable supplies	£79,000		
Deregistration threshold, taxable supplies	£77,000		
		Turnover to join	**Turnover to leave**
Annual accounting scheme		£1.35M	£1.6M
Cash accounting scheme		£1.35M	£1.6M
Flat rate scheme		£150,000	£230,000

CGT individuals 2013/14

For full details see pages 17–34

Annual exemption		£10,900
Taxable @		
	Qualifying for entrepreneurs' relief	10%
	Taxable up to the basic rate limit	18%
	Taxable above the basic rate (40% / 45%)	28%

Capital allowances 2013/14 (a)

For full details see pages 6–16

Cars writing-down allowances		**CO_2 emissions not exceed 130g/km**	**CO_2 emissions above 130g/km**
		General pool	**Special rate pool**
	Expenditure after 5.4.13 (31.3.13 for CT)	18%	8%
		General pool	**Special rate pool**
Plant & machinery writing down allowances		18%	8%
Annual investment allowance			
	Rate	100%	
	Limit for expenditure after 31.12.12 and before 1.1.15	£250,000	
		Expenditure before	
First year allowances @ rate of 100% available on	Energy saving equipment		
	Certain cars/ refuelling equipment	1.4.15	
	Environment-friendly equipment		
	Zero-emission goods vehicles	1.4.15 (6.4.15 for IT)	
	Equipment for use in designated areas of enterprise zones	1.4.17	

(a) For expenditure after 5.4.09 (31.3.09 for CT) but before 6.4.13 (1.4.13) cars with CO_2 emissions exceeding 160g/km are allocated to the special rate pool. All other cars being allocated to the general pool. The 18% / 8% (previously 20%/10%) rates shown above apply to the general / special rate pools for chargeable periods beginning on or after 6.4.12 (1.4.12 for CT).

Bank interest rates

Date	Base Rate %
20 March 1985	13.5
29 March	13
2 April	13.125
12 April	12.875
19 April	12.625
12 June	12.5
15 July	12
29 July	11.5
9 January 1986	12.5
19 March	11.5
9 April	11
21 April	10.5
14 October	11
10 March 1987	10.5
18 March	10
29 April	9.5
11 May	9
7 August	10
26 October 1987	9.5
5 November	9
4 December	8.5
2 February 1988	9
17 March	8.5
11 April	8
1 May	7.5
3 June	8
6 June	8.5
22 June	9
28 June	9.5
4 July	10
18 July	10.5
26 August	12
25 November	13
24 May 1989	14
5 October	15
8 October 1990	14

Date	Base Rate %
14 February 1991	13.5
27 February	13
22 March	12.5
12 April	12
24 May	11.5
12 July	11
4 September	10.5
5 May 1992	10
16 September	12
17/18 September	10
22 September	9
16/19 October	8
13 November 1992	7
26 January 1993	6
23 November	5.5
8 February 1994	5.25
12 September	5.75
7 December	6.25
2 February 1995	6.75
13 December	6.5
19 January 1996	6.25
8 March	6
6 June	5.75
30 October	6
6 May 1997	6.25
6 June	6.5
10 July	6.75
7 August	7
6 November	7.25
4 June 1998	7.5
8 October	7.25
5 November	6.75
10 December	6.25
7 January 1999	6
4 February	5.5
8 April	5.25

Date	Base Rate %
10 June	5
8 September	5.25
4 November	5.5
13 January 2000	5.75
10 February	6
8 February 2001	5.75
5 April	5.5
10 May	5.25
2 August	5
18 September	4.75
4 October	4.5
8 November	4
6 February 2003	3.75
10 July	3.5
6 November	3.75
5 February 2004	4
6 May	4.25
10 June	4.5
5 August	4.75
4 August 2005	4.5
3 August 2006	4.75
9 November	5
11 January 2007	5.25
10 May	5.5
5 July	5.75
6 December	5.5
7 February 2008	5.25
10 April	5
8 October	4.5
6 November	3
4 December	2
8 January 2009	1.5
5 February	1
5 March	0.5

Benefits in kind

Benefit provided	Directors and 'P11D' employees (see notes on page 5)	'Lower-paid' employees	Reference
Accommodation, supplies, etc. used in employment duties	Provision of accommodation, supplies or services used by an employee in performing the duties of the employment is not taxable provided that either (i) if the benefit is provided on premises occupied by the employer, any private use by the employee (or his family or household) is not significant; or (ii) in any other case, the sole purpose of providing the benefit is to enable the employee to perform those duties, any private use is not significant, and the benefit is not an 'excluded benefit' (i.e. the provision of a motor vehicle, boat or aircraft, or a benefit which involves the extension, conversion or alteration of any living accommodation or the construction, extension, conversion or alteration of a building or other structure on land adjacent to and enjoyed with living accommodation)	As aside	*ITEPA 2003, s 316*
Assets given to employees	If new, cost to employer less any part of cost made good by employee If used, greater of (i) market value at time of transfer and (ii) where asset (other than a car or a van) first applied for the provision of a benefit after 5.4.80 and a person has been chargeable to tax on its use, market value when first so applied less amounts charged to tax for use up to and including year of transfer	Market value	*ITEPA 2003, ss 203, 204, 206*
Buses to shops	The provision of buses for journeys of 10 miles or less from the workplace to shops, etc. on a working day is not taxable	As aside	*SI 2002 No 205*
Cheap loans			
(a) Interest free or beneficial rates	Taxable benefit on employer-related, cheap loans is the difference between interest paid and interest payable at 'official rate' below.	Not taxable	*ITEPA 2003, ss 174, 175, 181–187*
	Exception applies		
	(i) where all the employer-related loans (or all loans not qualifying for tax relief) do not exceed £5,000 (from 1.4.14 limit increases to £10,000);		*ITEPA 2003, s 180*
	(ii) where all the interest payable is or would be eligible for tax relief; and		*ITEPA 2003, ss 177–179*
	(iii) to ordinary commercial loans.		*ITEPA 2003, s 176*
	The 'official rate' (see notes on page 5) is		
	6.4.07–28.2.09 6.25%		*SI 2007 No 684*
	1.3.09–5.4.10 4.75%		*SI 2009 No 199*
	6.4.10–5.4.14 4%		*SI 2010 No 415*
(b) Waiver	Amount written off	Normally taxable	*ITEPA 2003, ss 188–190*
Christmas parties and annual functions	Not taxable if cost does not exceed £150 per head per tax year and open to staff generally. Otherwise fully taxable. Expenditure may be split between more than one function	Not taxable	*ITEPA 2003, s 264 SI 2003 No 1361*
Childcare provision	No liability arises (i) where the premises are not used wholly or mainly as a private dwelling and the provision is made available by the employer (or, where the scheme is provided under arrangements with other persons, by one or more of those persons); or (ii) in cases where (i) does not apply, on the first £55 per week of registered or approved childcare or, where the employee joins the scheme after 5 April 2011, the first £55 per week for a basic rate taxpayer, the first £28 for a higher rate taxpayer and the first £25 (£22 per week before 6 April 2013) for an additional rate taxpayer	Not taxable	*ITEPA 2003, ss 318–318D SI 2006 No 882*
Company cars/car fuel	See pages 76 to 78		
Company vans/van fuel	No benefit arises where a van is made available mainly for business travel and the terms on which it is made available prohibit private use other than for ordinary commuting; otherwise and for 2007/08 onwards the benefit is £3,000 (for 2006/07, the benefit is £500 or, if van over 4 years old at end of tax year, £350). Where the benefit charge applies for 2007/08 onwards and fuel for private travel is provided, there is an additional fuel benefit charge. For 2013/14 the charge is £564 (for 2010/11–2012/13 the charge is £550; for earlier years it is £500). For 2010/11–2014/15 the charge is reduced to nil for zero-emissions vans.	Not taxable	*ITEPA 2003, ss 154–164, 170*

Benefits in kind

Benefit provided	Directors and 'P11D' employees (see notes on page 5)	'Lower-paid' employees	Reference
Credit tokens	Cost to employer of money, goods or services obtained less any contribution from employee (except where used to obtain certain non-taxable benefits)	As aside	*ITEPA 2003, ss 90–96, 268–270, 363*
Cyclists' breakfasts	For 2012/13 and earlier years, breakfast provided for consumption of employees on arrival at workplace in recognition of having cycled to work is not taxable.	As aside	*SI 2002 No 205; SI 2012 No 1808*
Day subsistence	For 2009/10 onwards HMRC operate advisory benchmark scale rates for non-taxable day subsistence payments to employees' who incur allowable business travel expenses.		*HMRC Brief 24/09*
Disabled employees	No benefit arises on the provision of or payment for transport for disabled employees for ordinary commuting	As aside	*ITEPA 2003, ss 246, 247*
	No benefit arises on the provision of equipment, services or facilities to disabled employees to help them carry out their duties of employment		*SI 2002 No 1596*
Emergency service vehicles	No charge arises where an emergency vehicle is made available to a person employed in an emergency service where private use is prohibited otherwise than when on call	As aside	*ITEPA 2003, s 248A*
Employees' liability insurance	Not taxable	As aside	*ITEPA 2003, ss 346–350*
Expenses generally	Unless covered by specific exemptions elsewhere, all payments to an employee by reason of his employment in respect of expenses, including sums put at the employee's disposal and paid away by him, are taxable. Deduction is allowed for expenses the employee is obliged to incur which are either qualifying travelling expenses (broadly those necessarily incurred other than ordinary commuting or private travel) or other amounts incurred wholly, exclusively and necessarily in the performance of the duties of the employment	Not taxable	*ITEPA 2003, ss 70–72, 336–340*
Eye tests and corrective appliances	Not taxable provided that provision is required under health and safety legislation and is available as required to employees generally	As aside	*ITEPA 2003, s 320A FA 2006, s 62*
Fixed rate expenses	See pages 56 and 57		
Homeworkers	Employer contributions to additional household costs not taxable where employee works at home. Supporting evidence required if contributions exceed £4 per week (or £18 per month for monthly paid employees). For 2011/12 and earlier years the limit was £3 per week (£2 per week for 2007/08 and earlier years)	As aside	*ITEPA 2003, s 316A*
Incidental overnight expenses	Not taxable where employee stays away from home on business and payment from employer does not exceed £5 per night in the UK or £10 per night overseas	As aside	*ITEPA 2003, ss 240, 241*
Living accommodation (a) Representative	Employees – no liability where (i) necessary for proper performance of duties; (ii) customary to provide employee with accommodation; or (iii) special threat to employee's security Directors – (a) full-time working director whose interest in the company does not exceed 5%, as for employees above; (b) other directors, not taxable when (iii) above applies; otherwise as for beneficial below	Not taxable	*ITEPA 2003, ss 99, 100*
(b) Beneficial	Annual rental value (or actual rent if greater) less any sums made good by the employee. For leases of ten years or less commencing or extended after 21 April 2009, a premium is treated as actual rent spread over the lease term. Where the cost of providing accommodation exceeds £75,000 (and the charge under *ITEPA 2003, s 105* is not calculated on the full open market rental value), there is an additional charge at an annual rate, equivalent to the excess over £75,000 at the official rate for cheap loans (see above) at the beginning of the year of assessment (less any rent paid in excess of the benefit under *s 105*)	As aside	*ITEPA 2003, ss 102–105B* *ITEPA 2003, ss 106, 107*
	Where there is multiple occupation in a period, the total amount charged cannot exceed that chargeable if the property was available to one person throughout		*ITEPA 2003, s 108*
	An exemption applies in respect of occupation of an overseas property owned by a company that is owned by individuals and whose only activities are incidental to its ownership of the property, provided that the property is the company's only or main asset and is not funded by a connected company.		*ITEPA 2003, ss 100A, 100B*

Benefits in kind

Benefit provided	Directors and 'P11D' employees (see notes on page 5)	'Lower-paid' employees	Reference
Living expenses			
(a) Company's property			
(i) Representative	Cost to company subject to a maximum of 10% of net earnings	Normally not taxable	*ITEPA 2003, ss 313–315*
(ii) Beneficial	Normally cost to employer	Normally not taxable	
(b) Own accommodation	Normally cost to employer	Normally as aside	
Long service awards	Not taxable provided at least 20 years' service and cost to employer does not exceed £50 for each year of service. No similar award must have been made in the previous 10 years	As aside	*ITEPA 2003, s 323* *SI 2003 No 1361*
Medical check-ups	*2007/08 onwards.* One screening and one check-up each year not taxable. For 2007/08 and 2008/09, must be available to all employees or, in the case of check-ups, available to all employees identified in a screening as needing a check-up (but note that for both years, HMRC will not seek tax in respect of screenings or check-ups if they would not have been taxable under the previous rules). *2006/07.* Routine health checks and screenings for employees (or members of their family or household) not taxable	As aside	*ITEPA 2003, s 320B; SI 2002 No 205; SI 2007 No 2090; HMRC Employment Income Manual EIM 21765*
Medical insurance	Premium paid on behalf of employee taxable unless for treatment outside UK whilst employee performing his duties abroad	Not taxable	*ITEPA 2003, s 325*
Miners' free coal	Miners' free coal and coal allowances in lieu are not taxable	As aside	*ITEPA 2003, s 306*
Mobile telephones	Loan of one mobile phone to employee not taxable (and phones first loaned before 6 April 2006 not taxable) Exemption covers making the telephone available (without any transfer of property), line rental, and calls (business and private)	Not taxable	*ITEPA 2003, s 319* *FA 2006, s 60*
Parking spaces	Parking spaces at or near place of work for cars, bicycles, motorcycles and vans not taxable	Not taxable	*ITEPA 2003, s 237*
Pension advice	Not taxable if available to all employees and benefit does not exceed £150 per tax year	As aside	*SI 2002 No 205*
Public transport strikes	The provision of travel, accommodation and subsistence during public transport disruption caused by industrial action is not taxable	As aside	*ITEPA 2003, s 245*
Relocation expenses	Qualifying removal expenses and benefits up to £8,000 per move in connection with job-related residential moves are not taxable. Included are expenses of disposal, acquisition, abortive acquisition, transporting belongings, travelling and subsistence, bridging loans and duplicate expenses	As aside	*ITEPA 2003, ss 271–289*
Scholarships	Cost of any scholarship awarded (i) out of a trust fund etc. not satisfying a 25% distribution test; or (ii) because of employee's employment	Not taxable	*ITEPA 2003, ss 211–215*
Sports and recreational facilities	Not taxable	Not taxable	*ITEPA 2003, ss 261–263*
Subscriptions and fees	Not taxable where paid to professional bodies where employee has a contractual or professional requirement to be a member of the body	As aside	*ITEPA 2003, ss 343–345*
Third party entertaining	Not taxable where provided by a party unconnected with the employer and not for services provided in connection with employment	As aside	*ITEPA 2003, s 265*
Third party small gifts	Gifts of goods and non-cash vouchers up to £250 during the tax year not taxable where provided by a party unconnected with the employer and not for services provided in connection with employment	As aside	*ITEPA 2003, ss 270, 324 SI 2003 No 1361*
Training/counselling	Certain employee training costs, work-related training, and counselling services provided by employers are not taxable	As aside	*ITEPA 2003, ss 250–260, 310–312*
Transport to home	Transport and occasional late night journeys from work to home or following a failure of a car-sharing arrangement are not taxable	As aside	*ITEPA 2003, s 248*

Benefits in kind

Benefit provided	Directors and 'P11D' employees (see notes on page 5)	'Lower-paid' employees	Reference
Use of employer's assets (other than cars and vans)	Land at annual rental value; other assets at 20% of market value when first lent or rental charge to employer if higher. No benefit arises in respect of	Not taxable	*ITEPA 2003, ss 203–205*
	(i) use of computer equipment for private home use where equipment first made available before 6 April 2006 (provided use not restricted to directors and senior staff and cash equivalent of benefit does not exceed £500);		*ITEPA 2003, s 320* *FA 2006, s 61*
	(ii) use of works buses with a passenger seating capacity of at least 9 provided for employees (or their children) to travel to and from work;		*ITEPA 2003, s 242*
	(iii) bicycles and cycling safety equipment made available for employees to get between home and work		*ITEPA 2003, s 244*
	No benefit arises on purchase by employee at market value of computer or bicycle previously on loan		*FA 2005, s 17*
Vouchers			
(a) Cash vouchers	Amount for which voucher can be exchanged	Cashable value	*ITEPA 2003, ss 73–81, 95, 96*
(b) Non-cash vouchers	Cost to employer less any contribution from employee (except where used to obtain certain non-taxable benefits)	Cost to employer	*ITEPA 2003, ss 82–88, 95, 96, 268–270A, 362*
(c) Luncheon vouchers	Taxable other than 15p per working day before 6 April 2013	As aside	*ITEPA 2003, s 89; FA 2012, Sch 39 para 50*
(d) Transport vouchers	Cost to employer less any contribution from employee	As aside (note (c))	*ITEPA 2003, ss 82–86*
Welfare counselling	Not taxable (but excluding medical treatment and advice on finance (other than debt problems), tax, leisure or recreation, and legal advice)	As aside	*SI 2000 No 2080*
Workplace meals	Subsidised meals provided for staff generally at the workplace are not taxable. From 6 April 2011 this exemption does not apply if entitlement arises under salary sacrifice or flexible benefits arrangements	As aside	*ITEPA 2003, s 317*

Notes

(a) 'P11D' employees are those with emoluments, plus benefits etc. to be entered on form P11D (including VAT), at rate of £8,500 p.a. or more.

(b) The official rate is set in advance for the whole of the following tax year, subject to review if the typical mortgage rates were to *fall* sharply during a tax year. (IRPR 6/00, 25 January 2000).

(c) Transport vouchers provided for 'lower-paid' employees of passenger transport undertakings under arrangements in operation on 25 March 1982 are not taxable. [*ITEPA 2003, s 86*].

Capital allowances

Agricultural buildings

Expenditure after	Allowance	Reference
Initial allowance		
11 April 1978	20%	*CAA 1968, s 68(1) as amended by FA 1978, s 39(1)*
31 March 1986	Nil	*FA 1986, s 56, Sch 15*
31 October 1992 (note (d))	20%	*CAA 1990, s 124A*
31 October 1993	Nil	
Writing-down allowance (on cost)		
5 April 1946	10%	*CAA 1968, s 68*
31 March 1986 (note (b))	4%	*CAA 2001, s 373*

Notes

(a) Agricultural buildings allowances are **abolished** for income tax purposes for 2011/12 onwards and for corporation tax purposes for the financial year beginning 1 April 2011 onwards. *FA 2008, s 84*

(b) As a transitional measure, writing-down allowances are stepped down over the three financial or tax years prior to abolition. For 2008/09 (for corporation tax, the financial year beginning 1 April 2008) only 75% of the allowance is given. For 2009/10 (or financial year beginning 1 April 2009) only 50% is given and for 2010/11 (or financial year beginning 1 April 2010) only 25%. Where a chargeable period falls in more than one tax or financial year, time apportionment applies to determine the amount of the allowance. *FA 2008, s 85*

(c) Maximum allowance for farmhouse is on one third of expenditure. *CAA 2001, s 369(3)(4)*

(d) The initial allowance of 20% was given on new agricultural buildings where the contract was made between 1 November 1992 and 31 October 1993 inclusive and the building brought into use by 31 December 1994.

Business premises renovation

Expenditure after	Allowance	Reference
Initial allowance		
10 April 2007	100%	*CAA 2001, ss360A–360Z4* *FA 2005, s 92, Sch 6*

Notes

(a) Only for renovation or conversion of business properties that have been vacant for at least a year and are situated in any of the disadvantaged areas of the UK designated as Enterprise Areas.

(b) Where the initial allowance is not claimed or not claimed in full, a writing-down allowance of 25% on the cost is given.

(c) Allowances are available for expenditure incurred before 6 April 2017 (1 April 2017 for corporation tax).

Dredging

Expenditure after	Allowance	Reference
Initial allowance		
16 January 1966	15%	*CAA 1968, s 67(1)(a)*
31 March 1986	Nil	*FA 1985, s 61*
Writing-down allowance (on cost)		
5 April 1956	2%	*FA 1956, s 17(1)(b)*
5 November 1962	4%	*CAA 2001, s 487*

Dwelling-houses let on assured tenancies

Expenditure after	Allowance	Reference
Initial allowance		
9 March 1982	75%	*FA 1982, Sch 12 paras 1, 2*
13 March 1984	50%	
31 March 1985	25%	
31 March 1986	Nil	*FA 1984, s 58, Sch 12 para 3*
Writing-down allowance (on cost)		
After 9 March 1982 and before 1 April 1992	4%	*CAA 2001, s 508*

Notes

(a) Maximum qualifying expenditure is £60,000 on a construction in Greater London and £40,000 elsewhere. *CAA 2001, s 511(3)*

Flat conversion

Expenditure after	Allowance	Reference
Initial allowance		
10 May 2001	100%	*CAA 2001, ss 393A–393W*
5 April 2013 (see note c)	NIL	*FA 2012, Sch 39*

Notes

(a) Only for renovation or conversion of certain vacant or storage space above shops and other commercial premises to provide low-value flats for rent.

(b) Where the initial allowance is not claimed or not claimed in full, a writing-down allowance of 25% on the cost is given.

(c) Flat conversion allowances are abolished for expenditure incurred on or after 6 April 2013 (1 April 2013 for corporation tax). The entitlement to writing-down allowances on unrelieved expenditure brought forward ceases with effect from the same dates. [*FA 2012, Sch 39 paras 36–38*].

Capital allowances

Hotels

Expenditure after	Allowance	Reference
Initial allowances (note (c))		
11 April 1978	20%	*FA 1978, Sch 6 para 1*
31 March 1986	Nil	*FA 1985, s 66*
31 October 1992 (note (d))	20%	*CAA 1990, s 2A*
31 October 1993	Nil	
Writing-down allowances (on cost)		
11 April 1978 (note (b))	4%	*CAA 2001, ss 271, 279, 310*

Notes

(a) Allowances for hotels are **abolished** for income tax purposes for 2011/12 onwards and for corporation tax purposes for the financial year beginning 1 April 2011 onwards. *FA 2008, s 84*

(b) As a transitional measure, writing-down allowances are stepped down over the three financial or tax years prior to abolition. For 2008/09 (for corporation tax, the financial year beginning 1 April 2008) only 75% of the allowance is given. For 2009/10 (or financial year beginning 1 April 2009) only 50% is given and for 2010/11 (or financial year beginning 1 April 2010) only 25%. Where a chargeable period falls in more than one tax or financial year, time apportionment applies to determine the amount of the allowance. *FA 2008, s 85*

(c) An initial allowance of 100% is given on expenditure incurred or contracted for within ten years of the inclusion of the site in an enterprise zone. *CAA 2001, ss 298, 306*

(d) The initial allowance of 20% was given on new hotels where the contract was made between 1 November 1992 and 31 October 1993 inclusive and the hotel was brought into use by 31 December 1994.

Industrial buildings and sports pavilions

Expenditure after	Allowance		Reference
Initial allowance (note (c))			
17 February 1956	10%		*FA 1956, s 15*
14 April 1958	15%		*FA 1958, s 15(1)(5)*
7 April 1959	15%		*FA 1959, s 21(1)(2), Sch 4*
	15%	(where no investment allowance)	
16 January 1966	15%		*FA 1966, s 35*
5 April 1970	30%		
	40%	(if in development or intermediate area or NI)	*FA 1970, s 15(1)*
21 March 1972	40%		*FA 1972, s 67(2)(d)*
12 November 1974	50%		*FA 1975, s 13*
10 March 1981	75%		*FA 1981, s 73*
13 March 1984	50%		
31 March 1985	25%		
31 March 1986	Nil		*FA 1984, s 58, Sch 12 para 1*
31 October 1992 (note (g))	20%		*CAA 1990, s 2A*
31 October 1993	Nil		
Writing-down allowance (on cost)			
5 April 1946	2%		*ITA 1945, s 2* *ITA 1952, s 266(1)* *CAA 1968, s 2(2)*
5 November 1962 (note (b))	4%		*CAA 2001, s 310*

Notes

(a) Industrial buildings allowances and allowances for buildings in enterprise zones are **abolished** for income tax purposes for 2011/12 onwards and for corporation tax purposes for the financial year beginning 1 April 2011 onwards. *FA 2008, s 84*

(b) As a transitional measure, writing-down allowances are stepped down over the three financial or tax years prior to abolition. For 2008/09 (for corporation tax, the financial year beginning 1 April 2008) only 75% of the allowance is given. For 2009/10 (or financial year beginning 1 April 2009) only 50% is given and for 2010/11 (or financial year beginning 1 April 2010) only 25%. Where a chargeable period falls in more than one tax or financial year, time apportionment applies to determine the amount of the allowance. *FA 2008, s 85*

(c) An initial allowance of 100% is given on expenditure incurred or contracted for within ten years of the inclusion of the site in an enterprise zone. *CAA 2001, ss 298, 306*

(d) An initial allowance of 100% was given for expenditure incurred on 'small workshops' (internal floor space 2,500 square feet or less) after 26 March 1980 and before 27 March 1983. *FA 1980, s 75, Sch 13*

(e) An initial allowance of 100% was given for expenditure incurred after 26 March 1983 and before 27 March 1985 on 'very small workshops' i.e. units not exceeding 1,250 square feet or which, in a converted building, exceed that area but where the average size of all units in the building does not exceed 1,250 square feet. *FA 1982, s 73* *FA 1983, s 31*

(f) Where the allowances in (a) and (c) above are not claimed or not claimed in full, a writing-down allowance of 25% on the cost is given. *FA 1980, ss 74, 75, Sch 13* *CAA 2001, s 310*

(g) The initial allowance of 20% was given on new industrial buildings where the contract was made between 1 November 1992 and 31 October 1993 inclusive and the building was brought into use by 31 December 1994.

Know-how

Expenditure after	Allowance	Reference
Writing-down allowance		
31 March 1986	25% (on tax wdv)	*CAA 2001, s 458*

Capital allowances

Mineral extraction

Expenditure after	Allowance		Reference
Initial allowance			
5 April 1944	10%		*ITA 1945, s 26*
5 April 1952	Nil		*ITA 1952, s 306*
14 April 1953	40%		*FA 1953, s 16(3)*
6 April 1954	Nil		*FA 1954, s 16(4)*
	40%	(where no investment allowance)	
17 February 1956	40%		*FA 1956, s 15(1)*
7 April 1959	20%		*FA 1959, s 21(2)*
	40%	(where no investment allowance)	
16 January 1966	40%		*FA 1966, s 35* *CAA 1968, s 56(2)*
31 March 1986	Nil		*FA 1986, s 55, Schs 13, 14*
Writing-down allowance			
Before 1 April 1986	Residue of expenditure $\times \dfrac{A}{A+B}$ (subject to a minimum of 5% of residue of expenditure) where A = current output B = potential future output		*CAA 1968, s 57*
After 31 March 1986	25% (on tax wdv) 10% on minerals and mineral rights		*CAA 2001, s 418*

Notes

(a) An allowance of 100% was given on expenditure incurred after 26 October 1970 and before 1 April 1986 on the construction of works in a development area or in Northern Ireland. *FA 1971, s 52*

(b) After 31 March 1986, relief for land was abolished. Allowances are due on the residue of unrelieved expenditure incurred before 1 April 1986. *FA 1986, s 55, Schs 13, 14*

(c) A 100% first-year allowance is available for certain expenditure incurred after 16 April 2002 wholly for the purposes of a North Sea Oil ring-fence trade or on plant and machinery for use in such a trade. *CAA 2001, s 416D*

Motor cars suitable for private use

Not normally eligible for annual investment or first-year allowances (but see page 9, note (f))

Expenditure after	Allowance
Writing-down allowance	
5 April 2009 (31 March 2009 for CT)	
—chargeable periods ending after 5.4.12 (31.3.12 for CT)	18% where CO_2 emissions do not exceed the limit in note (b); otherwise 8%
—chargeable periods ending before 6.4.12 (1.4.12 for CT)	20% where CO_2 emissions do not exceed the limit in note (b); otherwise 10%
11 March 1992	maximum £3,000

Notes

(a) Expenditure incurred after 5 April 2009 (31 March 2009 for corporation tax) is allocated either to the main pool, or where the 8% or 10% rate applies, to the special rate pool, unless there is private use of the car. [*CAA 2001, ss 104A, 104AA*]. For chargeable periods beginning before 6 April 2012 and ending on or after that date (or, for corporation tax purposes, beginning before 1 April 2012 and ending on or after that date) a hybrid rate of WDAs applies, calculated by time apportionment of the 20% and 18% rates (or the 10% and 8% rates). For expenditure before 1/6 April 2013 limit is 160g/km and 130g/km for expenditure thereafter.

(b) The change in emissions is based on the date of expenditure rather than the chargeable period. For expenditure on or after 1/6 April 2013 the limit is 130g/km. For expenditure before 1/6 April 2013 the limit is 160g/km.

(c) Expenditure exceeding £12,000 incurred before 6 April 2009 (1 April 2009 for corporation tax) is allocated to a single asset pool (unless qualifying for first-year allowances). Writing-down allowances are given at the general rate, subject to the above annual maximum limit. Any expenditure remaining in such a single asset pool at the end of the first chargeable period ending on or after 5 April 2014 (31 March 2014 for corporation tax) will be transferred to the main pool, the annual maximum ceasing to apply thereafter. [*CAA 2001, ss 74, 75*].

Patent rights

Expenditure after	Allowance	Reference
Writing-down allowance		
31 March 1986	25% (on tax wdv)	*CAA 2001, s 472*

Research and development

Expenditure after	Allowance	Reference
Allowance in year 1		
5 November 1962	100%	*CAA 2001, s 441*

Capital allowances

Plant and machinery

	Expenditure after	before	Rate
Annual investment allowance (note (a))			
— for IT purposes	5.4.08		100%
— for CT purposes	31.3.08		100%
Annual investment allowance (note (a))			
			Limit
	31.12.12	1.1.15	£250,000
	31.3/5.4.12	1.1.13	£25,000
	31.3/5.4.10	1.4/6.4.12	£100,000
	31.3/5.4.08	1.4/6.4.10	£50,000
First-year allowances			Rate
(a) General (note (b))			
— for IT purposes	5.4.09	6.4.10	40%
— for CT purposes	31.3.09	1.4.10	40%
(b) Small/medium-sized businesses			
— generally for IT purposes (note (k))	1.7.98	6.4.08	40%
— generally for CT purposes (note (k))	1.7.98	1.4.08	40%
(c) Small businesses			
— generally for IT purposes (note (l))	5.4.06	6.4.08	50%
— generally for CT purposes (note (l))	31.3.04	1.4.05	50%
	31.3.06	1.4.08	50%
(d) Energy-saving equipment (note (c))	31.3.01		100%
(e) Certain cars/refuelling equipment (note (d))	16.4.02	1.4.15	100%
(f) Environment-friendly equipment (note (e))	31.3.03		100%
(g) Zero-emission goods vehicles (note (g))			
— for IT purposes	5.4.10	6.4.15	100%
— for CT purposes	1.4.10	1.4.15	100%
(h) Equipment for use in designated areas of enterprise zones (note (g))	31.3.12	1.4.17	100%
Writing-down allowances (WDAs) (note (h))			
(a) General (expenditure after 26.10.70)			
— chargeable periods ending after 5.4.12 (31.3.12 for CT)			18%
— chargeable periods ending after 5.4.08 (31.3.08 for CT)			20%
— chargeable periods ending before 6.4.08 (1.4.08 for CT)			25%
(b) Long-life assets (expenditure after 26.10.70)			
— chargeable periods ending before 6.4.08 (1.4.08 for CT)			6%
(c) Special rate expenditure			
— chargeable periods ending after 5.4.12 (31.3.12 for CT)			8%
— chargeable periods ending before 6.4.12 (1.4.12 for CT)			10%
(d) Foreign leased assets (expenditure after 9.3.82 and before 1.4.06)			10%

Notes

(a) Qualifying expenditure up to the threshold above incurred in a chargeable period qualifies for the annual investment allowance at 100%. The change in limit normally applies for expenditure incurred before 1st April for corporation tax and 6th April for income tax. From 1 January 2015 the AIA limit is expected to revert to £25,000. The limit is proportionately increased or decreased where the chargeable period is longer or shorter than a year. A group of companies (defined as for company law purposes) can only receive a single allowance. This restriction also applies to certain related businesses or companies. Expenditure on cars does not qualify. [*CAA 2001, ss 51A–51N; FA 2010, s 5; FA 2011, s 11; FA 2013, ss 7, 70*].

(b) Qualifying expenditure in the period attracts a FYA of 40%. This does not apply to expenditure on:
- (i) thermal insulation,
- (ii) integral features (see (h) below),
- (iii) long-life assets (see (h) below),
- (iv) cars,
- (v) plant or machinery for leasing.

From 1 April 2013 expenditure on ships and railway assets can qualify for FYA [*FA 2009, s 24*].

(c) Expenditure on designated energy-saving plant or machinery, in accordance with the Energy Technology Criteria and Product Lists, attracts a FYA of 100%. 100% FYAs are available even if the assets are leased or let on hire. [*CAA 2001, ss 45A–45C*]. See List E on page 12.

(d) Expenditure in the period attracts a FYA of 100% on:
- (i) new (not second-hand) cars first registered after 16 April 2002 which are either electrically-propelled or emit not more than 95g/km of carbon dioxide (110 g/km for expenditure before 1 April 2013; 120 g/km for expenditure incurred before 1 April 2008), or
- (ii) new plant or machinery for use in a refuelling station for the refuelling of vehicles with natural gas, hydrogen fuel or (for expenditure on or after 1 April 2008) biogas.

Assets qualify even if leased or let on hire. [*CAA 2001, ss 45D, 45E, 46*]. For expenditure incurred after 31 March 2013 cars provided for leasing no longer qualify for the FYA. It is proposed that FA 2015 will extend the 100% FYA to 31 March 2018 but at the same time reduce the qualifying threshold for low emission cars to 75g/km.

(e) Expenditure incurred on designated environmentally-friendly plant and machinery attracts a FYA of 100%. Details of the qualifying technologies and products are published in the Water Technology Criteria and Products List (see www.eca.gov.uk). [*CAA 2001, s 45H*]. See List F on page 12.

(f) Expenditure in the period attracts a FYA of 100% on new (not second-hand) vehicles which cannot produce carbon dioxide emissions when driven and which are of a design primarily suited to the conveyance of goods or burden. This is limited to expenditure of 85 million euros per undertaking (as defined) over the five years. [*CAA 2001, ss 45DA, 212T; F(No 3)A 2010, Sch 7 paras 3, 6*].

(g) Expenditure in the period incurred by a trading company attracts a FYA of 100% on new (not second-hand) plant or machinery which represents investment and not replacement expenditure and which is not transport or transport equipment for use in a transport business. This is limited to expenditure of 125 million euros per investment project. The asset must not be held for use in an area outside of the designated assisted area for a period of five years. [*CAA 2001, ss 45K–45N; FA 2012, Sch 11 para 3*].

(h) From 29 May 2013, FA 2013, s 73 puts beyond doubt that a business cannot claim capital allowances on capital expenditure on plant or machinery which is covered by a contribution from another business.

Capital allowances

(i) WDAs are calculated on a reducing balance basis. WDAs are calculated on a reducing balance basis. When the rate changes during a chargeable period a hybrid rate of WDAs applies, calculated by time apportionment of the new and old rates. For chargeable periods beginning on or after 6 April 2008 (1 April 2008 for CT purposes), a WDA of up to £1,000 can be claimed in respect of the main pool and/or the special rate pool where the unrelieved expenditure in the pool concerned is £1,000 or less.
The long-life asset rate applies to expenditure of more than £100,000 p.a. on plant and machinery with an expected working life when new of at least 25 years. It does not apply to plant and machinery which is:
(i) second-hand where the rate applied to the vendor because the original expenditure pre-dated these rules;
(ii) in a building used wholly or mainly as, or for purposes ancillary to, a dwelling-house, retail shop, showroom, hotel or office;
(iii) cars; or
(iv) sea-going ships and railway assets purchased before 1 January 2011.
For companies, the £100,000 *de minimis* limit is divided by one plus the number of associated companies (if any). [*CAA 2001, ss 90–104, Sch 3 para 20*].
The special rate applies to expenditure on :
(i) Long-life assets;
(ii) Integral features of a building and thermal insulation of a building incurred on or after 6 April 2008 (1 April 2008 for CT purposes);
(iii) Expenditure on long life asset incurred before the date in (ii) above but not allocated to a pool until a chargeable period beginning on or after that date.
(iv) Expenditure on motor cars incurred on or after 6 April 2009 (1 April 2009 (see page 8));
(v) Expenditure on cushion gas incurred on or after 1 April 2010; and
(vi) Expenditure on solar panels incurred on or after 6 April 2012 (1 April 2012).
The rate also applies to long-life assets pooled before 6/1 April 2008 for chargeable periods ending on or after 5 April 2008 (31 March 2008), subject to the above transitional rule. [*CAA 2001, s 104A; FA 2008, s 83*].
Integral features of a building are:
(i) Electrical systems,
(ii) Cold water systems,
(iii) Space or water heating systems,
(iv) Powered ventilation systems,
(v) Air cooling or purification, and any floor or ceiling comprised in such systems
(vi) Lifts,
(vii) Escalators and moving walkways, and
(viii) External solar shading.
[*CAA 2001, ss 33A, 33B*].

(j) A medium-sized business is one satisfying any 2 of the following conditions:
(i) turnover £22.8m or less;
(ii) assets £11.4m or less;
(iii) employees 250 or less.
A small business is one satisfying any 2 of the following conditions:
(i) turnover £5.6m or less;
(ii) assets £2.8m or less;
(iii) employees 50 or less.

(k) For expenditure incurred on or after 1 April 2008, a company can surrender a tax loss attributable to FYAs within categories (c) or (d) above in exchange for a cash payment from the Government. The cash payment is equal to 19% of the loss surrendered, subject to an upper limit of the greater of £250,000 and the company's PAYE and NIC liability for the period concerned. [*CAA 2001, s 262A, Sch A1; SI 2013/464*].

(l) Qualifying expenditure in the period by small and medium-sized businesses (see (i) above) attracts a FYA of 40% (but see (l) below for enhanced FYAs for small companies only). This does not apply to expenditure on plant and machinery for leasing or letting on hire, cars (but see (d) above), sea-going ships, railway assets or long-life assets (see (h) above). [*CAA 2001, ss 44, 46–49*].

(m) Expenditure incurred by small businesses (see (i) above) in the period attracts a FYA of 50%. The conditions are the same as those outlined under (k) above. Outside of the period, the FYAs revert to 40% as for small and medium-sized businesses. [*FA 2004, s 142; FA 2006, s 30; FA 2007, s 37*].

Expenditure on
(a) the provision of a building (including assets incorporated, or normally incorporated, in the building),
(b) the provisions of certain structures and assets or works involving the alteration of land, and
(c) the acquisition of any interest in land

does not qualify for plant and machinery allowances. [*CAA 2001, ss 21, 22, 24*].

Subject to certain conditions, these provisions do not apply to
(i) thermal insulation of industrial buildings; fire safety; safety at sports grounds (for expenditure incurred before 6 April 2013 (1 April 2013 for CT)); personal security; integral features; software and rights to software; films; or
(ii) expenditure on assets in List C.

See List A for assets treated as buildings and not qualifying as plant or machinery. [*CAA 2001, ss 21, 23*].

See List B for other assets specifically excluded from being plant or machinery. [*CAA 2001, ss 22, 23*].

See List C for assets not excluded from being plant or machinery. [*CAA 2001, s 23*].

See List D for activities which are qualifying activities for plant and machinery allowances. [*CAA 2001, s 15*].

See List E for classes of plant and machinery specified in the Energy Technology Criteria List.

See List F for classes of plant and machinery specified in the Water Technology Criteria List.

List G, reproduced by kind permission of Edward Magrin FTII, is a list of expenditure which *should*, subject to business use, be regarded as plant or machinery. The list has been compiled from case law (UK and foreign), Commissioners' decisions and HMRC practice. It is not exhaustive.

See also HMRC Brief 3/10 which includes a list of items specific to the pig industry which may qualify as plant or machinery.

Whether expenditure on items within List C or List D qualifies for capital allowances will depend upon the facts of the case as applied to existing case law.

List A Assets treated as buildings

(1) Walls, floors, ceilings, doors, gates, shutters, windows and stairs.
(2) Mains services, and systems, for water, electricity and gas.
(3) Waste disposal systems.
(4) Sewerage and drainage systems.
(5) Shafts or other structures in which lifts, hoists, escalators and moving walkways are installed.
(6) Fire safety systems.

List B Excluded structures and other assets

(1) A tunnel, bridge, viaduct, aqueduct, embankment or cutting.
(2) A way, hard standing (such as a pavement), road, railway, tramway, a park for vehicles or containers, or an airstrip or runway.
(3) An inland navigation, including a canal or basin or a navigable river.
(4) A dam, reservoir or barrage, including any sluices, gates, generators and other equipment associated with the dam, reservoir or barrage.
(5) A dock, harbour, wharf, pier, marina or jetty or any other structure in or at which vessels may be kept, or merchandise or passengers may be shipped or unshipped.
(6) Any dike, sea wall, weir or drainage ditch.
(7) Any structure not within items 1 to 6 other than
  (a) a structure (but not a building) within the meaning of 'industrial building',
  (b) a structure in use for the purposes of an undertaking for the extraction, production, processing or distribution of gas, and
  (c) a structure in use for the purposes of a trade which consists in the provision of telecommunication, television or radio services.

List C Assets not excluded from being plant or machinery

Note that items 1 to 16 do not include any assets whose principle purpose is to insulate or enclose the interior of a building, or to provide an interior wall, floor or ceiling intended to remain permanently in place. See also note (j) on page 9 for certain assets within items 2, 3 and 6 which qualify as integral features.

(1) Machinery (including devices for providing motive power) not within any other item in this list.
(2) Electrical systems (including lighting systems) and cold water, gas and sewerage systems provided mainly
  (a) to meet the particular requirements of the qualifying activity, or
  (b) to serve particular plant or machinery used for the purposes of the qualifying activity.
(3) Space or water heating systems; powered systems of ventilation, air cooling or air purification; and any floor or ceiling comprised in such systems.
(4) Manufacturing or processing equipment; storage equipment (including cold rooms); display equipment; and counters, checkouts and similar.
(5) Cookers, washing machines, dishwashers, refrigerators and similar equipment; washbasins, sinks, baths, showers, sanitary ware and similar equipment; and furniture and furnishings.
(6) Lifts, hoists, escalators and moving walkways.
(7) Sound insulation provided mainly to meet the particular requirements of the qualifying activity.
(8) Computer, telecommunication and surveillance systems (including their wiring or other links).
(9) Refrigeration or cooling equipment.
(10) Fire alarm systems; sprinkler and other equipment for extinguishing or containing fires.
(11) Burglar alarm systems.
(12) Strong rooms in bank or building society premises; safes.
(13) Partition walls, where moveable and intended to be moved in the course of the qualifying activity.
(14) Decorative assets provided for the enjoyment of the public in hotel, restaurant or similar trades.
(15) Advertising hoardings; signs, displays and similar.
(16) Swimming pools (including diving boards, slides and structures on which such boards or slides are mounted).
(17) Any glasshouse constructed so that the required environment (namely, air, heat, light, irrigation and temperature) for the growing of plants is provided automatically by means of devices forming an integral part of its structure.
(18) Cold stores.
(19) Caravans provided mainly for holiday lettings.
(20) Buildings provided for testing aircraft engines run within the buildings.
(21) Moveable buildings intended to be moved in the course of the qualifying activity.
(22) The alteration of land for the purpose only of installing plant or machinery.
(23) The provision of dry docks.
(24) The provision of any jetty or similar structure provided mainly to carry plant or machinery.

(25) The provision of pipelines or underground ducts or tunnels with a primary purpose of carrying utility conduits.
(26) The provision of towers to support floodlights.
(27) The provision of
(a) any reservoir incorporated into a water treatment works, or
(b) any service reservoir of treated water for supply within any housing estate or other particular locality.
(28) The provision of
(a) silos provided for temporary storage, or
(b) storage tanks.
(29) The provision of slurry pits or silage clamps.
(30) The provision of fish tanks or fish ponds.
(31) The provision of rails, sleepers and ballast for a railway or tramway.
(32) The provision of structures and other assets for providing the setting for any ride at an amusement park or exhibition.
(33) The provision of fixed zoo cages.

List D Qualifying Activities

Each of the following is a qualifying activity for the purposes of plant and machinery allowances but to the extent only that the profits or gains from the activity are, or (if there were any) would be, chargeable to tax.

(a) A trade.
(b) An ordinary property or Schedule A business.
(c) A furnished holiday lettings business.
(d) An overseas property business.
(e) A profession or vocation.
(f) A concern listed in *ITTOIA, s 12(4), CTA 2009, s 39(4)* (mines, transport undertakings etc).
(g) The management of an investment company.
(h) Special leasing of plant or machinery i.e. the hiring out of plant or machinery otherwise than in the course of another qualifying activity.
(i) An employment or office.

Where a person's qualifying activity falls within (b), (d) or (h) above, plant or machinery for use in a dwelling house is not qualifying expenditure. [*CAA 2001, s 35*].

Where a qualifying activity falls within (i) above, expenditure is qualifying expenditure only if the plant or machinery is necessarily provided for use in the performance of the duties of the employment or office. [*CAA 2001, ss 36, 80*].

List E Energy-saving plant and machinery

The Energy Technology Criteria List specifies the following technology classes as eligible for first-year allowances as energy-saving equipment. See page 9 note (e).

(1) Combined heat and power.
(2) Lighting.
(3) Pipework insulation.
(4) Boilers.
(5) Motors and drives.
(6) Refrigeration
(7) Thermal screens (for expenditure incurred before 7 September 2006).
(8) Heat pumps.
(9) Radiant and warm air heaters.
(10) Compressed air equipment.
(11) Solar thermal systems.
(12) Automatic monitoring and targeting equipment.
(13) Air to air energy recovery equipment.
(14) (For expenditure incurred before 8 October 2010) compact heat exchangers.
(15) Heating, ventilation and air conditioning equipment (for expenditure incurred before 4 August 2009, air conditioning zone controls).
(16) (For expenditure incurred on or after 4 August 2009) uninterruptible power supplies.
(17) High speed hand air dryers.

The equipment must meet the energy-saving criteria set out in that List and, in the case of classes (4) to (16), must be of a type specified in (and not removed from) or which has been accepted for inclusion in, the Energy Technology Product List. [*CAA 2001, s 45A; SI 2001 No 2541*].

For expenditure incurred on or after 6 April 2012 (1 April 2012 for corporation tax purposes) FYAs are not available in respect of expenditure on plant or machinery which generates electricity or heat, or produces biogas or biofuels, that attract tariff payments under the feed-in tariffs scheme or renewable heat incentive scheme introduced by the Department of Energy and Climate Change. This restriction applies to expenditure incurred on or after 6 April 2014 (1 April 2014) for combined heat and power equipment installations.

List F Environmentally-friendly plant and machinery

The Water Technology Criteria List specifies the following technology classes as eligible for first-year allowances as environmentally-friendly equipment. See page 9 note (e).

(1) Meters and monitoring equipment.
(2) Flow controllers.
(3) Leakage detection equipment.
(4) Efficient toilets.
(5) Efficient taps.
(6) Rainwater harvesting equipment.
(7) Water reuse systems (for expenditure before 11 August 2008, efficient membrane filtration systems for the treatment of waste water for recovery and reuse only).
(8) Cleaning in place equipment.
(9) Efficient showers.
(10) (For expenditure incurred on or after 7 September 2006) efficient washing machines.
(11) (For expenditure incurred on or after 7 September 2006) small scale slurry and sludge dewatering equipment.
(12) (For expenditure incurred on or after 16 August 2007) vehicle wash waste reclaim units.
(13) (For expenditure incurred on or after 16 August 2007) water efficient industrial cleaning equipment.
(14) (For expenditure incurred on or after 16 August 2007) water management equipment for mechanical seals (for expenditure before 11 August 2008, waste management for mechanical seals).

The equipment must meet the environmental criteria set out in that List and must be of a type specified in (and not removed from) or which has been accepted for inclusion in, the Water Technology Product List. [*CAA 2001, s 45H; SI 2003 No 2076*].

List G items which can qualify as plant or machinery based on case law, Revenue practice etc.

Acid chambers
Acoustic treatment of e.g. room ducts (specialised installations)
Advertising signs, billboards, hoardings and roller boards
Aerials
Air compressors and services
Air conditioning including ducting and vents
Air lines
Alterations to a building re: plant installation e.g. ventilating ducts
Amusement slides
Annealing ovens
Aquarium tanks
Arc and gas welding plant
Architects and professional fees related to a number of items including plant (part may qualify)
Armco barriers
Art works at a museum etc.
Artificial manure manufacturing plant

Bacon curing plant
Baffles
Baker's plant
Ball feeders and specialist tennis equipment
Banana ripening plant
Baths
Battery chargers
Beehives
Bicycle holders
Biscuit making plant
Bitumen laminating plant
Blast furnace
Blast tunnels
Blinds, curtains, blind boxes and pelmets
Boat shed jetties
Bobbin tamping machines
Boiler plants and auxiliaries
Boilers
Bowling alleys including ball return tracks, gutters, pit signals and terminals
Bowser tanks
Brewing plant including pipes, condenser and expansion
Brick elevators (portable)
Brick kilns
Bullet resistant screens
Burglar alarms
Buzz bars

Cable TV provision and ducting
Cable, both overhead and underground
Cable car systems
Calorifiers
Cameras
Canopy – where certain conditions met e.g. serves purpose of advertising
Canteen fittings and equipment
Capital contribution to a sewerage authority in the UK
Car park illumination
Carpets and other loose floor coverings
Car wash apparatus and housing
Cash dispensers
Casting pit
Cat walks
Catalysts (granuals)
Cathode filling machines
Ceilings – false, but only when performing a function distant from setting e.g. an integral part of a ventilation or air conditioning system
Central dictation systems
Charcoal burning kilns
Checkouts
Chillers
Cleaning cradles (including tracks and anchorages)
Clock installations
Coal carbonising apparatus
Coal hulks
Coffee making machines
Compressed air plant and piping
Computers and associated attachments together with specialised flooring and ceilings
Conduit for security alarm systems
Construction costs of erecting plant on site
Contribution to plant purchased by others (certain conditions must be met)
Conveyor installations and equipment
Cooking baths
Cooking, conveying and servicing equipment
Cooler rooms
Cooling furnaces
Cooling-water systems for (i) drinking and (ii) air-conditioning
Counters and fittings
Court floors – indoor and outdoor (certain cases only)
Cradles and fire balconies (demountable)
Crane gantries and towers
Curing barns e.g. tobacco and peanuts
Cyclic reforming apparatus

Dam (certain situations where not made of earth)
Dark rooms (demountable)
Derricks
Designs and blueprints
Dips for sheep and cattle
Dispensers
Disposal units with all live feeds, wastes and flues
Distillery plant and brewery apparatus including casks
Distribution systems
Documents hoist and other hoists and doors
Door closers
Draglines and buckets
Drilling plant
Drop hammers
Dry dock
Dry riser installation
Dryers

Capital allowances items qualifying as plant or machinery

Dumbwaiters
Dust extraction equipment
Dyehouse – specially designed
Dynamos

Electric dodgems
Electric fences
Electrically operated doors
Electrically operated roller shutters
Electrical sub-stations and generators
Electrical wiring closely related to an accepted piece of plant e.g. to smoke detectors
Electrical wiring and sockets in connection with particular trades e.g. TV shops and departments where the numbers of sockets are more than is normal for the size of the shop or department
Electronic scoring equipment
Electronic timing devices
Emergency lighting
Escalators and travelators
Excavating costs re: plant installation
Exchange losses when linked to capital expenditure
Extinguishers

Fairground and similar amusements
Fans
Fascia lettering
Fermentation chambers
Fire blankets and alarms
Fire protection systems and sprinklers
Fires
Fire safety equipment to comply with the requirements of a fire authority
Fish farming equipment
Fish ponds at garden centres and fish farms
Fitted desks, writing tables and screens
Fixed site caravans in a motor village
Flight simulators and trainers
Floating docks, pontoons and marinas
Floodlighting
Floor covering
Flooring (demountable)
Flooring (raised but only where incorporating special features necessary for trade)
Foreign currency fluctuation relating to expenditure (in certain cases)
Forges
Freezer rooms and chambers
Furnaces

Gamma irradiation apparatus
Gangways
Gantries
Gas bells
Gas installations after incoming main
General control and supervisory systems
Generators
Glasshouse (if of sophisticated design with e.g. a computer system monitoring and controlling such matters as temperature, humidity, ventilation and screens)
Goods and bullion lifts and doors
Grain silos
Gramophones and juke boxes
Grill work (removable)
Gymnasium equipment

Hand dryers
Heating installations, fittings, pipes and radiators
Hoists
Holding bay for oxygen steelmaking installation
Hoses and hose reels
Hot water services and related plumbing
Humidification buildings (specialist)
Hydraulic elevated platforms and hoists e.g. for car parking trade
Hydraulic presses

Ice making apparatus
Immersion and instant water heaters
Incinerators
Installation costs re: plant
Inter-com installations
Internal signs

Kennels (moveable)
Kitchen equipment
Knives and lasts

Launches for ships
Laundry equipment and services
Letter-boxes
Lifts and lift shafts
Light fittings and lamps (certain trades e.g. hotels re ambience)
Lighting protection systems
Livestock pens and cages
Loudspeakers
Lockers
Locks (certain situations)
Loose floor coverings and doormats
Loose furniture
LPG cylinders

Mannequin display figures
Mechanical hand dryers
Mechanical gates
Mechanical vehicle barriers
Mechanical ventilation systems
Merry-go-rounds
Mezzanine storage platforms (moveable)
Milking machinery and refrigeration storage facilities
Mining machinery
Mirrors
Model steam trains, permanent way and other equipment for carrying passengers
Moveable partitions (where required by trade)
Murals (certain trades e.g. hotels re ambience)
Museums – items displayed

Name plates
Navigation apparatus (both on and offshore)

Offshore accommodation modules and helidecks
Oil rigs, well linings and platforms

Capital allowances items qualifying as plant or machinery

Organic peroxides expansion cell block
Ornaments (certain trades e.g. hotels re ambience)
Outside tennis fencing
Ovens

Paper combining plant
Passenger lifts and doors
Payment for cancellation of options (in certain cases)
PBX
Personnel – location and call systems
Photofinish equipment
Pictures (certain trades e.g. hotels re ambience)
Pig unit (purpose built), automatic feeding etc.
Pipelines
Planetarium and space theatre domes
Plant housing (special circumstances)
Pneumatic tube conveying systems
Poles, cables, conductors and switch boards for the distribution of electricity
Portable toilet
Portakabins, huts of a nomadic type moved from site to site (e.g. the construction industry)
Pottery – works equipment and kiln
Poultry house – specially designed
Power cables
Power installations
Powering barrel mills
Prawn farming ponds
Professional fees specially related to an item of plant acquired
Projecting signs
Protective structures closely related to accepted items of plant
Public address and piped music systems
Pulleys
Pumps
Purifiers

Racking, cupboards and shelving (removable)
Radar installations
Radiators
Radio, television and data receivers
Radio, television and data transmission installations
Railway track including sleepers and ballast
Refinery
Refrigerated fruit juice dispensers
Refrigeration installations and cold stores
Refrigeration plant
Refuse collecting and disposal systems (including chutes and incinerators)
Reinforcing plant
Reticulation services installed in a factory if certain conditions are met
Retorts and associated structures
Revolving mechanical doors
Rock crushing machines
Roller shutter doors
Roofing – cost of strengthening roofs to support plant such as cranes and hoists

Safes, night safes and enclosures
Safety equipment and screens
Salmon farming apparatus
Sanitary installations such as lavatories, urinals and pans together with pipeline fittings
Sauna and jacuzzi
Screens and fire safety curtains – cinemas
Screens in a window display (moveable)
Sculptures (certain trades e.g. hotels re ambience)
Seats
Security assets and devices
Security gates to cash loading area (removable)
Security screens and lobbies
Sewer pipes in relation to e.g. factory or a large hotel
Shafts
Showers and baths
Shutters (mechanical)
Silage storage bunkers
Silos e.g. slurry blending and mixing and cement storage
Skating surface – synthetic
Skidpans and special surface tracks
Sleeping units for workers which are portable and taken from site to site
Slicing and wrapping machines
Smelters
Smoke detectors and heat detectors
Soda water fountains
Soft furnishings
Software purchased at the same time as the hardware re a computer system
Software with a life of more than 2 years
Solar energy systems
Special acoustical or suspended ceilings (in certain cases)
Special buildings which cannot be used as ordinary buildings e.g. boiler house, concrete shells housing plant, wind tunnels and anechoic chambers
Special foundations or reinforced flooring for plant
Special housing around plant
Special lighting related to the trade
Splashbacks (where not part of a wholly-tiled wall or floor)
Sports stadia expenditure re a safety certificate
Spray booth
Sprinkler systems
Squash courts – directly related to certain trading activities e.g. amusement park
Staff lockers
Stage lights and scenery
Stand (racecourse and similar trades (but only if certain conditions are met))
Starting gantries and stalls
Steam and other trains, permanent way and other equipment for carrying passengers or goods
Steam vats
Storage racks
Storage tanks and bins
Stoves
Stream services and condensate return systems
Strong rooms (demountable)
Strong room doors

Capital allowances items qualifying as plant or machinery

Swimming pools directly related to certain trading activities e.g. amusement or caravan park
Switchboards
Switchgear

Tanks (for brine, cream etc.)
Tapestries (certain trades e.g. hotels re ambience)
Tea and coffee dispensers
Telegraph poles
Telephone booths and kiosks
Telephone equipment and conduits
Teleprinters
Telex systems
Tennis courts – directly related to certain trading activities e.g. amusement or caravan park
Testing tanks
Thermal insulation re industrial buildings
Ticket issuing and collecting machines
Toll booths
Totalisator equipment
Towel dispensers
Towel rails
Traffic control apparatus
Tramway rails
Transformers
Transportation costs of plant
Trellis
Trickle irrigation equipment in glasshouses
Trolley parks
Turnstiles
Turntables

Vacuum cleaning installations
Vats e.g. for cyanide
Vaults
Vents
Vibration control
Video equipment

WC partitions (if demountable venestra type)
Wall decor (certain trades e.g. hotels re ambience)
Wash basins including drains
Water slide and associated equipment
Water softening installations
Water tower
Water treatment and filtration
Weighbridge
Welfare facilities
Wells
Wet and dry risers
Wharves – certain situations
Winches
Wind tunnels
Windmills
Window display lighting e.g. shops
Window displays (moveable)
Window panels, lighting and sockets for a shop front
Wiring and trunking to accepted items of plant

X-ray apparatus

Zoo cages (fixed)

Capital gains tax

Annual exemptions

(a) Individuals, personal representatives for the year of death and following two years and trusts for disabled person (as defined) [*TCGA 1992, s 3, Sch 1 para 1*]

2013/14	£10,900	*SI 2013 No 662*
2012/13	£10,600	*FA 2012, 34*
2011/12	£10,600	*FA 2011, s 8*
2010/11	£10,100	*SI 2010 No 923*
2009/10	£10,100	*SI 2009 No 824*
2008/09	£9,600	*SI 2008 No 708*
2007/08	£9,200	*SI 2007 No 942*

In respect of qualifying trusts above, where one person creates more than one settlement, the exemption above is divided by the number of settlements created after 9 March 1981, subject to a minimum of 10% of the annual exemption.

For 2008/09 onwards, an individual who claims to use the remittance basis for a tax year is not entitled to the capital gains tax annual exemption for that year. This does not apply if the individual's unremitted foreign income and gains for the year are less than £2,000.

(b) Settlements other than trusts covered in (a) above [*TCGA 1992, s 3, Sch 1 para 2*]

2013/14	£5,450	*SI 2013 No 662*
2012/13	£5,300	*FA 2012, 34*
2011/12	£5,300	*FA 2011, s 8*
2010/11	£5,050	*SI 2010 No 923*
2009/10	£5,050	*SI 2009 No 824*
2008/09	£4,800	*SI 2008 No 708*
2007/08	£4,600	*SI 2007 No 942*

In respect of settlements made after 6 June 1978, where one person creates more than one settlement, the exemption above is divided by the number of settlements created, subject to a minimum of 10% of the annual exemption for individuals.

Annual rates [*TCGA 1992, s 4; F(No 2)A 2010, Sch 1*]

Subject, for 2007/08 and earlier years, to taper relief in certain cases, gains are chargeable as follows

2011/12–2013/14	*Individuals*: treating gains as the top slice of taxable income: 18% up to basic rate limit; 28% above basic rate limit (subject to entrepreneurs' relief (see page 18)) *Settlements and personal representatives*: 28% (subject to entrepreneurs' relief (see page 18))
2010/11	*Individuals — gains after 22 June 2010*: treating gains made after that date as the top slice of taxable income: 18% up to basic rate limit; 28% above basic rate limit (subject to entrepreneurs' relief (see page 18)) *Individuals — gains before 23 June 2010*: 18% *Settlements and personal representatives*: 18% for gains before 23 June 2010, 28% for gains after 22 June 2010 (subject to entrepreneurs' relief (see page 18))
2008/09–2009/10	18%
2005/06–2007/08	*Individuals*: treating gain as the top slice of taxable income: 10% up to starting rate limit; 20% up to basic rate limit; 40% above basic rate limit *Settlements where settlor retains an interest*: chargeable on settlor at own rate(s) *Settlements for vulnerable persons*: taxed as if gains were those of the beneficiary *All other settlements and personal representatives*: 40% *Settlements where settlor retains an interest*: chargeable on settlor at own rate(s) *All other settlements and personal representatives*: 40%

Business expansion scheme [*TCGA 1992, s 150*]

In respect of shares issued after 18 March 1986 and before 1 January 1994 a disposal of scheme shares is exempt provided the scheme relief has been given and not withdrawn and other conditions are satisfied.

Charities, etc, gifts to [*TCGA 1992, s 257*]

Disposals (not at arm's length) to charities or bodies within *IHTA 1984, Sch 3* by way of gift or at a consideration not exceeding allowable expenditure are deemed to be made for a consideration giving neither a gain nor a loss. See also page 61.

FA 2012, s 49 provides relief from 1 April 2012, via a tax reduction, for taxpayers who donate pre-eminent objects, or collections of objects, to the nation. Individuals may qualify for a reduction in capital gains tax (and/or income tax) liability equal to 30% of the value of the objects. For corporation tax purposes the reduction is potentially 20% of the value. The cultural gift scheme is administered by the Arts Council and launched on 12 March 2013.

Chattels (other than currency) [*TCGA 1992, s 45, s 262*]

Maximum exempt proceeds	
1989/90 onwards	£6,000

Marginal relief applies to limit any gain to five-thirds of the excess over the above maximum. For the purposes of loss relief, a disposal for less than the maximum is deemed to be made for that maximum.

Chattels which are wasting assets are exempt whatever the consideration received, but this exemption is restricted or eliminated to the extent that the asset has been or could have been the subject of a capital allowance.

Child trust funds [*SI 2004 No 1450*]

No tax is chargeable on the account provider, his nominee or the child on gains on account investments. The child is treated as having sold all the account investments, and as having reacquired them in his personal capacity, for their market value, immediately before attaining the age of 18. See also page 61.

Capital gains tax

Dwelling houses *[TCGA 1992, ss 222–226B]*

A proportion of the gain accruing to an individual on the disposal of a dwelling house which has been his main residence is exempt given by the fraction

$$\frac{\text{length of the period of ownership after 31.3.82 during which the dwelling-house was the individual'sonly or main residence (but in any case inclusive of the last 36months)}}{\text{the length of the period of ownership after 31.3.82}}$$

Certain periods of absence during which the individual had no other residence available for relief (including any period or periods not exceeding three years) are included in the denominator provided both before and after the period there was a time when the dwelling house was the individual's only or main residence.

Where the dwelling house has been let at any time as residential accommodation, the gain otherwise chargeable by reason of the letting is exempt up to the lower of £40,000 and the amount of the gain otherwise exempt under these provisions.

Employee shareholder shares *[FA 2013, sch 23; SI 2013 No 1755]*

For shares received from 1 September 2013, subject to meeting certain conditions, gains on the disposal of employee shareholder shares worth up to £50,000 on acquisition are exempt from capital gains tax. The share identification rules are amended, where relevant, to enable the employee to determine which proportion of the shares disposed of are treated as exempt employee shareholder shares.

Enterprise investment scheme *[TCGA 1992, ss 150A–150D, Schs 5B, 5BA]*

A disposal of shares on which EIS income tax relief has been given and not withdrawn is exempt. Any loss (net of income tax relief) on a disposal of EIS shares may be relieved against income or capital gains. A chargeable gain arising on disposal of any assets can be deferred by a subscription for shares under the EIS made one year before or three years after the disposal. Deferral is possible regardless of whether or not the EIS investment qualifies for income tax relief or the subscriber is connected with the company, but is restricted to cash subscriptions for new eligible shares in qualifying companies. See also page 62.

Entrepreneurs' relief *[TCGA 1992, ss 169H–169S; F(No 2)A 2010, Sch 1; FA 2013, Sch 24]*

Entrepreneurs' relief applies to disposals by an individual on or after 6 April 2008 of:

- all or part of a trade carried on alone or in partnership;
- assets of such a trade following cessation; or
- shares or securities in the individual's 'personal trading company' (as defined).

Where a disposal of shares or of an interest in the assets of a partnership qualifies for relief, an associated disposal of assets owned by the individual and used by the company or partnership also qualifies for relief.

Trustees can claim relief where a qualifying beneficiary has an interest in the business concerned.

The relief is available where the relevant conditions are met throughout a period of one year and for gains arising after 22 June 2010 operates by charging the qualifying gains to CGT at 10%. Previously, the relief operated by reducing the amount of qualifying gains by four-ninths (so that the gains were effectively charged to CGT at 10%). Relief is subject to a lifetime limit of gains of £10 million (£5 million for disposals before 6 April 2011; £2 million for disposals before 23 June 2010; £1 million for disposals before 6 April 2010), but disposals before 6 April 2008 do not normally count towards the limit. Relief given to trustees counts towards the limit of the qualifying beneficiary.

Transitional rules apply to allow relief to be claimed in certain circumstances where a gain made before 6 April 2008 is deferred and becomes chargeable on or after that date.

Entrepreneurs' relief is extended to a disposal by an employee or officer of a trading company of shares in that company (or same trading group) where the shares were acquired via an enterprise management incentive scheme. Relief applies from 6 April 2013 where the shares were acquired on or after 6 April 2012. The option must have been granted at least one year before the date of disposal and the individual must have been employed or an officer throughout the year ending with the date of disposal.

Gifts *[TCGA 1992, ss 165–169G, 260, Sch 7]*

Where an individual makes a disposal not at arm's length (e.g. a gift) of a qualifying business asset, then, on a joint claim by the transferor and transferee, the unrelieved gain of the transferor is held over and the transferee's acquisition cost is reduced by a similar amount. Where any consideration exceeds the allowable expenditure, the held-over gain is the unrelieved gain less the excess. Qualifying business assets are

(a) assets used for the purposes of the trade, profession or vocation carried on by the transferor or his personal company; and

(b) shares or securities of a trading company which is the transferor's personal company or whose shares etc. are not listed. (Transfers of shares or securities *to a company* are excluded.)

Where a transferor makes a disposal not at arm's length of any asset which is a chargeable transfer under *IHTA 1984*, similar hold-over rules apply as above.

Government securities ('gilts') *[TCGA 1992, s 115]*

Disposals by individuals and trustees are exempt.

High value property disposals by companies etc (non-natural persons) *[TCGA 1992, s 2B; FA 2013, Sch 25]*

A capital gains tax charge arises on the disposal on or after 6 April 2013 of a high value property by a non-natural person. Gains since 6 April 2013 are taxed at 28%. This applies to both UK and non-UK resident non-natural persons. The rules are linked to the annual tax on enveloped dwellings see page 77.

Capital gains tax

Indexation [*TCGA 1992, ss 53–57, 109*]

Indexation allowance is abolished for disposals on or after 6 April 2008 by individuals, trustees and personal representatives (but not companies). For disposals before that date by such persons, the allowance is only given up to April 1998 and is not available for assets acquired after 31 March 1998.

For companies, the allowance continues and is computed by multiplying each item of allowable expenditure by

$$\frac{RD - RI}{RI} \text{ where}$$

RD = the RPI for month of disposal

RI = the RPI for the later of March 1982 or month expenditure incurred (but no later than March 1998 for individuals etc.)

See page 98 for RPI values.

For disposals before 6 April 2008 by individuals etc. of assets acquired on or before 31 March 1998, the following percentages can be used to calculate the indexation allowance for acquisitions in the month shown.

	Jan	Feb	Mar	Apr	May	Jun	Jul	Aug	Sep	Oct	Nov	Dec
1982	—	—	104.7	100.6	99.2	98.7	98.6	98.5	98.7	97.7	96.7	97.1
1983	96.8	96.0	95.6	92.9	92.1	91.7	90.6	89.8	88.9	88.3	87.6	87.1
1984	87.2	86.5	85.9	83.4	82.8	82.3	82.5	80.8	80.4	79.3	78.8	78.9
1985	78.3	76.9	75.2	71.6	70.8	70.4	70.7	70.3	70.4	70.1	69.5	69.3
1986	68.9	68.3	68.1	66.5	66.2	66.3	66.7	66.2	65.4	65.2	63.8	63.2
1987	62.6	62.0	61.6	59.7	59.6	59.6	59.7	59.3	58.8	58.0	57.3	57.4
1988	57.4	56.8	56.2	53.7	53.1	52.5	52.4	50.7	50.0	48.5	47.8	47.4
1989	46.5	45.4	44.8	42.3	41.4	40.9	40.8	40.4	39.5	38.4	37.2	36.9
1990	36.1	35.3	33.9	30.0	28.8	28.3	28.2	26.9	25.8	24.8	25.1	25.2
1991	24.9	24.2	23.7	22.2	21.8	21.3	21.5	21.3	20.8	20.4	19.9	19.8
1992	19.9	19.3	18.9	17.1	16.7	16.7	17.1	17.1	16.6	16.2	16.4	16.8
1993	17.9	17.1	16.7	15.6	15.2	15.3	15.6	15.1	14.6	14.7	14.8	14.6
1994	15.1	14.4	14.1	12.8	12.4	12.4	12.9	12.4	12.1	12.0	11.9	11.4
1995	11.4	10.7	10.2	9.1	8.7	8.5	9.1	8.5	8.0	8.5	8.5	7.9
1996	8.3	7.8	7.3	6.6	6.3	6.3	6.7	6.2	5.7	5.7	5.7	5.3
1997	5.3	4.9	4.6	4.0	3.6	3.2	3.2	2.6	2.1	1.9	1.9	1.6
1998	1.9	1.4	1.1									

Losses. Indexation allowance can only be used to reduce or extinguish a gain. It cannot increase or create a capital loss.

Assets acquired before 1 April 1982. Indexation allowance for an asset held on 31 March 1982 is calculated by reference to its market value on that date rather than its cost. The allowance can be claimed on the original cost if this is to the taxpayer's advantage.

Individual savings accounts ('ISAs') [*SI 1998 No 1870; SI 2013 No 1743*]

Investors are entitled to exemption from capital gains tax on their investments. There is no lock-in period and withdrawals may be made at any time without loss of tax relief. Where investments are withdrawn *in specie*, the investor is deemed to have made a disposal and reacquisition at market value. From 5 August 2013, an individual may invest their ISA allowance directly into qualifying SME equity markets and any gains arising from the growth of the investment would be tax free. This will be achieved by expanding the range of ISA qualifying investments to include company shares admitted to trading on a recognised stock exchange in the EEA. See also page 60.

Capital gains tax

Lease depreciation table [*TCGA 1992, Sch 8 para 1(3)–(6)*]

This table relates to leases of land which have 50 years or less to run (short leases)

Years	Percentage	Years	Percentage	Years	Percentage
50 or more	100	33	90.280	16	64.116
49	99.657	32	89.354	15	61.617
48	99.289	31	88.371	14	58.971
47	98.902	30	87.330	13	56.167
46	98.490	29	86.226	12	53.191
45	98.059	28	85.053	11	50.038
44	97.595	27	83.816	10	46.695
43	97.107	26	82.496	9	43.154
42	96.593	25	81.100	8	39.399
41	96.041	24	79.622	7	35.414
40	95.457	23	78.055	6	31.195
39	94.842	22	76.399	5	26.722
38	94.189	21	74.635	4	21.983
37	93.497	20	72.770	3	16.959
36	92.761	19	70.791	2	11.629
35	91.981	18	68.697	1	5.983
34	91.156	17	66.470	0	0

The fraction of expenditure (original cost and additional expenditure being treated separately) which is not allowed is calculated from the table above as follows

$$\frac{P(1) - P(3)}{P(1)} \text{ or } \frac{P(2) - P(3)}{P(2)}$$

where the percentages for the duration of the lease are

P(1) at acquisition

P(2) at the time of any additional expenditure

P(3) at disposal

If the duration of the lease is not an exact number of years, the percentage is that for the whole number of years plus one-twelfth of the difference between that and the next higher number for each odd month, counting an odd fourteen days or more as one month.

Miscellaneous

The following is a summary of other important exemptions from capital gains tax not covered separately in this section.

(a) **Betting, lottery etc.** Winnings from betting or lotteries of games with prizes are not chargeable gains, and no chargeable gain accrues on the disposal of rights to such winnings obtained by participating [*TCGA 1992, s 51(1)*].

(b) **Damages and compensation.** Sums received as compensation or damages for any wrong or injury suffered by an individual in his person or in his trade, employment, profession or vocation are not chargeable gains. [*TCGA 1992, s 51(2)*; HMRC ESC D33]. Compensation from foreign governments for assets confiscated, destroyed or expropriated is, subject to conditions, exempt. [HMRC ESC D50].

(c) **Debts.** A debt, other than a debt on a security, disposed of by the original creditor or his personal representative or legatee is exempt. [*TCGA 1992, s 251(1)*].

(d) **Decorations.** A decoration for valour or gallantry is exempt unless acquired by the vendor for money or money's worth. [*TCGA 1992, s 268*].

(e) **Foreign currency** acquired for an individual's (or his dependant(s) personal expenditure outside the UK is exempt. [*TCGA 1992, s 269*]. For disposals on or after 6 April 2012, all gains on withdrawals of money from foreign currency bank accounts by individuals, trustees and personal representatives are exempt.

(f) **Insurance policies.** A gain on the disposal of the rights conferred by a non-life insurance policy is exempt, subject to a restriction in certain cases where the policy is for loss or depreciation of assets which could themselves give rise to a chargeable gain. [*TCGA 1992, s 204*].

(g) **Motor cars etc.** [*TCGA 1992, s 263*].

(h) **Qualifying corporate bonds** are exempt. [*TCGA 1992, s 115*].

(i) **Renewables obligations certificates.** A gain on the disposal by an individual on or after 6 April 2007 of a certificate issued under *Electricity Act 1989, s 32B* is, subject to conditions, exempt. [*TCGA 1992, s 263AZA*].

(j) **Right to receive interest on deposit of victim of Nazi persecution.** A gain on the disposal of a right to receive interest eligible for income tax exemption under *ITTOIA 2005, s 756A* is not a chargeable gain. [*TCGA 1992, s 268A*].

(k) **Savings certificates, schemes and accounts etc.** No chargeable gain arises on the disposal of savings certificates and non-marketable securities issued under *National Loans Acts 1939* and *1968*. [*TCGA 1992, s 121*].

(l) **Settlements.** With certain exceptions, no chargeable gain accrues on the disposal of an interest created by or arising under a settlement by the original beneficiary or any other person. [*TCGA 1992, s 76*].

(m) **Substantial shareholdings of companies.** A gain on a disposal by a company of shares is exempt if, subject to further conditions, throughout a continuous twelve-month period beginning not more than two years before the disposal, the company held a substantial shareholding (broadly, at least a 10% interest) in the company whose shares are the subject of the disposal. [*TCGA 1992, Sch 7AC*].

Capital gains tax

Negligible value securities

HMRC have accepted that certain quoted securities have become of negligible value within *TCGA 1992, s 24(2)*. The effect is that, on a claim, the claimant is treated as having sold, and immediately reacquired, the shares for a consideration equal to the amount specified in the claim. The following is a list of securities so accepted in recent years.

Company	Security	Effective date
Alexandra Plc	Ord 10p	29/07/10
Bradford & Bingley Plc	All	29/09/08
Carter & Carter Group Plc	Ord 4p	14/04/08
Endeavors Plc	Ord	26/09/08
Ennstone Plc	Ord 25p	02/04/09
Entertainment Rights Plc	Ord	01/04/09
Erinaceous Group Plc	Ord 0.5p	23/03/10
Gaskell Plc	Ord 5p	22/11/07
Hampson Industries Plc	Ord 25p	04/12/12
Heywood Williams Group Plc	Ord	18/11/09
Jarvis Plc	Ord 5p	26/03/10
Lambert Howarth Group Plc	Ord 10p	24/12/07
Land of Leather Holdings Plc	Ord 10p	12/01/09
Leveraged Income Fund	Zero Div Pref Ord	03/12/07
Litho Supplies Plc	Ord	21/07/10
London Scottish Bank Plc	10p Ord	08/01/10
Marchpole Holdings Plc	Ord	01/07/09
Mice Group Plc	Ord	20/12/07
Mouchel Group Plc	Ord	28/08/12
Northern Rock Plc	All	22/02/08
Premier UK Dual Return Trust Plc	0.1p Capital	16/01/09
Regent Inns Plc	Ord	10/12/10
Vanco Plc	Ord 5p	29/07/08
Waterford Wedgwood UK Plc	Stock units	29/04/10
Woolworths Group Plc	Ord	26/02/09
World Trade Systems Plc	Ord	2008/09

Payment of tax

Under self-assessment, any CGT liability is taken into account in arriving at the final payment (or repayment) of IT and CGT due on 31 January following the year of assessment. See page 65.

Personal equity plans [*TCGA 1992, s 151; SI 1986 No 1948; SI 1989 No 469*]

No capital gains tax liability (or relief for losses) on the sale of investments under the plan. Where investments are withdrawn *in specie*, the investor is deemed to have made a disposal and reacquisition at market value. Continuing PEPs are brought within the Individual Savings Account rules from 6 April 2008. See also page 63.

Personal representatives (HMRC Statement of Practice SP 2/04)

HMRC have agreed that expenditure based on the following scale (for deaths after 5 April 2004) may be added to the market values of assets at the date of death (as an estimate of the legal and accountancy costs in preparing the inheritance tax account and obtaining probate etc.) in computing chargeable gains on disposal

Gross value of estate	Allowable expenditure
(a) Up to £50,000	1.8% of probate value of assets sold
(b) £50,001–£90,000	£900 — divided among all the assets in the estate in proportion to their probate values
(c) £90,001–£400,000	1% of probate value of assets sold
(d) £400,001–£500,000	£4,000 — divided as in (b) above
(e) £500,001–£1,000,000	0.8% of probate value of assets sold
(f) £1,000,001–£5,000,000	£8,000 — divided as in (b) above
(g) Over £5,000,000	0.16% of probate value of assets sold (maximum £10,000)

Rebasing to 31 March 1982 [*TCGA 1992, ss 35, 36*]

Gains and losses on disposals after 5 April 1988 of assets held on 31 March 1982 are computed by reference to their 31 March 1982 value rather than original cost. However, for disposals by companies and disposals before 6 April 2008 by individuals, trustees or personal representatives, a gain or loss cannot be greater than would have been the case if the rules relating to pre-6 April 1988 disposals had applied, unless a global election is made for 31 March 1982 value to apply irrevocably to all assets held on that date.

Rollover relief (replacement of business assets) [*TCGA1992, ss 152–160*]

A person disposing of a qualifying asset used exclusively for the purposes of a trade who uses the proceeds to purchase other qualifying assets so used may claim to defer the CGT payable by deducting the otherwise chargeable gain from the cost of new assets. Qualifying assets are

(a) land and buildings occupied and used for the purposes of the trade;
(b) fixed plant and machinery;
(c) ships, aircraft and hovercraft;
(d) satellites, space stations and spacecraft;
(e) goodwill;
(f) milk and potato quotas;
(g) ewe and suckler cow premium quotas;
(h) fish quotas; and
(i) payment entitlement under the single payment scheme.

Partial relief is available where not all the disposal proceeds are applied in acquiring new qualifying assets. As regards companies only, items (e) to (j) do not apply.

Seed enterprise investment scheme *[TCGA 1992, ss 150E-150G, Sch 5BB; FA 2012, Sch 6 paras 2-5; FA 2013, s 57]*

A disposal of shares on which SEIS income tax relief has been given and not withdrawn is exempt. Chargeable gains arising on disposals of any assets in 2012/13 can be deferred by a subscription for shares under the SEIS made in 2012/13, up to a maximum relief of £100,000. Deferral is possible only where the SEIS investment qualifies for income tax relief (and such relief is claimed). The relief is also extended to 2013/14 but only half of the reinvested amount can be set against chargeable gains. The relief applies to shares treated as issued in 2012/13 or 2013/14 as a result of a carry back claim. See also page 64.

Share identification rules *[TCGA 1992, ss 104–106A; FA 2008, Sch 2]*

For disposals on or after 6 April 2008 by individuals, trustees or personal representatives, shares and securities of the same class in the same company are normally identified with acquisitions in the following order:

- acquisitions on the same day as the disposal;
- acquisitions within 30 days after the day of disposal;
- shares comprised in a single pool incorporating all other shares of the same class, whenever acquired.

Exceptions to the normal share identification rules above:

(1) EMI shares – For disposals within the 30-day period on or after 6 April 2013, shares which are not relevant EMI shares are identified before those which are relevant EMI shares. Otherwise shares are identified with relevant EMI shares first on a first in/first out basis and such shares do not form part of the single pool.

(2) Employee shareholder shares – From 1 September 2013 and where relevant, an employee may determine what proportion of the shares disposed of are treated as exempt employee shareholder shares.

Disposals by such persons on or before 5 April 2008 are identified with acquisitions in the following order:

- same day acquisitions (subject to special rules distinguishing shares acquired after 5 April 2002 from approved employee share option schemes from other shares acquired on the same day);
- acquisitions within the following 30 days (see also below);
- previous acquisitions after 5 April 1998 on a last in/first out basis;
- any pooled shares acquired after 1982 and in the pool at 5 April 1998;
- any shares held at 5 April 1982;
- any shares acquired on or before 6 April 1965 on a last in/first out basis;
- (if shares disposed of still not fully matched) subsequent acquisitions.

The 30-day matching rule above also applied (in priority to pooling and otherwise than for corporation tax purposes) to disposals and reacquisitions between 17 March 1998 and 5 April 1998 inclusive.

For acquisitions after 21 March 2006, the 30-day rule does not apply where the person making the disposal is, or is treated as, neither resident nor ordinarily resident in the UK at the time of acquisition.

For the purposes of corporation tax on chargeable gains, disposals of shares etc. are identified with acquisitions in the following order:

- same day acquisitions;
- acquisitions within the previous nine days on a first in/first out basis;
- the pool of shares acquired after 31 March 1982;
- any shares held at 31 March 1982;
- any shares acquired on or before 6 April 1965 on a last in/first out basis;
- (if shares disposed of still not fully matched) subsequent acquisitions.

These rules are modified for disposals of shares before 5 December 2005 if the company acquired shares of the same class within a short period and held not less than 2% of the number issued.

Venture capital trusts *[TCGA 1992, ss 151A, 151B, Sch 5C]*

An individual's disposals of shares in VCTs are exempt from capital gains tax provided the shares were not *acquired* in excess of the permitted investment limit for any tax year. See page 65.

Capital gains tax

Taper relief *[TCGA 1992, s 2A, Sch A1; FA 2008, Sch 2]*

For disposals after 5 April 1998 and before 6 April 2008 by individuals, trustees and personal representatives, chargeable gains are reduced (tapered) according to the number of complete years after 5 April 1998 for which the asset has been held, as below. Taper relief is abolished for gains accruing, or treated as accruing, on or after 6 April 2008.

*Number of complete years after 5.4.98 for which asset held**	*Percentage of gain relieved*			
	Business assets			*Non-business assets*
	Disposals after 5.4.02	*Disposals after 5.4.00*	*Disposals after 5.4.98*	*All disposals*
0	—	—	—	—
1	50	12.5	7.5	—
2	75	25	15	—
3	75	50	22.5	5
4	75	75	30	10
5	75	75	37.5	15
6	75	75	45	20
7	75	75	52.5	25
8	75	75	60	30
9	75	75	67.5	35
10 or more	75	75	75	40

* Including, for disposals of business assets before 6.4.00 and all disposals of non-business assets, one bonus year where the asset was held on 17.3.98.

A 'business asset' is

- an asset used for the purposes of a trade carried on (alone or in partnership) by the taxpayer or, after 5 April 2004, any individual, trustee or personal representative; or
- an asset used for the purposes of a trade carried on by a 'qualifying company' (alone or, after 5 April 2004, in partnership); or
- after 5 April 2000, an asset used for the purposes of any office or employment (full-time or part-time) held by the taxpayer with a person carrying on a trade; or
- before 6 April 2000, an asset held for the purposes of a qualifying office or employment to which the taxpayer is required to devote substantially the whole of his time; or
- shares or securities in a qualifying company.

After 5 April 2000, a '*qualifying company*' is a trading company etc. where *either* the company is unlisted (which includes an AIM company) *or* the taxpayer is an employee (full-time or part-time) of the company or a fellow group company (in which case the requirement that the company be a *trading* company etc. is dropped, provided the taxpayer's interest in the company, including connected person holdings, is no more than 10%) *or* the taxpayer can exercise at least 5% of the voting rights. Before 6 April 2000, a '*qualifying company*' is a trading company (or holding company of a trading group) in which the taxpayer holds shares entitling him to at least 5% of the voting rights where he is a full-time employee or 25% otherwise.

Taper relief applies to gains after all deductions other than the annual exemption. Losses are set against pre-tapered gains in the most beneficial way possible. Where applicable, the combined period of holding by spouses is taken into account.

Capital gains indexation allowances for companies (April 2011 – April 2013)

Month of acquisition	2011									2012												2013			
	Apr	May	June	July	Aug	Sept	Oct	Nov	Dec	Jan	Feb	Mar	Apr	May	June	July	Aug	Sept	Oct	Nov	Dec	Jan	Feb	Mar	Apr
1982																									
Mar	1.951	1.961	1.961	1.954	1.972	1.995	1.996	2.002	2.014	1.996	2.020	2.031	2.053	2.051	2.044	2.047	2.059	2.074	2.092	2.092	2.107	2.094	2.117	2.131	2.141
Apr	1.892	1.902	1.902	1.896	1.913	1.936	1.937	1.943	1.954	1.937	1.960	1.971	1.992	1.991	1.984	1.987	1.999	2.013	2.031	2.031	2.045	2.033	2.055	2.069	2.079
May	1.872	1.882	1.882	1.875	1.893	1.915	1.916	1.922	1.933	1.916	1.939	1.950	1.971	1.970	1.962	1.966	1.977	1.992	2.009	2.009	2.024	2.011	2.033	2.047	2.057
June	1.864	1.874	1.874	1.867	1.885	1.907	1.908	1.914	1.925	1.908	1.931	1.942	1.963	1.961	1.954	1.958	1.969	1.983	2.001	2.001	2.015	2.003	2.025	2.038	2.048
July	1.863	1.873	1.873	1.867	1.884	1.906	1.907	1.913	1.924	1.907	1.930	1.941	1.962	1.961	1.953	1.957	1.968	1.983	2.000	2.000	2.014	2.002	2.024	2.038	2.047
Aug	1.862	1.872	1.872	1.866	1.883	1.905	1.906	1.912	1.923	1.906	1.929	1.940	1.961	1.960	1.952	1.956	1.967	1.982	1.999	1.999	2.013	2.001	2.023	2.037	2.046
Sept	1.864	1.874	1.874	1.867	1.885	1.907	1.908	1.914	1.925	1.908	1.931	1.942	1.963	1.961	1.954	1.958	1.969	1.983	2.001	2.001	2.015	2.003	2.025	2.038	2.048
Oct	1.850	1.859	1.859	1.853	1.870	1.892	1.893	1.899	1.910	1.893	1.917	1.927	1.948	1.947	1.940	1.943	1.954	1.969	1.986	1.986	2.000	1.988	2.010	2.023	2.033
Nov	1.836	1.845	1.845	1.839	1.856	1.878	1.879	1.885	1.896	1.879	1.902	1.913	1.934	1.932	1.925	1.929	1.940	1.954	1.971	1.971	1.986	1.974	1.995	2.009	2.018
Dec	1.841	1.851	1.851	1.845	1.861	1.883	1.885	1.891	1.901	1.885	1.908	1.918	1.939	1.938	1.931	1.934	1.945	1.960	1.977	1.977	1.991	1.979	2.001	2.014	2.024
1983																									
Jan	1.837	1.847	1.847	1.841	1.858	1.880	1.881	1.887	1.898	1.881	1.904	1.915	1.935	1.934	1.927	1.931	1.942	1.956	1.973	1.973	1.987	1.975	1.997	2.010	2.020
Feb	1.825	1.835	1.835	1.829	1.846	1.867	1.869	1.875	1.886	1.869	1.892	1.902	1.923	1.922	1.914	1.918	1.929	1.943	1.960	1.960	1.975	1.963	1.984	1.998	2.007
Mar	1.820	1.830	1.830	1.824	1.841	1.862	1.863	1.869	1.880	1.863	1.886	1.897	1.918	1.916	1.909	1.913	1.924	1.938	1.955	1.955	1.969	1.957	1.979	1.992	2.002
Apr	1.781	1.791	1.791	1.785	1.801	1.823	1.824	1.830	1.840	1.824	1.846	1.857	1.877	1.876	1.869	1.872	1.883	1.897	1.914	1.914	1.928	1.916	1.938	1.951	1.960
May	1.769	1.779	1.779	1.773	1.790	1.811	1.812	1.818	1.828	1.812	1.834	1.845	1.865	1.864	1.857	1.860	1.871	1.885	1.902	1.902	1.916	1.904	1.925	1.938	1.948
June	1.763	1.772	1.772	1.766	1.783	1.804	1.805	1.811	1.822	1.805	1.828	1.838	1.858	1.857	1.850	1.854	1.864	1.878	1.895	1.895	1.909	1.897	1.918	1.931	1.941
July	1.748	1.757	1.757	1.752	1.768	1.789	1.790	1.796	1.807	1.790	1.812	1.823	1.843	1.842	1.835	1.838	1.849	1.863	1.879	1.879	1.893	1.882	1.903	1.916	1.925
Aug	1.736	1.745	1.745	1.739	1.756	1.777	1.778	1.784	1.794	1.778	1.800	1.811	1.830	1.829	1.822	1.826	1.836	1.850	1.867	1.867	1.881	1.869	1.890	1.903	1.912
Sept	1.724	1.733	1.733	1.727	1.743	1.764	1.766	1.771	1.782	1.766	1.788	1.798	1.818	1.817	1.810	1.813	1.824	1.838	1.854	1.854	1.868	1.856	1.877	1.890	1.899
Oct	1.714	1.723	1.723	1.718	1.734	1.755	1.756	1.762	1.772	1.756	1.778	1.788	1.808	1.807	1.800	1.803	1.814	1.828	1.844	1.844	1.858	1.846	1.867	1.880	1.889
Nov	1.705	1.714	1.714	1.708	1.724	1.745	1.746	1.752	1.762	1.746	1.768	1.778	1.798	1.797	1.790	1.793	1.804	1.818	1.834	1.834	1.848	1.836	1.857	1.870	1.879
Dec	1.698	1.707	1.707	1.701	1.717	1.738	1.739	1.745	1.755	1.739	1.761	1.771	1.791	1.790	1.783	1.786	1.796	1.810	1.826	1.826	1.840	1.829	1.849	1.862	1.871
1984																									
Jan	1.699	1.708	1.708	1.703	1.719	1.739	1.741	1.746	1.757	1.741	1.762	1.773	1.792	1.791	1.784	1.788	1.798	1.812	1.828	1.828	1.842	1.830	1.851	1.864	1.873
Feb	1.688	1.697	1.697	1.692	1.708	1.728	1.729	1.735	1.745	1.729	1.751	1.762	1.781	1.780	1.773	1.776	1.787	1.800	1.817	1.817	1.830	1.819	1.839	1.852	1.861
Mar	1.680	1.689	1.689	1.683	1.699	1.720	1.721	1.726	1.737	1.721	1.742	1.753	1.772	1.771	1.764	1.768	1.778	1.792	1.808	1.808	1.821	1.810	1.830	1.843	1.852
Apr	1.644	1.653	1.653	1.648	1.663	1.684	1.685	1.691	1.701	1.685	1.706	1.716	1.736	1.735	1.728	1.731	1.741	1.755	1.771	1.771	1.784	1.773	1.793	1.806	1.815
May	1.634	1.643	1.643	1.638	1.654	1.674	1.675	1.681	1.691	1.675	1.696	1.706	1.726	1.724	1.718	1.721	1.731	1.745	1.760	1.760	1.774	1.763	1.783	1.795	1.804
June	1.628	1.637	1.637	1.631	1.647	1.667	1.668	1.674	1.684	1.668	1.689	1.700	1.719	1.717	1.711	1.714	1.724	1.738	1.753	1.753	1.767	1.756	1.776	1.788	1.797
July	1.631	1.640	1.640	1.634	1.650	1.670	1.671	1.677	1.687	1.671	1.692	1.703	1.722	1.721	1.714	1.717	1.727	1.741	1.756	1.756	1.770	1.759	1.779	1.791	1.800
Aug	1.606	1.615	1.615	1.610	1.625	1.645	1.646	1.652	1.662	1.646	1.667	1.677	1.696	1.695	1.689	1.692	1.702	1.715	1.731	1.731	1.744	1.733	1.753	1.765	1.774
Sept	1.601	1.610	1.610	1.604	1.620	1.640	1.641	1.647	1.657	1.641	1.662	1.672	1.691	1.690	1.683	1.687	1.697	1.710	1.725	1.725	1.739	1.728	1.748	1.760	1.769
Oct	1.585	1.594	1.594	1.588	1.604	1.624	1.625	1.630	1.640	1.625	1.646	1.656	1.674	1.673	1.667	1.670	1.680	1.693	1.709	1.709	1.722	1.711	1.731	1.743	1.752
Nov	1.577	1.586	1.586	1.581	1.596	1.616	1.617	1.622	1.632	1.617	1.638	1.648	1.666	1.665	1.659	1.662	1.672	1.685	1.700	1.700	1.714	1.703	1.722	1.734	1.743
Dec	1.579	1.588	1.588	1.583	1.598	1.618	1.619	1.624	1.634	1.619	1.640	1.650	1.669	1.667	1.661	1.664	1.674	1.687	1.703	1.703	1.716	1.705	1.725	1.737	1.746

Capital gains indexation allowances for companies (April 2011 – April 2013)

Month of acquisition	2011 Apr	May	June	July	Aug	Sept	Oct	Nov	Dec	2012 Jan	Feb	Mar	Apr	May	June	July	Aug	Sept	Oct	Nov	Dec	2013 Jan	Feb	Mar	Apr
1985																									
Jan	1.570	1.579	1.579	1.573	1.589	1.608	1.610	1.615	1.625	1.610	1.630	1.640	1.659	1.658	1.651	1.654	1.664	1.678	1.693	1.693	1.706	1.695	1.715	1.727	1.736
Feb	1.550	1.558	1.558	1.553	1.568	1.588	1.589	1.594	1.604	1.589	1.609	1.619	1.638	1.637	1.630	1.633	1.643	1.656	1.671	1.671	1.684	1.674	1.693	1.705	1.714
Mar	1.526	1.534	1.534	1.529	1.544	1.564	1.565	1.570	1.580	1.565	1.585	1.595	1.613	1.612	1.606	1.609	1.619	1.631	1.647	1.647	1.659	1.649	1.668	1.680	1.689
Apr	1.473	1.482	1.482	1.476	1.491	1.510	1.511	1.516	1.526	1.511	1.531	1.541	1.559	1.558	1.551	1.554	1.564	1.577	1.591	1.591	1.604	1.593	1.612	1.624	1.632
May	1.462	1.470	1.470	1.465	1.480	1.499	1.500	1.505	1.514	1.500	1.520	1.529	1.547	1.546	1.540	1.543	1.552	1.565	1.580	1.580	1.592	1.582	1.601	1.612	1.621
June	1.457	1.465	1.465	1.460	1.475	1.493	1.494	1.500	1.509	1.494	1.514	1.524	1.542	1.541	1.534	1.537	1.547	1.559	1.574	1.574	1.587	1.576	1.595	1.607	1.615
July	1.461	1.470	1.470	1.464	1.479	1.498	1.499	1.504	1.514	1.499	1.519	1.528	1.546	1.545	1.539	1.542	1.552	1.564	1.579	1.579	1.591	1.581	1.600	1.611	1.620
Aug	1.455	1.463	1.463	1.458	1.473	1.491	1.492	1.498	1.507	1.492	1.512	1.522	1.540	1.539	1.532	1.535	1.545	1.557	1.572	1.572	1.585	1.574	1.593	1.605	1.613
Sept	1.456	1.464	1.464	1.459	1.474	1.493	1.494	1.499	1.508	1.494	1.514	1.523	1.541	1.540	1.534	1.537	1.546	1.559	1.573	1.573	1.586	1.576	1.594	1.606	1.614
Oct	1.452	1.461	1.461	1.455	1.470	1.489	1.490	1.495	1.504	1.490	1.510	1.519	1.537	1.536	1.530	1.533	1.542	1.555	1.569	1.569	1.582	1.571	1.590	1.602	1.610
Nov	1.444	1.452	1.452	1.447	1.461	1.480	1.481	1.486	1.496	1.481	1.501	1.510	1.528	1.527	1.521	1.524	1.533	1.546	1.560	1.560	1.573	1.563	1.581	1.593	1.601
Dec	1.441	1.449	1.449	1.444	1.458	1.477	1.478	1.483	1.493	1.478	1.498	1.507	1.525	1.524	1.518	1.521	1.530	1.543	1.557	1.557	1.570	1.559	1.578	1.589	1.598
1986																									
Jan	1.435	1.444	1.444	1.438	1.453	1.472	1.473	1.478	1.487	1.473	1.493	1.502	1.520	1.518	1.512	1.515	1.525	1.537	1.552	1.552	1.564	1.554	1.573	1.584	1.592
Feb	1.426	1.435	1.435	1.430	1.444	1.463	1.464	1.469	1.478	1.464	1.483	1.493	1.510	1.509	1.503	1.506	1.515	1.528	1.542	1.542	1.555	1.544	1.563	1.574	1.583
Mar	1.423	1.432	1.432	1.426	1.441	1.459	1.460	1.466	1.475	1.460	1.480	1.489	1.507	1.506	1.500	1.503	1.512	1.525	1.539	1.539	1.551	1.541	1.560	1.571	1.579
Apr	1.400	1.408	1.408	1.403	1.417	1.436	1.437	1.442	1.451	1.437	1.456	1.465	1.483	1.482	1.476	1.479	1.488	1.500	1.515	1.515	1.527	1.517	1.535	1.546	1.555
May	1.396	1.404	1.404	1.399	1.413	1.431	1.432	1.438	1.447	1.432	1.452	1.461	1.478	1.477	1.471	1.474	1.484	1.496	1.510	1.510	1.522	1.512	1.531	1.542	1.550
June	1.397	1.405	1.405	1.400	1.414	1.433	1.434	1.439	1.448	1.434	1.453	1.462	1.480	1.479	1.473	1.476	1.485	1.497	1.511	1.511	1.524	1.513	1.532	1.543	1.551
July	1.404	1.412	1.412	1.407	1.421	1.440	1.441	1.446	1.455	1.441	1.460	1.469	1.487	1.486	1.480	1.483	1.492	1.504	1.519	1.519	1.531	1.521	1.539	1.550	1.559
Aug	1.396	1.404	1.404	1.399	1.414	1.432	1.433	1.438	1.447	1.433	1.452	1.462	1.479	1.478	1.472	1.475	1.484	1.496	1.511	1.511	1.523	1.513	1.531	1.542	1.551
Sept	1.384	1.393	1.393	1.388	1.402	1.420	1.421	1.426	1.435	1.421	1.440	1.450	1.467	1.466	1.460	1.463	1.472	1.484	1.498	1.498	1.511	1.500	1.519	1.530	1.538
Oct	1.381	1.389	1.389	1.384	1.398	1.416	1.417	1.422	1.432	1.417	1.437	1.446	1.463	1.462	1.456	1.459	1.468	1.480	1.495	1.495	1.507	1.497	1.515	1.526	1.534
Nov	1.361	1.369	1.369	1.364	1.378	1.396	1.397	1.402	1.411	1.397	1.416	1.425	1.442	1.441	1.435	1.438	1.447	1.459	1.474	1.474	1.486	1.476	1.494	1.505	1.513
Dec	1.353	1.361	1.361	1.356	1.370	1.388	1.389	1.394	1.403	1.389	1.408	1.417	1.434	1.433	1.427	1.430	1.439	1.451	1.465	1.465	1.477	1.467	1.485	1.496	1.505
1987																									
Jan	1.344	1.352	1.352	1.347	1.361	1.379	1.380	1.385	1.394	1.380	1.399	1.408	1.425	1.424	1.418	1.421	1.430	1.442	1.456	1.456	1.468	1.458	1.476	1.487	1.495
Feb	1.335	1.343	1.343	1.338	1.352	1.370	1.371	1.375	1.384	1.371	1.389	1.398	1.415	1.414	1.408	1.411	1.420	1.432	1.446	1.446	1.458	1.448	1.466	1.477	1.485
Mar	1.330	1.338	1.338	1.333	1.347	1.365	1.366	1.371	1.380	1.366	1.385	1.394	1.411	1.410	1.404	1.407	1.416	1.427	1.441	1.441	1.453	1.443	1.461	1.472	1.480
Apr	1.303	1.310	1.310	1.306	1.319	1.337	1.338	1.343	1.352	1.338	1.357	1.365	1.382	1.381	1.375	1.378	1.387	1.399	1.413	1.413	1.424	1.415	1.432	1.443	1.451
May	1.300	1.308	1.308	1.303	1.317	1.335	1.336	1.341	1.349	1.336	1.354	1.363	1.380	1.379	1.373	1.376	1.385	1.396	1.410	1.410	1.422	1.412	1.430	1.441	1.448
June	1.300	1.308	1.308	1.303	1.317	1.335	1.336	1.341	1.349	1.336	1.354	1.363	1.380	1.379	1.373	1.376	1.385	1.396	1.410	1.410	1.422	1.412	1.430	1.441	1.448
July	1.303	1.310	1.310	1.306	1.319	1.337	1.338	1.343	1.352	1.338	1.357	1.365	1.382	1.381	1.375	1.378	1.387	1.399	1.413	1.413	1.424	1.415	1.432	1.443	1.451
Aug	1.296	1.304	1.304	1.299	1.312	1.330	1.331	1.336	1.345	1.331	1.350	1.358	1.375	1.374	1.368	1.371	1.380	1.392	1.405	1.405	1.417	1.407	1.425	1.436	1.444
Sept	1.289	1.297	1.297	1.292	1.306	1.323	1.324	1.329	1.338	1.324	1.343	1.352	1.368	1.367	1.361	1.364	1.373	1.385	1.398	1.398	1.410	1.400	1.418	1.429	1.437
Oct	1.278	1.286	1.286	1.281	1.294	1.312	1.313	1.318	1.327	1.313	1.331	1.340	1.357	1.356	1.350	1.353	1.362	1.373	1.387	1.387	1.398	1.389	1.406	1.417	1.425
Nov	1.267	1.275	1.275	1.270	1.283	1.301	1.302	1.307	1.315	1.302	1.320	1.329	1.345	1.344	1.338	1.341	1.350	1.362	1.375	1.375	1.387	1.377	1.395	1.405	1.413
Dec	1.269	1.277	1.277	1.272	1.286	1.303	1.304	1.309	1.318	1.304	1.322	1.331	1.348	1.347	1.341	1.344	1.352	1.364	1.378	1.378	1.389	1.379	1.397	1.408	1.415

Capital gains indexation allowances for companies (April 2011 – April 2013)

Month of acquisition	2011 Apr	May	June	July	Aug	Sept	Oct	Nov	Dec	2012 Jan	Feb	Mar	Apr	May	June	July	Aug	Sept	Oct	Nov	Dec	2013 Jan	Feb	Mar	Apr
1988																									
Jan	1.269	1.277	1.277	1.272	1.286	1.303	1.304	1.309	1.318	1.304	1.322	1.331	1.348	1.347	1.341	1.344	1.352	1.364	1.378	1.378	1.389	1.379	1.397	1.408	1.415
Feb	1.260	1.268	1.268	1.263	1.277	1.294	1.295	1.300	1.309	1.295	1.313	1.322	1.338	1.338	1.332	1.335	1.343	1.355	1.368	1.368	1.380	1.370	1.388	1.398	1.406
Mar	1.252	1.259	1.259	1.255	1.268	1.285	1.286	1.291	1.300	1.286	1.305	1.313	1.329	1.329	1.323	1.326	1.334	1.346	1.359	1.359	1.371	1.361	1.378	1.389	1.397
Apr	1.216	1.223	1.223	1.218	1.232	1.249	1.250	1.254	1.263	1.250	1.267	1.276	1.292	1.291	1.285	1.288	1.297	1.308	1.321	1.321	1.333	1.323	1.340	1.351	1.358
May	1.207	1.215	1.215	1.210	1.223	1.240	1.241	1.246	1.254	1.241	1.259	1.267	1.283	1.282	1.277	1.280	1.288	1.299	1.313	1.313	1.324	1.315	1.331	1.342	1.349
June	1.199	1.206	1.206	1.202	1.215	1.232	1.233	1.237	1.246	1.233	1.250	1.259	1.275	1.274	1.268	1.271	1.280	1.291	1.304	1.304	1.315	1.306	1.323	1.333	1.341
July	1.197	1.204	1.204	1.200	1.213	1.230	1.231	1.235	1.244	1.231	1.248	1.257	1.273	1.272	1.266	1.269	1.277	1.289	1.302	1.302	1.313	1.304	1.321	1.331	1.338
Aug	1.172	1.180	1.180	1.175	1.188	1.205	1.206	1.210	1.219	1.206	1.223	1.232	1.247	1.247	1.241	1.244	1.252	1.263	1.276	1.276	1.287	1.278	1.295	1.305	1.312
Sept	1.162	1.170	1.170	1.165	1.178	1.195	1.196	1.200	1.208	1.196	1.213	1.221	1.237	1.236	1.231	1.233	1.242	1.253	1.266	1.266	1.277	1.268	1.284	1.294	1.302
Oct	1.141	1.148	1.148	1.143	1.156	1.173	1.174	1.178	1.186	1.174	1.191	1.199	1.215	1.214	1.208	1.211	1.219	1.230	1.243	1.243	1.254	1.245	1.261	1.271	1.279
Nov	1.131	1.138	1.138	1.134	1.146	1.163	1.164	1.168	1.176	1.164	1.181	1.189	1.205	1.204	1.198	1.201	1.209	1.220	1.233	1.233	1.244	1.235	1.251	1.261	1.268
Dec	1.125	1.132	1.132	1.128	1.141	1.157	1.158	1.162	1.170	1.158	1.175	1.183	1.199	1.198	1.192	1.195	1.203	1.214	1.227	1.227	1.238	1.228	1.245	1.255	1.262
1989																									
Jan	1.112	1.119	1.119	1.114	1.127	1.143	1.144	1.149	1.157	1.144	1.161	1.169	1.185	1.184	1.178	1.181	1.189	1.200	1.213	1.213	1.223	1.214	1.231	1.241	1.248
Feb	1.097	1.104	1.104	1.099	1.112	1.128	1.129	1.133	1.141	1.129	1.146	1.154	1.169	1.168	1.163	1.165	1.174	1.184	1.197	1.197	1.208	1.199	1.215	1.225	1.232
Mar	1.087	1.094	1.094	1.090	1.102	1.118	1.119	1.124	1.132	1.119	1.136	1.144	1.159	1.159	1.153	1.156	1.164	1.175	1.187	1.187	1.198	1.189	1.205	1.215	1.222
Apr	1.051	1.058	1.058	1.053	1.066	1.081	1.082	1.087	1.094	1.082	1.099	1.107	1.122	1.121	1.115	1.118	1.126	1.136	1.149	1.149	1.159	1.150	1.166	1.176	1.183
May	1.038	1.045	1.045	1.041	1.053	1.069	1.070	1.074	1.082	1.070	1.086	1.094	1.109	1.108	1.103	1.105	1.113	1.123	1.136	1.136	1.146	1.137	1.153	1.163	1.170
June	1.031	1.038	1.038	1.034	1.046	1.062	1.062	1.067	1.075	1.062	1.079	1.087	1.101	1.101	1.095	1.098	1.106	1.116	1.128	1.128	1.139	1.130	1.146	1.155	1.162
July	1.029	1.036	1.036	1.032	1.044	1.060	1.061	1.065	1.073	1.061	1.077	1.085	1.100	1.099	1.094	1.096	1.104	1.114	1.126	1.126	1.137	1.128	1.144	1.153	1.160
Aug	1.024	1.031	1.031	1.027	1.039	1.054	1.055	1.060	1.067	1.055	1.072	1.079	1.094	1.093	1.088	1.091	1.098	1.109	1.121	1.121	1.131	1.123	1.138	1.148	1.155
Sept	1.010	1.017	1.017	1.013	1.025	1.040	1.041	1.045	1.053	1.041	1.057	1.065	1.080	1.079	1.074	1.076	1.084	1.094	1.106	1.106	1.117	1.108	1.123	1.133	1.140
Oct	0.995	1.002	1.002	0.997	1.009	1.025	1.026	1.030	1.037	1.026	1.042	1.049	1.064	1.063	1.058	1.060	1.068	1.078	1.090	1.090	1.100	1.092	1.107	1.117	1.123
Nov	0.978	0.985	0.985	0.981	0.992	1.008	1.008	1.013	1.020	1.008	1.024	1.032	1.046	1.046	1.041	1.043	1.051	1.061	1.073	1.073	1.083	1.074	1.089	1.099	1.105
Dec	0.973	0.980	0.980	0.976	0.987	1.003	1.003	1.008	1.015	1.003	1.019	1.027	1.041	1.040	1.035	1.038	1.045	1.056	1.067	1.067	1.077	1.069	1.084	1.093	1.100
1990																									
Jan	0.962	0.968	0.968	0.964	0.976	0.991	0.992	0.996	1.003	0.992	1.008	1.015	1.029	1.028	1.023	1.026	1.033	1.044	1.055	1.055	1.065	1.057	1.072	1.081	1.088
Feb	0.950	0.957	0.957	0.953	0.964	0.979	0.980	0.984	0.992	0.980	0.996	1.003	1.017	1.017	1.012	1.014	1.022	1.032	1.043	1.043	1.053	1.045	1.060	1.069	1.076
Mar	0.931	0.937	0.937	0.933	0.945	0.960	0.960	0.965	0.972	0.960	0.976	0.984	0.998	0.997	0.992	0.994	1.002	1.012	1.023	1.023	1.033	1.025	1.040	1.049	1.055
Apr	0.874	0.880	0.880	0.876	0.887	0.902	0.902	0.906	0.914	0.902	0.918	0.925	0.938	0.938	0.933	0.935	0.942	0.952	0.963	0.963	0.973	0.965	0.979	0.988	0.994
May	0.857	0.864	0.864	0.860	0.871	0.885	0.886	0.890	0.897	0.886	0.901	0.908	0.922	0.921	0.916	0.918	0.926	0.935	0.946	0.946	0.956	0.948	0.962	0.971	0.977
June	0.850	0.856	0.856	0.852	0.863	0.878	0.878	0.882	0.890	0.878	0.893	0.901	0.914	0.913	0.908	0.911	0.918	0.927	0.938	0.938	0.948	0.940	0.954	0.963	0.969
July	0.849	0.855	0.855	0.851	0.862	0.876	0.877	0.881	0.888	0.877	0.892	0.899	0.912	0.912	0.907	0.909	0.916	0.926	0.937	0.937	0.946	0.938	0.953	0.961	0.968
Aug	0.830	0.836	0.836	0.832	0.843	0.857	0.858	0.862	0.869	0.858	0.873	0.880	0.893	0.892	0.888	0.890	0.897	0.906	0.917	0.917	0.927	0.919	0.933	0.941	0.948
Sept	0.813	0.819	0.819	0.815	0.826	0.840	0.841	0.845	0.852	0.841	0.855	0.862	0.875	0.875	0.870	0.872	0.879	0.889	0.899	0.899	0.909	0.901	0.915	0.923	0.930
Oct	0.799	0.805	0.805	0.801	0.812	0.826	0.827	0.830	0.837	0.827	0.841	0.848	0.861	0.860	0.856	0.858	0.865	0.874	0.885	0.885	0.894	0.886	0.900	0.909	0.915
Nov	0.803	0.809	0.809	0.805	0.816	0.830	0.831	0.835	0.842	0.831	0.845	0.852	0.865	0.865	0.860	0.862	0.869	0.878	0.889	0.889	0.898	0.891	0.905	0.913	0.919
Dec	0.804	0.811	0.811	0.807	0.818	0.831	0.832	0.836	0.843	0.832	0.847	0.854	0.867	0.866	0.861	0.864	0.871	0.880	0.891	0.891	0.900	0.892	0.906	0.915	0.921

Capital gains indexation allowances for companies (April 2011 – April 2013)

Month of acquisition	2011 Apr	May	June	July	Aug	Sept	Oct	Nov	Dec	2012 Jan	Feb	Mar	Apr	May	June	July	Aug	Sept	Oct	Nov	Dec	2013 Jan	Feb	Mar	Apr
1991																									
Jan	0.800	0.806	0.806	0.803	0.813	0.827	0.828	0.832	0.839	0.828	0.843	0.849	0.863	0.862	0.857	0.859	0.866	0.876	0.886	0.886	0.896	0.888	0.902	0.910	0.916
Feb	0.791	0.797	0.797	0.793	0.804	0.817	0.818	0.822	0.829	0.818	0.833	0.840	0.853	0.852	0.847	0.850	0.856	0.866	0.876	0.876	0.885	0.878	0.892	0.900	0.906
Mar	0.784	0.790	0.790	0.786	0.797	0.811	0.811	0.815	0.822	0.811	0.826	0.833	0.846	0.845	0.840	0.842	0.849	0.858	0.869	0.869	0.878	0.871	0.884	0.893	0.899
Apr	0.761	0.767	0.767	0.763	0.774	0.787	0.788	0.792	0.799	0.788	0.802	0.809	0.822	0.821	0.817	0.819	0.826	0.835	0.845	0.845	0.854	0.847	0.860	0.869	0.875
May	0.756	0.762	0.762	0.758	0.769	0.782	0.783	0.787	0.793	0.783	0.797	0.804	0.816	0.816	0.811	0.813	0.820	0.829	0.840	0.840	0.849	0.841	0.855	0.863	0.869
June	0.748	0.754	0.754	0.750	0.761	0.774	0.775	0.779	0.785	0.775	0.789	0.796	0.808	0.808	0.803	0.805	0.812	0.821	0.831	0.831	0.840	0.833	0.846	0.855	0.861
July	0.752	0.758	0.758	0.754	0.765	0.778	0.779	0.783	0.789	0.779	0.793	0.800	0.812	0.812	0.807	0.809	0.816	0.825	0.836	0.836	0.845	0.837	0.851	0.859	0.865
Aug	0.748	0.754	0.754	0.750	0.761	0.774	0.775	0.779	0.785	0.775	0.789	0.796	0.808	0.808	0.803	0.805	0.812	0.821	0.831	0.831	0.840	0.833	0.846	0.855	0.861
Sept	0.741	0.747	0.747	0.744	0.754	0.767	0.768	0.772	0.779	0.768	0.782	0.789	0.802	0.801	0.796	0.799	0.805	0.814	0.825	0.825	0.834	0.826	0.840	0.848	0.854
Oct	0.735	0.741	0.741	0.737	0.748	0.761	0.762	0.765	0.772	0.762	0.776	0.782	0.795	0.794	0.790	0.792	0.799	0.808	0.818	0.818	0.827	0.819	0.833	0.841	0.847
Nov	0.729	0.735	0.735	0.731	0.741	0.754	0.755	0.759	0.765	0.755	0.769	0.776	0.788	0.788	0.783	0.785	0.792	0.801	0.811	0.811	0.820	0.813	0.826	0.834	0.840
Dec	0.727	0.733	0.733	0.730	0.740	0.753	0.754	0.758	0.764	0.754	0.768	0.775	0.787	0.786	0.782	0.784	0.791	0.800	0.810	0.810	0.819	0.811	0.825	0.833	0.839
1992																									
Jan	0.729	0.735	0.735	0.731	0.741	0.754	0.755	0.759	0.765	0.755	0.769	0.776	0.788	0.788	0.783	0.785	0.792	0.801	0.811	0.811	0.820	0.813	0.826	0.834	0.840
Feb	0.720	0.726	0.726	0.722	0.732	0.745	0.746	0.750	0.756	0.746	0.760	0.767	0.779	0.778	0.774	0.776	0.783	0.792	0.802	0.802	0.811	0.803	0.817	0.825	0.831
Mar	0.715	0.721	0.721	0.717	0.727	0.740	0.741	0.745	0.751	0.741	0.755	0.762	0.774	0.773	0.769	0.771	0.778	0.786	0.797	0.797	0.805	0.798	0.811	0.819	0.825
Apr	0.689	0.695	0.695	0.691	0.701	0.714	0.715	0.718	0.725	0.715	0.728	0.735	0.747	0.746	0.742	0.744	0.751	0.759	0.769	0.769	0.778	0.771	0.784	0.792	0.798
May	0.683	0.688	0.688	0.685	0.695	0.708	0.709	0.712	0.719	0.709	0.722	0.729	0.741	0.740	0.736	0.738	0.744	0.753	0.763	0.763	0.772	0.765	0.777	0.785	0.791
June	0.683	0.688	0.688	0.685	0.695	0.708	0.709	0.712	0.719	0.709	0.722	0.729	0.741	0.740	0.736	0.738	0.744	0.753	0.763	0.763	0.772	0.765	0.777	0.785	0.791
July	0.689	0.695	0.695	0.691	0.701	0.714	0.715	0.718	0.725	0.715	0.728	0.735	0.747	0.746	0.742	0.744	0.751	0.759	0.769	0.769	0.778	0.771	0.784	0.792	0.798
Aug	0.688	0.693	0.693	0.690	0.700	0.713	0.713	0.717	0.724	0.713	0.727	0.734	0.746	0.745	0.741	0.743	0.749	0.758	0.768	0.768	0.777	0.770	0.783	0.790	0.796
Sept	0.681	0.687	0.687	0.684	0.694	0.707	0.707	0.711	0.717	0.707	0.721	0.727	0.740	0.739	0.735	0.737	0.743	0.752	0.762	0.762	0.770	0.763	0.776	0.784	0.790
Oct	0.675	0.681	0.681	0.678	0.688	0.701	0.701	0.705	0.711	0.701	0.715	0.721	0.733	0.733	0.728	0.731	0.737	0.746	0.756	0.756	0.764	0.757	0.770	0.778	0.783
Nov	0.678	0.684	0.684	0.680	0.690	0.703	0.704	0.707	0.714	0.704	0.717	0.724	0.736	0.735	0.731	0.733	0.739	0.748	0.758	0.758	0.767	0.759	0.772	0.780	0.786
Dec	0.684	0.690	0.690	0.686	0.696	0.709	0.710	0.713	0.720	0.710	0.723	0.730	0.742	0.741	0.737	0.739	0.746	0.754	0.764	0.764	0.773	0.766	0.779	0.787	0.792
1993																									
Jan	0.700	0.706	0.706	0.702	0.712	0.725	0.726	0.730	0.736	0.726	0.740	0.746	0.759	0.758	0.753	0.756	0.762	0.771	0.781	0.781	0.790	0.782	0.796	0.803	0.809
Feb	0.689	0.695	0.695	0.691	0.701	0.714	0.715	0.718	0.725	0.715	0.728	0.735	0.747	0.746	0.742	0.744	0.751	0.759	0.769	0.769	0.778	0.771	0.784	0.792	0.798
Mar	0.683	0.688	0.688	0.685	0.695	0.708	0.709	0.712	0.719	0.709	0.722	0.729	0.741	0.740	0.736	0.738	0.744	0.753	0.763	0.763	0.772	0.765	0.777	0.785	0.791
Apr	0.667	0.673	0.673	0.669	0.679	0.692	0.693	0.696	0.703	0.693	0.706	0.713	0.725	0.724	0.720	0.722	0.728	0.737	0.747	0.747	0.755	0.748	0.761	0.769	0.775
May	0.661	0.667	0.667	0.663	0.673	0.686	0.687	0.690	0.697	0.687	0.700	0.707	0.719	0.718	0.714	0.716	0.722	0.731	0.741	0.741	0.749	0.742	0.755	0.763	0.768
June	0.662	0.668	0.668	0.665	0.674	0.687	0.688	0.691	0.698	0.688	0.701	0.708	0.720	0.719	0.715	0.717	0.723	0.732	0.742	0.742	0.750	0.743	0.756	0.764	0.770
July	0.666	0.672	0.672	0.668	0.678	0.691	0.692	0.695	0.701	0.692	0.705	0.711	0.724	0.723	0.719	0.721	0.727	0.736	0.746	0.746	0.754	0.747	0.760	0.768	0.773
Aug	0.659	0.665	0.665	0.661	0.671	0.684	0.684	0.688	0.694	0.684	0.698	0.704	0.716	0.715	0.711	0.713	0.720	0.728	0.738	0.738	0.747	0.740	0.752	0.760	0.766
Sept	0.652	0.658	0.658	0.654	0.664	0.677	0.677	0.681	0.687	0.677	0.691	0.697	0.709	0.708	0.704	0.706	0.712	0.721	0.731	0.731	0.739	0.732	0.745	0.753	0.758
Oct	0.653	0.659	0.659	0.655	0.665	0.678	0.678	0.682	0.688	0.678	0.692	0.698	0.710	0.709	0.705	0.707	0.714	0.722	0.732	0.732	0.740	0.733	0.746	0.754	0.760
Nov	0.655	0.661	0.661	0.657	0.667	0.680	0.681	0.684	0.691	0.681	0.694	0.701	0.713	0.712	0.708	0.710	0.716	0.725	0.734	0.734	0.743	0.736	0.749	0.756	0.762
Dec	0.652	0.658	0.658	0.654	0.664	0.677	0.677	0.681	0.687	0.677	0.691	0.697	0.709	0.708	0.704	0.706	0.712	0.721	0.731	0.731	0.739	0.732	0.745	0.753	0.758

Capital gains indexation allowances for companies (April 2011 – April 2013)

Month of acquisition	2011 Apr	May	June	July	Aug	Sept	Oct	Nov	Dec	2012 Jan	Feb	Mar	Apr	May	June	July	Aug	Sept	Oct	Nov	Dec	2013 Jan	Feb	Mar	Apr
1994																									
Jan	0.659	0.665	0.665	0.661	0.671	0.684	0.684	0.688	0.694	0.684	0.698	0.704	0.716	0.715	0.711	0.713	0.720	0.728	0.738	0.738	0.747	0.740	0.752	0.760	0.766
Feb	0.650	0.655	0.655	0.652	0.662	0.674	0.675	0.678	0.685	0.675	0.688	0.695	0.707	0.706	0.702	0.704	0.710	0.719	0.728	0.728	0.737	0.730	0.742	0.750	0.756
Mar	0.645	0.651	0.651	0.647	0.657	0.669	0.670	0.674	0.680	0.670	0.684	0.690	0.702	0.701	0.697	0.699	0.705	0.714	0.724	0.724	0.732	0.725	0.738	0.745	0.751
Apr	0.626	0.631	0.631	0.628	0.637	0.650	0.650	0.654	0.660	0.650	0.664	0.670	0.682	0.681	0.677	0.679	0.685	0.693	0.703	0.703	0.712	0.705	0.717	0.725	0.730
May	0.620	0.625	0.625	0.622	0.632	0.644	0.645	0.648	0.654	0.645	0.658	0.664	0.676	0.675	0.671	0.673	0.679	0.688	0.697	0.697	0.706	0.699	0.711	0.719	0.724
June	0.620	0.625	0.625	0.622	0.632	0.644	0.645	0.648	0.654	0.645	0.658	0.664	0.676	0.675	0.671	0.673	0.679	0.688	0.697	0.697	0.706	0.699	0.711	0.719	0.724
July	0.628	0.633	0.633	0.630	0.640	0.652	0.653	0.656	0.663	0.653	0.666	0.672	0.684	0.683	0.679	0.681	0.688	0.696	0.706	0.706	0.714	0.707	0.719	0.727	0.733
Aug	0.620	0.625	0.625	0.622	0.632	0.644	0.645	0.648	0.654	0.645	0.658	0.664	0.676	0.675	0.671	0.673	0.679	0.688	0.697	0.697	0.706	0.699	0.711	0.719	0.724
Sept	0.617	0.622	0.622	0.619	0.628	0.641	0.641	0.645	0.651	0.641	0.654	0.661	0.672	0.672	0.668	0.670	0.676	0.684	0.694	0.694	0.702	0.695	0.708	0.715	0.721
Oct	0.614	0.620	0.620	0.616	0.626	0.638	0.639	0.643	0.649	0.639	0.652	0.658	0.670	0.669	0.665	0.667	0.674	0.682	0.691	0.691	0.700	0.693	0.705	0.713	0.718
Nov	0.613	0.619	0.619	0.615	0.625	0.637	0.638	0.641	0.648	0.638	0.651	0.657	0.669	0.668	0.664	0.666	0.672	0.681	0.690	0.690	0.699	0.692	0.704	0.712	0.717
Dec	0.605	0.611	0.611	0.608	0.617	0.629	0.630	0.634	0.640	0.630	0.643	0.649	0.661	0.660	0.656	0.658	0.664	0.673	0.682	0.682	0.690	0.684	0.696	0.703	0.709
1995																									
Jan	0.605	0.611	0.611	0.608	0.617	0.629	0.630	0.634	0.640	0.630	0.643	0.649	0.661	0.660	0.656	0.658	0.664	0.673	0.682	0.682	0.690	0.684	0.696	0.703	0.709
Feb	0.596	0.601	0.601	0.598	0.607	0.619	0.620	0.624	0.630	0.620	0.633	0.639	0.651	0.650	0.646	0.648	0.654	0.662	0.672	0.672	0.680	0.673	0.686	0.693	0.698
Mar	0.589	0.595	0.595	0.591	0.601	0.613	0.614	0.617	0.623	0.614	0.626	0.633	0.644	0.643	0.639	0.641	0.647	0.656	0.665	0.665	0.673	0.666	0.679	0.686	0.692
Apr	0.573	0.579	0.579	0.575	0.585	0.597	0.597	0.601	0.607	0.597	0.610	0.616	0.628	0.627	0.623	0.625	0.631	0.639	0.648	0.648	0.656	0.650	0.662	0.669	0.674
May	0.567	0.572	0.572	0.569	0.578	0.590	0.591	0.594	0.600	0.591	0.604	0.610	0.621	0.620	0.616	0.618	0.624	0.632	0.642	0.642	0.650	0.643	0.655	0.662	0.668
June	0.565	0.570	0.570	0.567	0.576	0.588	0.589	0.592	0.598	0.589	0.601	0.607	0.619	0.618	0.614	0.616	0.622	0.630	0.640	0.640	0.648	0.641	0.653	0.660	0.666
July	0.572	0.577	0.577	0.574	0.584	0.596	0.596	0.600	0.606	0.596	0.609	0.615	0.626	0.626	0.622	0.624	0.630	0.638	0.647	0.647	0.655	0.649	0.661	0.668	0.673
Aug	0.564	0.569	0.569	0.566	0.575	0.587	0.588	0.591	0.597	0.588	0.600	0.606	0.618	0.617	0.613	0.615	0.621	0.629	0.638	0.638	0.646	0.640	0.652	0.659	0.664
Sept	0.556	0.562	0.562	0.558	0.568	0.580	0.580	0.584	0.590	0.580	0.593	0.599	0.610	0.610	0.606	0.608	0.614	0.622	0.631	0.631	0.639	0.632	0.644	0.651	0.657
Oct	0.565	0.570	0.570	0.567	0.576	0.588	0.589	0.592	0.598	0.589	0.601	0.607	0.619	0.618	0.614	0.616	0.622	0.630	0.640	0.640	0.648	0.641	0.653	0.660	0.666
Nov	0.565	0.570	0.570	0.567	0.576	0.588	0.589	0.592	0.598	0.589	0.601	0.607	0.619	0.618	0.614	0.616	0.622	0.630	0.640	0.640	0.648	0.641	0.653	0.660	0.666
Dec	0.555	0.561	0.561	0.557	0.567	0.579	0.579	0.583	0.589	0.579	0.592	0.598	0.609	0.608	0.605	0.607	0.612	0.620	0.630	0.630	0.638	0.631	0.643	0.650	0.656
1996																									
Jan	0.561	0.566	0.566	0.563	0.572	0.584	0.585	0.588	0.594	0.585	0.597	0.603	0.615	0.614	0.610	0.612	0.618	0.626	0.635	0.635	0.643	0.636	0.648	0.656	0.661
Feb	0.553	0.559	0.559	0.555	0.565	0.577	0.577	0.581	0.586	0.577	0.590	0.596	0.607	0.606	0.602	0.604	0.610	0.618	0.628	0.628	0.636	0.629	0.641	0.648	0.653
Mar	0.547	0.552	0.552	0.549	0.558	0.570	0.571	0.574	0.580	0.571	0.583	0.589	0.601	0.600	0.596	0.598	0.604	0.612	0.621	0.621	0.629	0.622	0.634	0.642	0.647
Apr	0.536	0.541	0.541	0.538	0.547	0.559	0.560	0.563	0.569	0.560	0.572	0.578	0.589	0.588	0.585	0.587	0.592	0.600	0.609	0.609	0.617	0.611	0.623	0.630	0.635
May	0.533	0.538	0.538	0.535	0.544	0.556	0.557	0.560	0.566	0.557	0.569	0.575	0.586	0.585	0.581	0.583	0.589	0.597	0.606	0.606	0.614	0.608	0.619	0.627	0.632
June	0.532	0.537	0.537	0.534	0.543	0.555	0.556	0.559	0.565	0.556	0.568	0.574	0.585	0.584	0.580	0.582	0.588	0.596	0.605	0.605	0.613	0.607	0.618	0.625	0.631
July	0.538	0.543	0.543	0.540	0.549	0.561	0.562	0.565	0.571	0.562	0.574	0.580	0.591	0.591	0.587	0.589	0.594	0.602	0.612	0.612	0.619	0.613	0.625	0.632	0.637
Aug	0.531	0.536	0.536	0.533	0.542	0.554	0.555	0.558	0.564	0.555	0.567	0.573	0.584	0.583	0.579	0.581	0.587	0.595	0.604	0.604	0.612	0.605	0.617	0.624	0.630
Sept	0.524	0.529	0.529	0.526	0.535	0.547	0.547	0.551	0.557	0.547	0.560	0.566	0.577	0.576	0.572	0.574	0.580	0.588	0.597	0.597	0.605	0.598	0.610	0.617	0.622
Oct	0.524	0.529	0.529	0.526	0.535	0.547	0.547	0.551	0.557	0.547	0.560	0.566	0.577	0.576	0.572	0.574	0.580	0.588	0.597	0.597	0.605	0.598	0.610	0.617	0.622
Nov	0.523	0.528	0.528	0.525	0.534	0.546	0.546	0.550	0.556	0.546	0.559	0.565	0.576	0.575	0.571	0.573	0.579	0.587	0.596	0.596	0.604	0.597	0.609	0.616	0.621
Dec	0.518	0.523	0.523	0.520	0.529	0.541	0.541	0.545	0.551	0.541	0.554	0.560	0.571	0.570	0.566	0.568	0.574	0.582	0.591	0.591	0.598	0.592	0.604	0.611	0.616

Capital gains indexation allowances for companies (April 2011 – April 2013)

Month of acquisition	2011 Apr	May	June	July	Aug	Sept	Oct	Nov	Dec	2012 Jan	Feb	Mar	Apr	May	June	July	Aug	Sept	Oct	Nov	Dec	2013 Jan	Feb	Mar	Apr
1997																									
Jan	0.518	0.523	0.523	0.520	0.529	0.541	0.541	0.545	0.551	0.541	0.554	0.560	0.571	0.570	0.566	0.568	0.574	0.582	0.591	0.591	0.598	0.592	0.604	0.611	0.616
Feb	0.512	0.517	0.517	0.514	0.523	0.535	0.535	0.539	0.545	0.535	0.548	0.554	0.565	0.564	0.560	0.562	0.568	0.575	0.585	0.585	0.592	0.586	0.597	0.605	0.610
Mar	0.508	0.514	0.514	0.510	0.519	0.531	0.532	0.535	0.541	0.532	0.544	0.550	0.560	0.560	0.556	0.558	0.564	0.571	0.580	0.580	0.588	0.582	0.593	0.600	0.606
Apr	0.500	0.505	0.505	0.502	0.511	0.522	0.523	0.526	0.532	0.523	0.535	0.541	0.552	0.551	0.547	0.549	0.555	0.562	0.571	0.571	0.579	0.573	0.584	0.591	0.596
May	0.494	0.499	0.499	0.496	0.505	0.516	0.517	0.520	0.526	0.517	0.529	0.535	0.546	0.545	0.541	0.543	0.549	0.556	0.565	0.565	0.573	0.567	0.578	0.585	0.590
June	0.488	0.493	0.493	0.490	0.499	0.510	0.511	0.514	0.520	0.511	0.523	0.529	0.540	0.539	0.535	0.537	0.543	0.550	0.559	0.559	0.567	0.561	0.572	0.579	0.584
July	0.488	0.493	0.493	0.490	0.499	0.510	0.511	0.514	0.520	0.511	0.523	0.529	0.540	0.539	0.535	0.537	0.543	0.550	0.559	0.559	0.567	0.561	0.572	0.579	0.584
Aug	0.479	0.484	0.484	0.481	0.490	0.501	0.502	0.505	0.510	0.502	0.514	0.519	0.530	0.529	0.526	0.527	0.533	0.541	0.550	0.550	0.557	0.551	0.562	0.569	0.574
Sept	0.471	0.476	0.476	0.473	0.482	0.493	0.494	0.497	0.503	0.494	0.506	0.512	0.522	0.522	0.518	0.520	0.525	0.533	0.542	0.542	0.549	0.543	0.554	0.561	0.566
Oct	0.470	0.475	0.475	0.471	0.480	0.492	0.492	0.495	0.501	0.492	0.504	0.510	0.520	0.520	0.516	0.518	0.524	0.531	0.540	0.540	0.547	0.541	0.552	0.559	0.564
Nov	0.469	0.474	0.474	0.471	0.479	0.491	0.491	0.494	0.500	0.491	0.503	0.509	0.519	0.519	0.515	0.517	0.523	0.530	0.539	0.539	0.546	0.540	0.551	0.558	0.563
Dec	0.465	0.470	0.470	0.467	0.476	0.487	0.488	0.491	0.496	0.488	0.499	0.505	0.516	0.515	0.511	0.513	0.519	0.526	0.535	0.535	0.543	0.536	0.548	0.554	0.559
1998																									
Jan	0.470	0.475	0.475	0.471	0.480	0.492	0.492	0.495	0.501	0.492	0.504	0.510	0.520	0.520	0.516	0.518	0.524	0.531	0.540	0.540	0.547	0.541	0.552	0.559	0.564
Feb	0.462	0.467	0.467	0.464	0.473	0.484	0.485	0.488	0.493	0.485	0.497	0.502	0.513	0.512	0.508	0.510	0.516	0.523	0.532	0.532	0.540	0.533	0.545	0.551	0.556
Mar	0.458	0.463	0.463	0.460	0.468	0.479	0.480	0.483	0.489	0.480	0.492	0.498	0.508	0.507	0.504	0.506	0.511	0.519	0.527	0.527	0.535	0.529	0.540	0.547	0.552
Apr	0.442	0.446	0.446	0.443	0.452	0.463	0.464	0.467	0.472	0.464	0.475	0.481	0.491	0.491	0.487	0.489	0.494	0.502	0.510	0.510	0.518	0.512	0.523	0.530	0.534
May	0.434	0.439	0.439	0.435	0.444	0.455	0.456	0.459	0.464	0.456	0.467	0.473	0.483	0.483	0.479	0.481	0.486	0.494	0.502	0.502	0.509	0.503	0.514	0.521	0.526
June	0.435	0.439	0.439	0.436	0.445	0.456	0.457	0.460	0.465	0.457	0.468	1.474	0.484	0.483	0.480	0.482	0.487	0.494	0.503	0.503	0.510	0.504	0.515	0.522	0.527
July	0.438	0.443	0.443	0.440	0.448	0.460	0.460	0.463	0.469	0.460	0.472	0.477	0.488	0.487	0.483	0.485	0.491	0.498	0.507	0.507	0.514	0.508	0.519	0.526	0.531
Aug	0.432	0.437	0.437	0.434	0.442	0.453	0.454	0.457	0.462	0.454	0.465	0.471	0.481	0.481	0.477	0.479	0.484	0.492	0.500	0.500	0.508	0.502	0.513	0.519	0.524
Sept	0.426	0.431	0.431	0.428	0.436	0.447	0.448	0.451	0.456	0.448	0.459	0.465	0.475	0.474	0.471	0.473	0.478	0.485	0.494	0.494	0.501	0.495	0.506	0.513	0.518
Oct	0.425	0.430	0.430	0.427	0.435	0.446	0.447	0.450	0.455	0.447	0.458	0.464	0.474	0.474	0.470	0.472	0.477	0.484	0.493	0.493	0.500	0.494	0.505	0.512	0.517
Nov	0.426	0.431	0.431	0.428	0.436	0.447	0.448	0.451	0.456	0.448	0.459	0.465	0.475	0.474	0.471	0.473	0.478	0.485	0.494	0.494	0.501	0.495	0.506	0.513	0.518
Dec	0.426	0.431	0.431	0.428	0.436	0.447	0.448	0.451	0.456	0.448	0.459	0.465	0.475	0.474	0.471	0.473	0.478	0.485	0.494	0.494	0.501	0.495	0.506	0.513	0.518
1999																									
Jan	0.435	0.439	0.439	0.436	0.445	0.456	0.457	0.460	0.465	0.457	0.468	0.474	0.484	0.483	0.480	0.482	0.487	0.494	0.503	0.503	0.510	0.504	0.515	0.522	0.527
Feb	0.432	0.437	0.437	0.434	0.442	0.453	0.454	0.457	0.462	0.454	0.465	0.471	0.481	0.481	0.477	0.479	0.484	0.492	0.500	0.500	0.508	0.502	0.513	0.519	0.524
Mar	0.428	0.433	0.433	0.430	0.439	0.450	0.450	0.453	0.459	0.450	0.462	0.467	0.478	0.477	0.473	0.475	0.481	0.488	0.497	0.497	0.504	0.498	0.509	0.516	0.520
Apr	0.419	0.424	0.424	0.421	0.429	0.440	0.441	0.444	0.449	0.441	0.452	0.458	0.468	0.467	0.464	0.465	0.471	0.478	0.487	0.487	0.494	0.488	0.499	0.505	0.510
May	0.415	0.420	0.420	0.417	0.426	0.437	0.437	0.440	0.446	0.437	0.449	0.454	0.464	0.464	0.460	0.462	0.467	0.475	0.483	0.483	0.490	0.484	0.495	0.502	0.507
June	0.415	0.420	0.420	0.417	0.426	0.437	0.437	0.440	0.446	0.437	0.449	0.454	0.464	0.464	0.460	0.462	0.467	0.475	0.483	0.483	0.490	0.484	0.495	0.502	0.507
July	0.420	0.425	0.425	0.422	0.430	0.441	0.442	0.445	0.450	0.442	0.453	0.459	0.469	0.468	0.465	0.466	0.472	0.479	0.488	0.488	0.495	0.489	0.500	0.506	0.511
Aug	0.416	0.421	0.421	0.418	0.427	0.437	0.438	0.441	0.447	0.438	0.450	0.455	0.465	0.465	0.461	0.463	0.468	0.476	0.484	0.484	0.491	0.485	0.496	0.503	0.508
Sept	0.410	0.415	0.415	0.412	0.421	0.431	0.432	0.435	0.440	0.432	0.443	0.449	0.459	0.458	0.455	0.457	0.462	0.469	0.478	0.478	0.485	0.479	0.490	0.496	0.501
Oct	0.408	0.413	0.413	0.410	0.418	0.429	0.429	0.432	0.438	0.429	0.441	0.446	0.456	0.456	0.452	0.454	0.459	0.467	0.475	0.475	0.482	0.476	0.487	0.494	0.498
Nov	0.406	0.411	0.411	0.408	0.416	0.427	0.428	0.431	0.436	0.428	0.439	0.445	0.455	0.454	0.451	0.452	0.458	0.465	0.473	0.473	0.481	0.475	0.485	0.492	0.497
Dec	0.401	0.406	0.406	0.403	0.411	0.422	0.423	0.426	0.431	0.423	0.434	0.439	0.449	0.449	0.445	0.447	0.452	0.460	0.468	0.468	0.475	0.469	0.480	0.487	0.491

Capital gains indexation allowances for companies (April 2011 – April 2013)

Month of acquisition	2011 Apr	May	June	July	Aug	Sept	Oct	Nov	Dec	2012 Jan	Feb	Mar	Apr	May	June	July	Aug	Sept	Oct	Nov	Dec	2013 Jan	Feb	Mar	Apr
2000																									
Jan	0.407	0.412	0.412	0.409	0.417	0.428	0.429	0.432	0.437	0.429	0.440	0.445	0.456	0.455	0.451	0.453	0.459	0.466	0.474	0.474	0.481	0.475	0.486	0.493	0.498
Feb	0.399	0.404	0.404	0.401	0.410	0.420	0.421	0.424	0.429	0.421	0.432	0.438	0.448	0.447	0.444	0.445	0.451	0.458	0.466	0.466	0.473	0.467	0.478	0.485	0.490
Mar	0.392	0.397	0.397	0.394	0.402	0.413	0.413	0.416	0.422	0.413	0.425	0.430	0.440	0.439	0.436	0.438	0.443	0.450	0.458	0.458	0.466	0.460	0.470	0.477	0.482
Apr	0.378	0.383	0.383	0.380	0.388	0.399	0.399	0.402	0.407	0.399	0.410	0.416	0.426	0.425	0.422	0.423	0.429	0.436	0.444	0.444	0.451	0.445	0.456	0.462	0.467
May	0.373	0.378	0.378	0.375	0.383	0.394	0.394	0.397	0.402	0.394	0.405	0.411	0.421	0.420	0.417	0.418	0.424	0.431	0.439	0.439	0.446	0.440	0.450	0.457	0.462
June	0.370	0.375	0.375	0.372	0.380	0.390	0.391	0.394	0.399	0.391	0.402	0.407	0.417	0.417	0.413	0.415	0.420	0.427	0.435	0.435	0.442	0.437	0.447	0.454	0.458
July	0.375	0.379	0.379	0.377	0.385	0.395	0.396	0.399	0.404	0.396	0.407	0.412	0.422	0.422	0.418	0.420	0.425	0.432	0.440	0.440	0.448	0.442	0.452	0.459	0.463
Aug	0.375	0.379	0.379	0.377	0.385	0.395	0.396	0.399	0.404	0.396	0.407	0.412	0.422	0.422	0.418	0.420	0.425	0.432	0.440	0.440	0.448	0.442	0.452	0.459	0.463
Sept	0.365	0.370	0.370	0.367	0.375	0.386	0.386	0.389	0.394	0.386	0.397	0.402	0.412	0.412	0.408	0.410	0.415	0.422	0.430	0.430	0.437	0.432	0.442	0.448	0.453
Oct	0.366	0.371	0.371	0.368	0.376	0.386	0.387	0.390	0.395	0.387	0.398	0.403	0.413	0.413	0.409	0.411	0.416	0.423	0.431	0.431	0.438	0.432	0.443	0.449	0.454
Nov	0.362	0.367	0.367	0.364	0.372	0.382	0.383	0.386	0.391	0.383	0.394	0.399	0.409	0.408	0.405	0.407	0.412	0.419	0.427	0.427	0.434	0.428	0.439	0.445	0.450
Dec	0.361	0.366	0.366	0.363	0.371	0.382	0.382	0.385	0.390	0.382	0.393	0.398	0.408	0.408	0.404	0.406	0.411	0.418	0.426	0.426	0.433	0.427	0.438	0.444	0.449
2001																									
Jan	0.370	0.375	0.375	0.372	0.380	0.390	0.391	0.394	0.399	0.391	0.402	0.407	0.417	0.417	0.413	0.415	0.420	0.427	0.435	0.435	0.442	0.437	0.447	0.454	0.458
Feb	0.363	0.367	0.367	0.365	0.373	0.383	0.384	0.387	0.392	0.384	0.395	0.400	0.410	0.409	0.406	0.408	0.413	0.420	0.428	0.428	0.435	0.429	0.440	0.446	0.451
Mar	0.361	0.366	0.366	0.363	0.371	0.382	0.382	0.385	0.390	0.382	0.393	0.398	0.408	0.408	0.404	0.406	0.411	0.418	0.426	0.426	0.433	0.427	0.438	0.444	0.449
Apr	0.354	0.359	0.359	0.356	0.364	0.374	0.375	0.378	0.383	0.375	0.386	0.391	0.401	0.400	0.397	0.399	0.404	0.411	0.419	0.419	0.426	0.420	0.430	0.437	0.441
May	0.346	0.350	0.350	0.347	0.355	0.366	0.366	0.369	0.374	0.366	0.377	0.382	0.392	0.392	0.388	0.390	0.395	0.402	0.410	0.410	0.417	0.411	0.421	0.428	0.432
June	0.344	0.349	0.349	0.346	0.354	0.364	0.365	0.368	0.373	0.365	0.376	0.381	0.390	0.390	0.386	0.388	0.393	0.400	0.408	0.408	0.415	0.409	0.420	0.426	0.431
July	0.353	0.357	0.357	0.354	0.362	0.373	0.373	0.376	0.381	0.373	0.384	0.389	0.399	0.399	0.395	0.397	0.402	0.409	0.417	0.417	0.424	0.418	0.429	0.435	0.440
Aug	0.347	0.352	0.352	0.349	0.357	0.367	0.368	0.371	0.376	0.368	0.379	0.384	0.394	0.393	0.390	0.391	0.397	0.403	0.411	0.411	0.418	0.413	0.423	0.429	0.434
Sept	0.342	0.347	0.347	0.344	0.352	0.363	0.363	0.366	0.371	0.363	0.374	0.379	0.389	0.388	0.385	0.387	0.392	0.399	0.407	0.407	0.414	0.408	0.418	0.424	0.429
Oct	0.345	0.349	0.349	0.347	0.355	0.365	0.365	0.368	0.373	0.365	0.376	0.382	0.391	0.391	0.387	0.389	0.394	0.401	0.409	0.409	0.416	0.410	0.421	0.427	0.431
Nov	0.350	0.355	0.355	0.352	0.360	0.370	0.371	0.374	0.379	0.371	0.382	0.387	0.397	0.396	0.393	0.395	0.400	0.407	0.415	0.415	0.422	0.416	0.426	0.433	0.437
Dec	0.352	0.356	0.356	0.354	0.362	0.372	0.373	0.375	0.381	0.373	0.384	0.389	0.399	0.398	0.394	0.396	0.401	0.408	0.416	0.416	0.423	0.418	0.428	0.434	0.439
2002																									
Jan	0.353	0.357	0.357	0.354	0.362	0.373	0.373	0.376	0.381	0.373	0.384	0.389	0.399	0.399	0.395	0.397	0.402	0.409	0.417	0.417	0.424	0.418	0.429	0.435	0.440
Feb	0.349	0.353	0.353	0.350	0.358	0.369	0.369	0.372	0.377	0.369	0.380	0.386	0.395	0.395	0.391	0.393	0.398	0.405	0.413	0.413	0.420	0.414	0.425	0.431	0.436
Mar	0.343	0.348	0.348	0.345	0.353	0.363	0.364	0.367	0.372	0.364	0.375	0.380	0.390	0.389	0.386	0.387	0.393	0.399	0.407	0.407	0.414	0.409	0.419	0.425	0.430
Apr	0.334	0.339	0.339	0.336	0.344	0.354	0.355	0.357	0.363	0.355	0.365	0.371	0.380	0.380	0.376	0.378	0.383	0.390	0.398	0.398	0.405	0.399	0.409	0.415	0.420
May	0.330	0.335	0.335	0.332	0.340	0.350	0.351	0.354	0.359	0.351	0.362	0.367	0.376	0.376	0.372	0.374	0.379	0.386	0.394	0.394	0.401	0.395	0.405	0.411	0.416
June	0.330	0.335	0.335	0.332	0.340	0.350	0.351	0.354	0.359	0.351	0.362	0.367	0.376	0.376	0.372	0.374	0.379	0.386	0.394	0.394	0.401	0.395	0.405	0.411	0.416
July	0.333	0.337	0.337	0.334	0.342	0.352	0.353	0.356	0.361	0.353	0.364	0.369	0.379	0.378	0.375	0.376	0.381	0.388	0.396	0.396	0.403	0.397	0.408	0.414	0.418
Aug	0.329	0.333	0.333	0.330	0.338	0.349	0.349	0.352	0.357	0.349	0.360	0.365	0.375	0.374	0.371	0.372	0.378	0.384	0.392	0.392	0.399	0.393	0.404	0.410	0.414
Sept	0.320	0.324	0.324	0.322	0.329	0.340	0.340	0.343	0.348	0.340	0.351	0.356	0.365	0.365	0.361	0.363	0.368	0.375	0.383	0.383	0.390	0.384	0.394	0.400	0.405
Oct	0.318	0.322	0.322	0.319	0.327	0.337	0.338	0.341	0.346	0.338	0.349	0.354	0.363	0.363	0.359	0.361	0.366	0.373	0.381	0.381	0.387	0.382	0.392	0.398	0.402
Nov	0.315	0.320	0.320	0.317	0.325	0.335	0.336	0.338	0.343	0.336	0.346	0.351	0.361	0.360	0.357	0.359	0.364	0.370	0.371	0.371	0.385	0.379	0.389	0.396	0.400
Dec	0.313	0.318	0.318	0.315	0.323	0.333	0.333	0.336	0.341	0.333	0.344	0.349	0.359	0.358	0.355	0.356	0.361	0.368	0.376	0.376	0.383	0.377	0.387	0.393	0.398

Capital gains indexation allowances for companies (April 2011 – April 2013)

Month of acquisition	2011 Apr	May	June	July	Aug	Sept	Oct	Nov	Dec	2012 Jan	Feb	Mar	Apr	May	June	July	Aug	Sept	Oct	Nov	Dec	2013 Jan	Feb	Mar	Apr
2003																									
Jan	0.314	0.318	0.318	0.316	0.323	0.334	0.334	0.337	0.342	0.334	0.345	0.350	0.359	0.359	0.355	0.357	0.362	0.369	0.377	0.377	0.383	0.378	0.388	0.394	0.399
Feb	0.307	0.312	0.312	0.309	0.317	0.327	0.327	0.330	0.335	0.327	0.338	0.343	0.352	0.352	0.349	0.350	0.355	0.362	0.370	0.370	0.376	0.371	0.381	0.387	0.392
Mar	0.303	0.307	0.307	0.305	0.312	0.322	0.323	0.326	0.331	0.323	0.334	0.339	0.348	0.347	0.344	0.346	0.351	0.357	0.365	0.365	0.372	0.366	0.376	0.382	0.387
Apr	0.294	0.298	0.298	0.295	0.303	0.313	0.313	0.316	0.321	0.313	0.324	0.329	0.338	0.338	0.334	0.336	0.341	0.348	0.355	0.355	0.362	0.357	0.366	0.373	0.377
May	0.291	0.296	0.296	0.293	0.301	0.311	0.311	0.314	0.319	0.311	0.322	0.327	0.336	0.336	0.332	0.334	0.339	0.345	0.353	0.353	0.360	0.354	0.364	0.370	0.375
June	0.293	0.297	0.297	0.295	0.302	0.312	0.313	0.315	0.320	0.313	0.323	0.328	0.338	0.337	0.334	0.335	0.340	0.347	0.355	0.355	0.361	0.356	0.366	0.372	0.376
July	0.293	0.297	0.297	0.295	0.302	0.312	0.313	0.315	0.320	0.313	0.323	0.328	0.338	0.337	0.334	0.335	0.340	0.347	0.355	0.355	0.361	0.356	0.366	0.372	0.376
Aug	0.291	0.295	0.295	0.292	0.300	0.310	0.311	0.313	0.318	0.311	0.321	0.326	0.335	0.335	0.331	0.333	0.338	0.345	0.352	0.352	0.359	0.354	0.363	0.369	0.374
Sept	0.284	0.289	0.289	0.286	0.294	0.304	0.304	0.307	0.312	0.304	0.315	0.319	0.329	0.328	0.325	0.327	0.332	0.338	0.346	0.346	0.352	0.347	0.357	0.363	0.367
Oct	0.284	0.288	0.288	0.285	0.293	0.303	0.303	0.306	0.311	0.303	0.314	0.319	0.328	0.327	0.324	0.326	0.331	0.337	0.345	0.345	0.352	0.346	0.356	0.362	0.366
Nov	0.283	0.287	0.287	0.285	0.292	0.302	0.303	0.305	0.310	0.303	0.313	0.318	0.327	0.327	0.323	0.325	0.330	0.337	0.344	0.344	0.351	0.345	0.355	0.361	0.366
Dec	0.277	0.282	0.282	0.279	0.287	0.296	0.297	0.300	0.305	0.297	0.307	0.312	0.322	0.321	0.318	0.319	0.324	0.331	0.338	0.338	0.345	0.340	0.349	0.355	0.360
2004																									
Jan	0.280	0.285	0.285	0.282	0.289	0.299	0.300	0.303	0.307	0.300	0.310	0.315	0.324	0.324	0.321	0.322	0.327	0.334	0.341	0.341	0.348	0.342	0.352	0.358	0.363
Feb	0.275	0.280	0.280	0.277	0.285	0.294	0.295	0.298	0.303	0.295	0.305	0.310	0.319	0.319	0.316	0.317	0.322	0.329	0.336	0.336	0.343	0.337	0.347	0.353	0.357
Mar	0.270	0.274	0.274	0.271	0.279	0.289	0.289	0.292	0.297	0.289	0.300	0.304	0.314	0.313	0.310	0.311	0.316	0.323	0.330	0.330	0.337	0.332	0.341	0.347	0.352
Apr	0.262	0.267	0.267	0.264	0.271	0.281	0.282	0.284	0.289	0.282	0.292	0.297	0.306	0.305	0.302	0.304	0.309	0.315	0.323	0.323	0.329	0.324	0.333	0.339	0.344
May	0.257	0.261	0.261	0.258	0.266	0.276	0.276	0.279	0.284	0.276	0.286	0.291	0.300	0.300	0.297	0.298	0.303	0.309	0.317	0.317	0.323	0.318	0.328	0.334	0.338
June	0.255	0.259	0.259	0.256	0.264	0.274	0.274	0.277	0.282	0.274	0.284	0.289	0.298	0.298	0.294	0.296	0.301	0.307	0.315	0.315	0.321	0.316	0.325	0.331	0.336
July	0.255	0.259	0.259	0.256	0.264	0.274	0.274	0.277	0.282	0.274	0.284	0.289	0.298	0.298	0.294	0.296	0.301	0.307	0.315	0.315	0.321	0.316	0.325	0.331	0.336
Aug	0.251	0.255	0.255	0.252	0.260	0.269	0.270	0.273	0.277	0.270	0.280	0.285	0.294	0.293	0.290	0.292	0.297	0.303	0.311	0.311	0.317	0.312	0.321	0.327	0.331
Sept	0.246	0.250	0.250	0.248	0.255	0.265	0.265	0.268	0.273	0.265	0.275	0.280	0.289	0.289	0.285	0.287	0.292	0.298	0.306	0.306	0.312	0.307	0.316	0.322	0.326
Oct	0.243	0.247	0.247	0.244	0.252	0.261	0.262	0.265	0.269	0.262	0.272	0.277	0.286	0.285	0.282	0.284	0.288	0.295	0.302	0.302	0.309	0.303	0.313	0.319	0.323
Nov	0.240	0.244	0.244	0.242	0.249	0.259	0.259	0.262	0.267	0.259	0.269	0.274	0.283	0.283	0.279	0.281	0.286	0.292	0.299	0.299	0.306	0.301	0.310	0.316	0.320
Dec	0.234	0.239	0.239	0.236	0.243	0.253	0.253	0.256	0.261	0.253	0.263	0.268	0.277	0.276	0.273	0.275	0.280	0.286	0.293	0.293	0.300	0.294	0.304	0.310	0.314
2005																									
Jan	0.241	0.245	0.245	0.242	0.250	0.259	0.260	0.263	0.267	0.260	0.270	0.275	0.284	0.283	0.280	0.282	0.286	0.293	0.300	0.300	0.307	0.301	0.311	0.317	0.321
Feb	0.236	0.241	0.241	0.238	0.245	0.255	0.255	0.258	0.263	0.255	0.265	0.270	0.279	0.278	0.275	0.277	0.282	0.288	0.295	0.295	0.302	0.296	0.306	0.312	0.316
Mar	0.230	0.235	0.235	0.232	0.239	0.249	0.249	0.252	0.257	0.249	0.259	0.264	0.273	0.272	0.269	0.271	0.276	0.282	0.289	0.289	0.296	0.290	0.300	0.306	0.310
Apr	0.223	0.228	0.228	0.225	0.232	0.242	0.242	0.245	0.249	0.242	0.252	0.257	0.266	0.265	0.262	0.264	0.268	0.275	0.282	0.282	0.288	0.283	0.292	0.298	0.302
May	0.221	0.225	0.225	0.222	0.230	0.239	0.240	0.242	0.247	0.240	0.249	0.254	0.263	0.263	0.259	0.261	0.266	0.272	0.279	0.279	0.285	0.280	0.290	0.295	0.299
June	0.220	0.224	0.224	0.221	0.228	0.238	0.238	0.241	0.246	0.238	0.248	0.253	0.262	0.261	0.258	0.260	0.264	0.271	0.278	0.278	0.284	0.279	0.288	0.294	0.298
July	0.220	0.224	0.224	0.221	0.228	0.238	0.238	0.241	0.246	0.238	0.248	0.253	0.262	0.261	0.258	0.260	0.264	0.271	0.278	0.278	0.284	0.279	0.288	0.294	0.298
Aug	0.217	0.221	0.221	0.219	0.226	0.235	0.236	0.238	0.243	0.236	0.246	0.250	0.259	0.259	0.255	0.257	0.262	0.268	0.275	0.275	0.281	0.276	0.286	0.291	0.295
Sept	0.214	0.218	0.218	0.215	0.223	0.232	0.233	0.235	0.240	0.233	0.242	0.247	0.256	0.255	0.252	0.254	0.258	0.265	0.272	0.272	0.278	0.273	0.282	0.288	0.292
Oct	0.213	0.217	0.217	0.214	0.221	0.231	0.231	0.234	0.238	0.231	0.241	0.246	0.255	0.254	0.251	0.252	0.257	0.263	0.271	0.271	0.277	0.272	0.281	0.287	0.291
Nov	0.211	0.215	0.215	0.212	0.220	0.229	0.229	0.232	0.237	0.229	0.239	0.244	0.253	0.252	0.249	0.251	0.255	0.261	0.269	0.269	0.275	0.270	0.279	0.285	0.289
Dec	0.208	0.212	0.212	0.209	0.216	0.226	0.226	0.229	0.233	0.226	0.236	0.241	0.249	0.249	0.246	0.247	0.252	0.258	0.265	0.265	0.272	0.266	0.276	0.281	0.285

Capital gains indexation allowances for companies (April 2011 – April 2013)

Month of acquisition	2011									2012												2013			
	Apr	May	June	July	Aug	Sept	Oct	Nov	Dec	Jan	Feb	Mar	Apr	May	June	July	Aug	Sept	Oct	Nov	Dec	Jan	Feb	Mar	Apr
2006																									
Jan	0.212	0.216	0.216	0.214	0.221	0.230	0.231	0.233	0.238	0.231	0.240	0.245	0.254	0.253	0.250	0.252	0.256	0.263	0.270	0.270	0.276	0.271	0.280	0.286	0.290
Feb	0.207	0.211	0.211	0.209	0.216	0.225	0.226	0.228	0.233	0.226	0.235	0.240	0.249	0.248	0.245	0.247	0.251	0.257	0.265	0.265	0.271	0.266	0.275	0.281	0.285
Mar	0.202	0.206	0.206	0.204	0.211	0.220	0.221	0.223	0.228	0.221	0.230	0.235	0.244	0.243	0.240	0.242	0.246	0.252	0.259	0.259	0.266	0.261	0.270	0.275	0.279
Apr	0.193	0.197	0.197	0.194	0.202	0.211	0.211	0.214	0.218	0.211	0.221	0.225	0.234	0.234	0.231	0.232	0.237	0.243	0.250	0.250	0.256	0.251	0.260	0.266	0.270
May	0.186	0.190	0.190	0.187	0.194	0.203	0.204	0.206	0.211	0.204	0.213	0.218	0.227	0.226	0.223	0.225	0.229	0.235	0.242	0.242	0.248	0.243	0.252	0.258	0.262
June	0.181	0.185	0.185	0.182	0.189	0.198	0.199	0.202	0.206	0.199	0.209	0.213	0.222	0.221	0.218	0.220	0.224	0.230	0.237	0.237	0.243	0.238	0.247	0.253	0.257
July	0.181	0.185	0.185	0.182	0.189	0.198	0.199	0.202	0.206	0.199	0.209	0.213	0.222	0.221	0.218	0.220	0.224	0.230	0.237	0.237	0.243	0.238	0.247	0.253	0.257
Aug	0.177	0.181	0.181	0.178	0.185	0.194	0.195	0.197	0.202	0.195	0.204	0.209	0.217	0.217	0.214	0.215	0.220	0.226	0.233	0.233	0.239	0.234	0.243	0.248	0.253
Sept	0.171	0.175	0.175	0.173	0.180	0.189	0.189	0.192	0.196	0.189	0.199	0.203	0.212	0.211	0.208	0.210	0.214	0.220	0.227	0.227	0.233	0.228	0.237	0.243	0.247
Oct	0.170	0.174	0.174	0.171	0.178	0.187	0.188	0.190	0.195	0.188	0.197	0.202	0.210	0.210	0.207	0.208	0.213	0.219	0.226	0.226	0.232	0.227	0.236	0.241	0.245
Nov	0.166	0.170	0.170	0.167	0.174	0.183	0.183	0.186	0.190	0.183	0.193	0.197	0.206	0.205	0.202	0.204	0.208	0.214	0.221	0.221	0.227	0.222	0.231	0.237	0.241
Dec	0.156	0.160	0.160	0.158	0.165	0.174	0.174	0.177	0.181	0.174	0.184	0.188	0.196	0.196	0.193	0.194	0.199	0.205	0.212	0.212	0.218	0.213	0.222	0.227	0.231
2007																									
Jan	0.163	0.167	0.167	0.164	0.171	0.180	0.181	0.183	0.188	0.181	0.190	0.194	0.203	0.202	0.199	0.201	0.205	0.211	0.218	0.218	0.224	0.219	0.228	0.234	0.238
Feb	0.154	0.158	0.158	0.156	0.162	0.171	0.172	0.174	0.179	0.172	0.181	0.186	0.194	0.194	0.191	0.192	0.196	0.202	0.209	0.209	0.215	0.210	0.219	0.225	0.228
Mar	0.147	0.151	0.151	0.148	0.155	0.164	0.164	0.167	0.171	0.164	0.174	0.178	0.186	0.186	0.183	0.184	0.189	0.195	0.202	0.202	0.207	0.203	0.211	0.217	0.221
Apr	0.141	0.145	0.145	0.143	0.149	0.158	0.159	0.161	0.166	0.159	0.168	0.172	0.181	0.180	0.177	0.179	0.183	0.189	0.196	0.196	0.202	0.197	0.205	0.211	0.215
May	0.137	0.141	0.141	0.138	0.145	0.154	0.154	0.157	0.161	0.154	0.163	0.168	0.176	0.176	0.173	0.174	0.178	0.184	0.191	0.191	0.197	0.192	0.201	0.206	0.210
June	0.131	0.135	0.135	0.132	0.139	0.148	0.148	0.151	0.155	0.148	0.157	0.162	0.170	0.169	0.166	0.168	0.172	0.178	0.185	0.185	0.191	0.186	0.194	0.200	0.204
July	0.137	0.141	0.141	0.139	0.146	0.154	0.155	0.157	0.162	0.155	0.164	0.168	0.177	0.176	0.173	0.175	0.179	0.185	0.192	0.192	0.197	0.193	0.201	0.207	0.211
Aug	0.131	0.135	0.135	0.132	0.139	0.148	0.148	0.151	0.155	0.148	0.157	0.162	0.170	0.169	0.166	0.168	0.172	0.178	0.185	0.185	0.191	0.186	0.194	0.200	0.204
Sept	0.127	0.131	0.131	0.128	0.135	0.144	0.144	0.147	0.151	0.144	0.153	0.158	0.166	0.165	0.163	0.164	0.168	0.174	0.181	0.181	0.187	0.182	0.190	0.196	0.200
Oct	0.122	0.126	0.126	0.124	0.130	0.139	0.139	0.142	0.146	0.139	0.148	0.153	0.161	0.160	0.157	0.159	0.163	0.169	0.176	0.176	0.181	0.177	0.185	0.191	0.194
Nov	0.118	0.122	0.122	0.119	0.126	0.134	0.135	0.137	0.142	0.135	0.144	0.148	0.156	0.156	0.153	0.155	0.159	0.165	0.171	0.171	0.177	0.172	0.181	0.186	0.190
Dec	0.111	0.115	0.115	0.113	0.119	0.128	0.128	0.131	0.135	0.128	0.138	0.142	0.150	0.149	0.147	0.148	0.152	0.158	0.165	0.165	0.170	0.165	0.174	0.179	0.183
2008																									
Jan	0.117	0.121	0.121	0.119	0.125	0.134	0.134	0.137	0.141	0.134	0.143	0.148	0.156	0.155	0.153	0.154	0.158	0.164	0.171	0.171	0.176	0.172	0.180	0.185	0.189
Feb	0.109	0.113	0.113	0.110	0.117	0.125	0.126	0.128	0.132	0.126	0.135	0.139	0.147	0.147	0.144	0.145	0.149	0.155	0.162	0.162	0.167	0.163	0.171	0.176	0.180
Mar	0.105	0.109	0.109	0.107	0.113	0.122	0.122	0.124	0.129	0.122	0.131	0.135	0.143	0.143	0.140	0.141	0.146	0.151	0.158	0.158	0.164	0.159	0.167	0.173	0.176
Apr	0.095	0.099	0.099	0.097	0.103	0.112	0.112	0.114	0.119	0.112	0.121	0.125	0.133	0.133	0.130	0.131	0.136	0.141	0.148	0.148	0.153	0.149	0.157	0.162	0.166
May	0.090	0.093	0.093	0.091	0.098	0.106	0.106	0.109	0.113	0.106	0.115	0.119	0.127	0.127	0.124	0.126	0.130	0.135	0.142	0.142	0.147	0.143	0.151	0.156	0.160
June	0.081	0.085	0.085	0.083	0.089	0.097	0.098	0.100	0.104	0.098	0.107	0.111	0.119	0.118	0.115	0.117	0.121	0.126	0.133	0.133	0.138	0.134	0.142	0.147	0.151
July	0.083	0.086	0.086	0.084	0.091	0.099	0.099	0.102	0.106	0.099	0.108	0.112	0.120	0.120	0.117	0.118	0.122	0.128	0.134	0.134	0.140	0.135	0.144	0.149	0.152
Aug	0.079	0.083	0.083	0.081	0.087	0.095	0.096	0.098	0.102	0.096	0.105	0.109	0.116	0.116	0.113	0.115	0.119	0.124	0.131	0.131	0.136	0.132	0.140	0.145	0.149
Sept	0.073	0.077	0.077	0.075	0.081	0.089	0.090	0.092	0.096	0.090	0.098	0.103	0.110	0.110	0.107	0.109	0.113	0.118	0.125	0.125	0.130	0.125	0.134	0.139	0.142
Oct	0.077	0.080	0.080	0.078	0.085	0.093	0.093	0.096	0.100	0.093	0.102	0.106	0.114	0.113	0.111	0.112	0.116	0.122	0.128	0.128	0.134	0.129	0.137	0.142	0.146
Nov	0.085	0.089	0.089	0.087	0.093	0.101	0.102	0.104	0.108	0.102	0.111	0.115	0.123	0.122	0.119	0.121	0.125	0.131	0.137	0.137	0.143	0.138	0.146	0.151	0.155
Dec	0.101	0.105	0.105	0.102	0.109	0.117	0.118	0.120	0.124	0.118	0.127	0.131	0.139	0.139	0.136	0.137	0.141	0.147	0.154	0.154	0.159	0.155	0.163	0.168	0.172

Capital gains indexation allowances for companies (April 2011 – April 2013)

Month of acquisition	2011 Apr	May	June	July	Aug	Sept	Oct	Nov	Dec	2012 Jan	Feb	Mar	Apr	May	June	July	Aug	Sept	Oct	Nov	Dec	2013 Jan	Feb	Mar	Apr
2009																									
Jan	0.116	0.119	0.119	0.117	0.124	0.132	0.133	0.135	0.139	0.133	0.142	0.146	0.154	0.154	0.151	0.152	0.157	0.162	0.169	0.169	0.175	0.170	0.178	0.184	0.188
Feb	0.109	0.113	0.113	0.110	0.117	0.125	0.126	0.128	0.132	0.126	0.135	0.139	0.147	0.147	0.144	0.145	0.149	0.155	0.162	0.162	0.167	0.163	0.171	0.176	0.180
Mar	0.109	0.113	0.113	0.111	0.117	0.126	0.126	0.129	0.133	0.126	0.135	0.140	0.148	0.147	0.144	0.146	0.150	0.156	0.162	0.162	0.168	0.163	0.172	0.177	0.181
Apr	0.108	0.112	0.112	0.110	0.116	0.125	0.125	0.128	0.132	0.125	0.134	0.139	0.147	0.146	0.143	0.145	0.149	0.155	0.161	0.161	0.167	0.162	0.171	0.176	0.180
May	0.102	0.105	0.105	0.103	0.109	0.118	0.118	0.121	0.125	0.118	0.127	0.132	0.140	0.139	0.136	0.138	0.142	0.148	0.154	0.154	0.160	0.155	0.164	0.169	0.172
June	0.098	0.102	0.102	0.100	0.106	0.115	0.115	0.118	0.122	0.115	0.124	0.128	0.136	0.136	0.133	0.134	0.139	0.144	0.151	0.151	0.157	0.152	0.160	0.165	0.169
July	0.098	0.102	0.102	0.100	0.106	0.115	0.115	0.118	0.122	0.115	0.124	0.128	0.136	0.136	0.133	0.134	0.139	0.144	0.151	0.151	0.157	0.152	0.160	0.165	0.169
Aug	0.093	0.097	0.097	0.095	0.101	0.110	0.110	0.112	0.117	0.110	0.119	0.123	0.131	0.131	0.128	0.129	0.133	0.139	0.146	0.146	0.151	0.146	0.155	0.160	0.164
Sept	0.089	0.092	0.092	0.090	0.097	0.105	0.105	0.108	0.112	0.105	0.114	0.118	0.126	0.126	0.123	0.124	0.129	0.134	0.141	0.141	0.146	0.142	0.150	0.155	0.159
Oct	0.085	0.089	0.089	0.087	0.093	0.101	0.102	0.104	0.108	0.102	0.111	0.115	0.123	0.122	0.119	0.121	0.125	0.131	0.137	0.137	0.143	0.138	0.146	0.151	0.155
Nov	0.082	0.086	0.086	0.084	0.090	0.098	0.099	0.101	0.105	0.099	0.108	0.112	0.120	0.119	0.116	0.118	0.122	0.127	0.134	0.134	0.139	0.135	0.143	0.148	0.152
Dec	0.075	0.079	0.079	0.077	0.083	0.091	0.092	0.094	0.098	0.092	0.100	0.105	0.112	0.112	0.109	0.111	0.115	0.120	0.127	0.127	0.132	0.128	0.136	0.141	0.144
2010																									
Jan	0.076	0.079	0.079	0.077	0.084	0.092	0.092	0.095	0.099	0.092	0.101	0.105	0.113	0.112	0.110	0.111	0.115	0.121	0.127	0.127	0.133	0.128	0.136	0.141	0.145
Feb	0.069	0.073	0.073	0.071	0.077	0.085	0.086	0.088	0.092	0.086	0.094	0.099	0.106	0.106	0.103	0.104	0.109	0.114	0.120	0.120	0.126	0.121	0.130	0.135	0.138
Mar	0.062	0.066	0.066	0.063	0.070	0.078	0.078	0.081	0.085	0.078	0.087	0.091	0.099	0.098	0.096	0.097	0.101	0.106	0.113	0.113	0.118	0.114	0.122	0.127	0.130
Apr	0.052	0.056	0.056	0.053	0.060	0.068	0.068	0.070	0.075	0.068	0.077	0.081	0.088	0.088	0.085	0.087	0.091	0.096	0.102	0.102	0.108	0.103	0.111	0.116	0.120
May	0.048	0.052	0.052	0.050	0.056	0.064	0.064	0.067	0.071	0.064	0.073	0.077	0.085	0.084	0.081	0.083	0.087	0.092	0.098	0.098	0.104	0.099	0.107	0.112	0.116
June	0.046	0.050	0.050	0.047	0.054	0.062	0.062	0.064	0.068	0.062	0.071	0.075	0.082	0.082	0.079	0.080	0.084	0.090	0.096	0.096	0.101	0.097	0.105	0.110	0.113
July	0.048	0.052	0.052	0.050	0.056	0.064	0.064	0.067	0.071	0.064	0.073	0.077	0.085	0.084	0.081	0.083	0.087	0.092	0.098	0.098	0.104	0.099	0.107	0.112	0.116
Aug	0.044	0.048	0.048	0.045	0.052	0.060	0.060	0.062	0.066	0.060	0.069	0.073	0.080	0.080	0.077	0.078	0.082	0.088	0.094	0.094	0.099	0.095	0.103	0.108	0.111
Sept	0.040	0.044	0.044	0.042	0.048	0.056	0.056	0.059	0.063	0.056	0.065	0.069	0.076	0.076	0.073	0.075	0.079	0.084	0.090	0.090	0.095	0.091	0.099	0.104	0.107
Oct	0.038	0.042	0.042	0.039	0.046	0.054	0.054	0.056	0.060	0.054	0.062	0.066	0.074	0.074	0.071	0.072	0.076	0.081	0.088	0.088	0.093	0.089	0.097	0.101	0.105
Nov	0.034	0.037	0.037	0.035	0.041	0.049	0.049	0.052	0.056	0.049	0.058	0.062	0.069	0.069	0.066	0.067	0.071	0.077	0.083	0.083	0.088	0.084	0.092	0.097	0.100
Dec	0.026	0.030	0.030	0.028	0.034	0.042	0.042	0.044	0.048	0.042	0.050	0.054	0.062	0.061	0.059	0.060	0.064	0.069	0.075	0.075	0.081	0.076	0.084	0.089	0.092
2011																									
Jan	0.024	0.027	0.027	0.025	0.031	0.039	0.039	0.041	0.045	0.039	0.048	0.052	0.059	0.059	0.056	0.057	0.061	0.066	0.072	0.072	0.078	0.073	0.081	0.086	0.090
Feb	0.013	0.017	0.017	0.015	0.021	0.029	0.029	0.031	0.035	0.029	0.037	0.041	0.048	0.048	0.045	0.047	0.051	0.056	0.062	0.062	0.067	0.063	0.070	0.075	0.079
Mar	0.008	0.012	0.012	0.009	0.015	0.023	0.024	0.026	0.030	0.024	0.032	0.036	0.043	0.043	0.040	0.041	0.045	0.050	0.056	0.056	0.062	0.057	0.065	0.070	0.073
Apr	—	0.003	0.003	0.001	0.007	0.015	0.015	0.017	0.021	0.015	0.023	0.027	0.035	0.034	0.032	0.033	0.037	0.042	0.048	0.048	0.053	0.049	0.056	0.061	0.064
May	—	—	0.000	0.000	0.004	0.011	0.012	0.014	0.018	0.012	0.020	0.024	0.031	0.031	0.028	0.029	0.033	0.038	0.044	0.044	0.049	0.045	0.053	0.057	0.061
June	—	—	—	0.000	0.004	0.011	0.012	0.014	0.018	0.012	0.020	0.024	0.031	0.031	0.028	0.029	0.033	0.038	0.044	0.044	0.049	0.045	0.053	0.057	0.061
July	—	—	—	—	0.006	0.014	0.014	0.016	0.020	0.014	0.022	0.026	0.033	0.033	0.030	0.032	0.035	0.040	0.046	0.046	0.052	0.047	0.055	0.060	0.063
Aug	—	—	—	—	—	0.008	0.008	0.010	0.014	0.008	0.016	0.020	0.027	0.027	0.024	0.025	0.029	0.034	0.040	0.040	0.045	0.041	0.049	0.053	0.057
Sept	—	—	—	—	—	—	0.000	0.003	0.006	0.000	0.008	0.012	0.019	0.019	0.016	0.018	0.021	0.026	0.032	0.032	0.037	0.033	0.041	0.045	0.049
Oct	—	—	—	—	—	—	—	0.002	0.006	0.000	0.008	0.012	0.019	0.018	0.016	0.017	0.021	0.026	0.032	0.032	0.037	0.033	0.040	0.045	0.048
Nov	—	—	—	—	—	—	—	—	0.004	0.000	0.006	0.010	0.017	0.016	0.014	0.015	0.019	0.024	0.030	0.030	0.035	0.031	0.038	0.043	0.046
Dec	—	—	—	—	—	—	—	—	—	0.000	0.002	0.006	0.013	0.013	0.010	0.011	0.015	0.020	0.026	0.026	0.031	0.027	0.034	0.039	0.042

Capital gains indexation allowances for companies (April 2011 – April 2013)

Month of acquisition	2011 Apr	May	June	July	Aug	Sept	Oct	Nov	Dec	2012 Jan	Feb	Mar	Apr	May	June	July	Aug	Sept	Oct	Nov	Dec	2013 Jan	Feb	Mar	Apr
2012																									
Jan	—	—	—	—	—	—	—	—	—	0.000	0.008	0.012	0.019	0.018	0.016	0.017	0.021	0.026	0.032	0.032	0.037	0.033	0.040	0.045	0.048
Feb	—	—	—	—	—	—	—	—	—	—	0.000	0.004	0.011	0.010	0.008	0.009	0.013	0.018	0.024	0.024	0.029	0.025	0.032	0.037	0.040
Mar	—	—	—	—	—	—	—	—	—	—	—	0.000	0.007	0.007	0.004	0.005	0.009	0.014	0.020	0.020	0.025	0.021	0.028	0.033	0.036
Apr	—	—	—	—	—	—	—	—	—	—	—	—	0.000	0.000	0.000	0.000	0.002	0.007	0.013	0.013	0.018	0.014	0.021	0.026	0.029
May	—	—	—	—	—	—	—	—	—	—	—	—	—	0.000	0.000	0.000	0.002	0.007	0.013	0.013	0.018	0.014	0.021	0.026	0.029
June	—	—	—	—	—	—	—	—	—	—	—	—	—	—	0.000	0.001	0.005	0.010	0.016	0.016	0.021	0.017	0.024	0.029	0.032
July	—	—	—	—	—	—	—	—	—	—	—	—	—	—	—	0.000	0.004	0.009	0.014	0.014	0.019	0.015	0.023	0.027	0.031
Aug	—	—	—	—	—	—	—	—	—	—	—	—	—	—	—	—	0.000	0.005	0.011	0.011	0.016	0.012	0.019	0.023	0.027
Sept	—	—	—	—	—	—	—	—	—	—	—	—	—	—	—	—	—	0.000	0.006	0.006	0.011	0.007	0.014	0.018	0.022
Oct	—	—	—	—	—	—	—	—	—	—	—	—	—	—	—	—	—	—	0.000	0.000	0.005	0.001	0.008	0.013	0.016
Nov	—	—	—	—	—	—	—	—	—	—	—	—	—	—	—	—	—	—	—	0.000	0.005	0.001	0.008	0.013	0.016
Dec	—	—	—	—	—	—	—	—	—	—	—	—	—	—	—	—	—	—	—	—	0.000	0.000	0.003	0.008	0.011
2013																									
Jan	—	—	—	—	—	—	—	—	—	—	—	—	—	—	—	—	—	—	—	—	—	0.000	0.007	0.012	0.015
Feb	—	—	—	—	—	—	—	—	—	—	—	—	—	—	—	—	—	—	—	—	—	—	0.000	0.004	0.008
Mar	—	—	—	—	—	—	—	—	—	—	—	—	—	—	—	—	—	—	—	—	—	—	—	0.000	0.003
Apr	—	—	—	—	—	—	—	—	—	—	—	—	—	—	—	—	—	—	—	—	—	—	—	—	0.000

Certificates of tax deposit

Rates of interest

Deposits of less than £100,000

Date	A	B
9 February — 5 April 2001	2¼%	1¼%
6 April — 2 August	2%	1%
3 August — 18 September	1½%	¾%
19 September — 4 October	1¼%	¾%
5 October — 8 November	1%	½%
9 November — 6 February 2003	½%	¼%
7 February — 10 July	¼%	Nil
11 July — 6 November	Nil	Nil
7 November — 5 February 2004	¼%	Nil
6 February — 6 May	½%	¼%
7 May — 10 June	¾%	¼%
11 June — 5 August	1%	½%
6 August — 4 August 2005	1¼%	½%
5 August — 3 August 2006	1%	½%
4 August — 9 November	1¾%	¾%
10 November — 10 May 2007	1½%	¾%
11 May — 5 July	2%	1%
6 July — 6 December	2¼%	1¹/₁₀%
7 December — 7 February 2008	3%	1½%
8 February — 10 April	2%	1%
11 April — 8 October	2%	1%
9 October — 6 November	2½%	1¼%
7 November — 4 December	1¾%	¾%
5 December —	0%	0%

Deposits of £100,000 or more

Date	A and held for Under 1 mth	1–3 mths	3–6 mths	6–9 mths	9–12 mths	B and held for under 1 mth	1–3 mths	3–6 mths	6–9 mths	9–12 mths
9 February — 5 April 2001	2¼%	4¾%	4¼%	4¼%	4%	1¼%	2½%	2¼%	2¼%	2%
6 April — 10 May	2%	4¼%	4%	3¾%	3½%	1%	2¼%	2%	2%	1¾%
11 May — 2 August	2%	4%	4%	3¾%	3¾%	1%	2%	2%	2%	2%
3 August — 18 September	1½%	4%	3¾%	3¾%	3¾%	¾%	2%	1⅞%	1⅞%	1⅞%
19 September — 4 October	1¼%	3½%	3¼%	3¼%	3%	¾%	1¾%	1¾%	1¾%	1½%
5 October — 8 November	1%	3¼%	3%	3%	3%	½%	1¾%	1½%	1½%	1½%
9 November — 6 February 2003	½%	2¾%	2½%	2¼%	2¼%	¼%	1½%	1¼%	1¼%	1¼%
7 February — 10 July	¼%	2¾%	2¼%	2¼%	2%	Nil	1¼%	1%	1%	1%
11 July — 6 November	Nil	2½%	2¼%	2%	2%	Nil	1¼%	1%	1%	1%
7 November — 5 February 2004	¼%	3%	3%	3%	3%	Nil	1½%	1½%	1½%	1½%
6 February — 6 May	½%	3%	3%	3%	3%	¼%	1½%	1½%	1½%	1½%
7 May — 10 June	¾%	3¼%	3¼%	3¼%	3¼%	¼%	1½%	1½%	1½%	1½%
11 June — 5 August	1%	3¾%	3½%	3¾%	3¾%	½%	1¾%	1¾%	1¾%	1¾%
6 August — 4 August 2005	1¼%	3¾%	3¾%	3¾%	3¾%	½%	1¾%	1¾%	1¾%	1¾%
5 August — 3 August 2006	1%	3½%	3¼%	3%	3%	½%	1¾%	1½%	1½%	1½%
4 August — 9 November	1¾%	4¼%	4¼%	4%	4%	¾%	2%	2%	2%	2%
10 November — 11 January 2007	1½%	4%	4%	3¾%	3¾%	¾%	2%	2%	1¾%	1¾%
12 January — 10 May	1½%	4¼%	4%	4%	4%	¾%	2%	2%	2%	2%
11 May — 5 July	2%	4¾%	4½%	4½%	4½%	1%	2¼%	2¼%	2¼%	2¼%
6 July — 6 December	2¼%	5%	4¾%	4¾%	4¾%	1¹/₁₀%	2½%	2¼%	2¼%	2¼%
7 December — 7 February 2008	3%	5½%	5%	4¾%	4½%	1½%	2¾%	2½%	2¼%	2¼%
8 February — 10 April	2%	4½%	4¼%	4%	3¾%	1%	2¼%	2%	2%	1½%
11 April — 8 October	2%	4¾%	4½%	4¼%	4¼%	1%	2¼%	2¼%	2%	2%
9 October — 6 November	2½%	5¼%	5%	5%	4¾%	1¼%	2½%	2½%	2½%	2¼%
7 November — 4 December	1¾%	4½%	4¼%	4¼%	4%	¾%	2¼%	2%	2%	2%
5 December — 8 January 2009	0%	2½%	2½%	2½%	2¼%	0%	1¼%	1¼%	1¼%	1%
9 January — 5 February	0%	1½ %	1¼%	1¼%	1¼%	0%	¾%	½	½%	½%
6 February — 5 March	0%	1%	1%	1%	¾%	0%	½%	½%	½%	¼%
6 March —	0%	¾%	¾%	¾%	¾%	0%	¼%	¼%	¼%	¼%

A = used to pay tax
B = withdrawn for cash

Notes

(a) Certificates may be used by taxpayers generally — that is to say companies, individuals, partnerships, personal representatives, trustees etc. for payment of tax and petroleum royalties but not PAYE, tax deducted from payments to construction subcontractors or VAT. Certificates are no longer available for purchase for use against corporation tax liabilities.

(b) The first deposit must be for a minimum of £500. Further deposits must be either at least £250 or enough to bring total deposits up to £500 (i.e. where total deposits have fallen below that amount).

(c) Interest accrues daily (without compounding) for a maximum of six years from the date of deposit to (i) the deemed due date for tax paid with deposits; or (ii) the day on which the deposit is withdrawn for cash. It is payable gross but taxable.

(d) Rates of interest on certificates are, for the first year, those applying on the date of deposit, and thereafter rates are realigned with current rates on each anniversary.

Corporation tax

Rates

Financial year	2013	2012	2011	2010	2009	2008	2007	2006
Full rate	23%	24%	26%	28%	28%	28%	30%	30%
Small profits rate	20%	20%	20%	21%	21%	21%	20%	19%
Upper profit limit	£300,000	£300,000	£300,000	£300,000	£300,000	£300,000	£300,000	£300,000
Marginal relief — upper profit limit	£1.5m	£1.5m	£1.5m	£1.5m	£1.5m	£1.5m	£1.5m	£1.5m
Marginal relief fraction	3/400	1/100	3/200	7/400	7/400	7/400	1/40	11/400
Effective marginal rate	23.75%	25%	27.5%	29.75%	29.75%	29.75%	32.5%	32.75%
Chargeable gains	(a) The whole of the chargeable gains (less allowable losses) is included in the taxable total profits. The rate of corporation tax applicable will be either the full rate, or the small profits rate (with marginal relief as appropriate)							
	(b) For authorised unit and investment trusts, gains are not chargeable. Gains on disposals of investment properties by UK real estate investment trusts are not chargeable							

Notes

(a) Where 'profits' of an accounting period exceed the upper profit limit for the small profits rate, but are less than the appropriate marginal relief upper profit limit, corporation tax is reduced by:

$$F(U - \text{augmented profits}) \times \frac{\text{taxable total profits}}{\text{augmented profits}}$$

where F is the marginal relief fraction and U is the marginal relief upper profit limit.

(b) 'Augmented profits' are total taxable profits plus franked investment income (other than from UK companies within the same group or owned by a consortium of which the recipient is a member). Adjusted taxable total profits excludes amounts which are chargeable to capital gains tax rather than corporation tax under TCGA 1992, s 2B (non-natural person and certain high value property see page 19 & 77).

(c) The upper profit limits and the marginal relief upper profit limits for the small profits rate are proportionately reduced for accounting periods of less than 12 months.

(d) Where a company has associated companies, the upper profit limits and the marginal relief upper profit limits for the small profits rate are divided by one plus the number of associated companies in the accounting period, including those associated for part only of the period but ignoring companies which have not traded at any time in the period.

(e) For the financial years 2014 and 2015 the full rate of corporation tax will be 21% and 20%. This is intended to result in the unification of the CT full rate with the small profits rate.

(f) For all years, the corporation tax rates applicable to North Sea oil and gas ring fence activities are as follows: main rate 30%; small profits rate 19%; marginal relief fraction 11/400.

(g) Subject to a phased introduction, an effective 10% rate of corporation tax (the 'patent box') applies to profits attributable to qualifying intellectual property made on or after 1 April 2013. See page 39.

Corporation tax

Payment of Corporation tax	Without assessment, no later than nine months and one day after the end of the accounting period (the 'due date'). **Instalments.** Subject to the exceptions below, a 'large company' (i.e. one whose taxable profits exceed £1.5m a year, divided by one plus the number of active associated companies if any) must pay its CT in four quarterly instalments on the basis of anticipated liabilities for the accounting period. For a company with a 12 month accounting period, the first two instalments are due on the 14th day of months 7 and 10 in the accounting period, the third is due 14 days after the end of the accounting period and the final instalment is due 3 months and 14 days after the end of the accounting period. *Exceptions.* (i) A company which would otherwise be large is not treated as such for an accounting period if its CT liability for that period does not exceed £10,000. (ii) A company is not large for an accounting period if it was not large in the 12 months preceding the accounting period and its profits for the accounting period do not exceed £10m, divided by one plus the number of active associated companies as at the end of the preceding accounting period. The limits of £1.5m, £10,000 and £10m are proportionately reduced for accounting periods of less than 12 months. *Groups* can enter into group payment arrangements provided the paying company enters into a standard contract at least two months prior to the first instalment payment due date.	*CTA 2009, s 8* *TMA 1970, s 59* *SI 1998 No 3175*
Income tax	Within 14 days of end of return period during which the income tax was deducted. Return periods end on 31 March, 30 June, 30 September, 31 December, at the end of each of the company's accounting periods.	*ITA 2007, ss 947–950*
Tax returns	Filing date is normally the later of (i) twelve months after the end of the return period; and (ii) three months after the receipt of Notice. Special rules apply where accounts are prepared for periods exceeding twelve months. Returns may not be amended more than twelve months after the filing date unless otherwise provided.	*FA 1998, Sch 18 paras 14, 15*
Interest on tax	See pages 69 and 70.	
Research and development	An 'SME' incurring R & D expenditure can claim to deduct 225% of the expenditure (200% for expenditure incurred before 1 April 2012; 175% before 1 April 2011; 150% before 1 August 2008) when computing its trading profit or loss. A company not yet in profit, or which has not started to trade, can claim relief up front as a cash payment (an 'R & D tax credit'). For expenditure incurred after 31 July 2008, these reliefs (together with vaccine research relief) are limited to €7.5m per project. For accounting periods ending before 1 April 2012 the SME had to incur R & D expenditure of at least £10,000 in a 12-month accounting period to qualify. An SME can also claim relief for expenditure on R & D contracted out to it by a large company or by any other person not carrying on a trade etc. and for R & D expenditure which is subsidised or to which the project limit above applies. The relief provides for a deduction equal to 130% of the expenditure (125% for expenditure incurred before 1 April 2008). For accounting periods ending before 1 April 2012 the relief is subject to the same minimum expenditure rules as above. An 'SME' is a company with fewer than 500 employees and either or both of annual turnover not exceeding €100m and annual balance sheet total not exceeding €86m. For expenditure incurred on or after 1 August 2008, the limits were fewer than 250 employees and either or both of turnover not exceeding €50m and balance sheet total not exceeding €43m. Large companies (i.e. companies which are not SMEs) incurring R & D expenditure (for accounting periods ending before 1 April 2012, of at least £10,000) can generally claim to deduct 130% of the expenditure (125% for expenditure incurred before 1 April 2008) from trading profits. Alternatively, for R& D expenditure on or after 1 April 2013 large companies can elect to claim a 10% above the line (ATL) credit. The ATL credit is claimable by all large companies including those who have no liability to corporation tax. The ATL credit is a taxable receipt and is paid net of tax to companies with no corporation tax liability. The ATL credit is paid at a higher percentage rate to those companies within ring fence activities. It is proposed that the ATL credit will replace the above relief (130%) from 1.4.16.	*CTA 2009, ss 1039–1142* *ICTA 1988, s 837A* *FA 2000, ss 68,69, Schs 19–21* *FA 2002, Schs 12, 13* *FA 2003, s 168, Sch 31* *FA 2007, s 50* *FA 2008, ss 26–29, Schs 8, 9* *FA 2011, s 43* *FA 2012, s 20, Sch 3* FA 2013, Sch 15

	Large companies can also claim a relief similar to that for SMEs above, including tax credits, for expenditure incurred on certain vaccine research. The relief is also available to SMEs for expenditure incurred before 1 April 2012. The rate of relief is 140% for large companies and 120% (140% for expenditure incurred before 1 April 2011) for SMEs. The rate for all companies was 150% before 1 August 2008. See also page 8.	
Creative industry tax reliefs: a) Film tax relief b) Relief for animation and high end television production and video games development	Qualifying expenditure may entitle the company to an additional deduction in computing taxable profits or where losses a payable tax credit. Part b) applies to expenditure from a date to be appointed (awaiting state aid approval).	CTA 2009, ss 1195–1207 CTA 2009, Parts 15A & 15B inserted by FA 2013, Schs 16,17 SI 2013 No 1817
Corporate venturing scheme	In respect of shares issued after 31 March 2000 and before 1 April 2010, an investing company can obtain 20% CT relief on amounts subscribed for ordinary shares in small higher-risk unquoted trading companies which are held for at least 3 years. Any chargeable gains on disposal of the shares can be deferred by reinvestment in another shareholding under the scheme; any allowable losses (net of the 20% relief) can be set against income if not deducted from chargeable gains. The investing company must not control the investee company or own or be entitled to acquire more than 30% of its ordinary shares. At least 20% of the investee company's ordinary shares must be owned by independent individuals.	*FA 2000, s 63, Sch 15* *FA 2001, s 64, Sch 16*
Community investment tax credit	Tax relief worth up to 25% of qualifying investments. See page 61.	*CTA 2010, ss 218–269* *FA 2002, s 57, Sch 16*
Charitable giving		
Gift aid scheme	Relief is available for qualifying donations to charity or to a community amateur sports club. Relief is given by deducting the amount of the donation from the company's total profits for the accounting period in which the payment is made. The donation is not taxable in the hands of the charity or club if applied to charitable purposes only.	*CTA 2010, ss 189–202* *ICTA 1988, ss 338–339*
Gifts in kind	Relief is available for gifts by companies to charities, community amateur sports clubs or educational establishments of goods produced or sold or of plant and machinery used in the donor's trade, etc.	*CTA 2009, ss 105–108* *ICTA 1988, ss 83A, 84* *CAA 2001, s 63(2)*
Gifts of land, shares and securities etc.	Relief is available where a company disposes of a freehold or leasehold interest in land, listed shares or securities, units in an authorised unit trust, etc. to a charity by way of gift or sale at an undervalue. The market value of the land, shares etc. on the date of disposal (plus, in the case of a gift, incidental disposal costs) less any consideration or value of benefits received by the donor or a connected person is deducted from the total profits of the company for the accounting period in which the disposal is made.	*CTA 2010, ss 189, 190, 203–216* *ICTA 1988, s 587B*
Gifts of pre-eminent objects to the nation	Under the cultural gift scheme from 1 April 2012, companies which donate pre-eminent objects, or collections of objects, to the nation may qualify for a tax reduction of 20% of the value of the objects.	*FA 2012, s 49*
Groups of companies		
Group relief	A company which is a member of a group of companies can surrender certain losses, etc. to be claimed by another member of the group against its own corporation tax liability. Companies are members of a group of companies for this purpose broadly if one is the 75% subsidiary of the other or both are 75% subsidiaries of a third company. The following are eligible for surrender as group relief: trading losses, non-trading loan relationship deficits, certain excess capital allowances on plant or machinery used for special leasing, management expenses, qualifying charitable donations, property business losses, non-trading losses on intangible fixed assets and qualifying overseas losses of non-resident companies.	*CTA 2010, ss 97–188* *ICTA 1988, ss 402–413* FA 2013, s 30

Corporation tax

Chargeable gains	Disposals of capital assets by one member of a group to another member are treated as if made at a 'no gain/no loss' disposal value. A 'group' for this purpose consists of a principal company, its 75% subsidiaries and those subsidiaries' 75% subsidiaries (and so on), but excluding any subsidiary which is not an effective 51% subsidiary of the principal company. Two members of a group can elect to transfer a gain or loss between them. A de-grouping charge will apply where a company leaves a group and owns a capital asset which has been transferred to it by another group member within the preceding six years.	*TCGA 1992, ss 170–171B, 179*
Patent box	For profits arising on or after 1 April 2013, a company can make an election under which its trading profits from patents and certain other intellectual property are effectively charged to corporation tax at 10%. The lower rate is given effect by way of a deduction in computing the trading profits of the company. The relief is being phased in, so that for financial year 2013 only 60% of the relevant profits qualify. The percentage is increased by 10 percentage points in each subsequent financial year until 100% of the profits qualify in financial year 2017.	*CTA 2010, ss 357A–357GE; FA 2012, s 19, Sch 2*

Double taxation treaties

Agreements covering taxes on income and capital gains

Country	SI or SR & O Number
Antigua and Barbuda	**1947 No 2865**
	1968 No 1096
Argentina	**1997 No 1777**
Armenia	**2011 No 2722**
Australia	**2003 No 3199**
Austria	**1970 No 1947**
	1979 No 117
	1994 No 768
	2010 No 2688
Azerbaijan	**1995 No 762**
Bahrain	**2012 No 3075**
Bangladesh	**1980 No 708**
Barbados	**2012 No 3076**
Belarus (see note (b))	**1986 No 224**
Belgium	**1987 No 2053**
	2010 No 2979
Belize	**1947 No 2866**
	1968 No 573
	1973 No 2097
Bolivia	**1995 No 2707**
Bosnia-Herzegovina (see note (d))	**1981 No 1815**
Botswana	**2006 No 1925**
British Virgin Islands	**2009 No 3013**
Brunei	**1950 No 1977**
	1968 No 306
	1973 No 2098
Bulgaria	**1987 No 2054**
Burma (see Myanmar)	
Canada	**1980 No 709**
	1980 No 1528
	1985 No 1996
	2003 No 2619
Cayman Islands	**2010 No 2973**
Chile	**2003 No 3200**
China	**1984 No 1826**
	1996 No 3164
	2011 No 2724
Croatia (see note (d))	**1981 No 1815**
Cyprus	**1975 No 425**
	1980 No 1529
Czech Republic (see note (c))	**1991 No 2876**
Denmark	**1980 No 1960**
	1991 No 2877
	1996 No 3165
Egypt	**1980 No 1091**
Estonia	**1994 No 3207**
Ethiopia	**2011 No 2725**
Falkland Islands	**1997 No 2985**
Faroes	**2007 No 3469**
Fiji	**1976 No 1342**
Finland	**1970 No 153**
	1980 No 710
	1985 No 1997
	1991 No 2878
	1996 No 3166
France	**2009 No 226**
Gambia	**1980 No 1963**
Georgia	**2004 No 3325**
	2010 No 2972
Germany	**2010 No 2975**
Ghana	**1993 No 1800**
Greece	**1954 No 142**
Grenada	**1949 No 361**
	1968 No 1867
Guernsey	**1952 No 1215**
	1994 No 3209
	2009 No 3011
Guyana	**1992 No 3207**
Hong Kong	**2010 No 2974**
Hungary	**1978 No 1056**
	2011 No 2726
Iceland	**1991 No 2879**
India	**1993 No 1801**
Indonesia	**1994 No 769**
Irish Republic	**1976 No 2151**
	1976 No 2152
	1995 No 764
	1998 No 3151
Isle of Man	**1955 No 1205**
	1991 No 2880
	1994 No 3208
	2009 No 228
Israel	**1963 No 616**
	1971 No 391
Italy	**1990 No 2590**
Ivory Coast	**1987 No 169**
Jamaica	**1973 No 1329**
Japan	**2006 No 1924**
Jersey	**1952 No 1216**
	1994 No 3210
	2009 No 3012
Jordan	**2001 No 3924**
Kazakhstan	**1994 No 3211**
	1998 No 2567
Kenya	**1977 No 1299**
Kiribati (and Tuvalu)	**1950 No 750**
	1968 No 309
	1974 No 1271
Korea (South)	**1996 No 3168**
Kuwait	**1999 No 2036**
Kyrgyzstan (see note (b))	
Latvia	**1996 No 3167**
Lesotho	**1997 No 2986**
Libya	**2010 No 243**
Liechtenstein	**2012 No 3077**
Lithuania	**2001 No 3925**
	2002 No 2847
Luxembourg	**1968 No 1100**
	1980 No 567
	1984 No 364
	2010 No 237
Macedonia	**2007 No 2127**
Malawi	**1956 No 619**
	1964 No 1401
	1968 No 1101
	1979 No 302
Malaysia	**1997 No 2987**
	2010 No 2971
Malta	**1995 No 763**
Mauritius	**1981 No 1121**
	1987 No 467
	2003 No 2620

Double taxation treaties

Country	SI or SR & O Number
	2011 No 2442
Mexico	**1994 No 3212**
	2010 No 2686
Moldova	**2008 No 1795**
Mongolia	**1996 No 2598**
Montenegro (see note (d))	**1981 No 1815**
Montserrat	**1947 No 2869**
	1968 No 576
	2011 No 1083
Morocco	**1991 No 2881**
Myanmar (Burma)	**1952 No 751**
Namibia	**1962 No 2352**
	1962 No 2788
	1967 No 1490
Netherlands	**2009 No 227**
New Zealand	**1984 No 365**
	2004 No 1274
	2008 No 1793
Nigeria	**1987 No 2057**
Norway	**2000 No 3247**
Oman	**1998 No 2568**
	2010 No 2687
Pakistan	**1987 No 2058**
Papua New Guinea	**1991 No 2882**
Philippines	**1978 No 184**
Poland	**2006 No 3323**

Country	SI or SR & O Number
Portugal	**1969 No 599**
Qatar	**2010 No 241**
	2011 No 1684
Romania	**1977 No 57**
Russian Federation	**1994 No 3213**
St. Kitts and Nevis	**1947 No 2872**
Saudi Arabia	**2008 No 1770**
Serbia (see note (d))	**1981 No 1815**
Sierra Leone	**1947 No 2873**
	1968 No 1104
Singapore	**1997 No 2988**
	2010 No 2685
	2012 No 3078
Slovak Republic (see note (c))	**1991 No 2876**
Slovenia	**2008 No 1796**
Solomon Islands	**1950 No 748**
	1968 No 574
	1974 No 1270
South Africa	**2002 No 3138**
	2011 No 2441
Spain	**1976 No 1919**
	1995 No 765
Sri Lanka	**1980 No 713**
Sudan	**1977 No 1719**
Swaziland	**1969 No 380**
Sweden	**1984 No 366**

Country	SI or SR & O Number
Switzerland	**1978 No 1408**
	1982 No 714
	1994 No 3215
	2007 No 3465
	2010 No 2689
	2012 No 3079
Taiwan	**2002 No 3137**
Tajikistan (see note (b))	**1986 No 224**
Thailand	**1981 No 1546**
Trinidad & Tobago	**1983 No 1903**
Tunisia	**1984 No 133**
Turkey	**1988 No 932**
Turkmenistan (see note (b))	**1986 No 224**
Tuvalu (and Kiribati)	**1950 No 750**
	1968 No 309
	1974 No 1271
Uganda	**1993 No 1802**
Ukraine	**1993 No 1803**
USA	**2002 No 2848**
Uzbekistan	**1994 No 770**
Venezuela	**1996 No 2599**
Vietnam	**1994 No 3216**
Yugoslavia (see note (d))	**1981 No 1815**
Zambia	**1972 No 1721**
	1981 No 1816
Zimbabwe	**1982 No 1842**

Notes

(a) Entries in bold are for main agreements. Entries in Roman are for amending protocols.

(b) The Agreement published as *SI 1986 No 224* (which also continued in force the Air Transport agreement published as *SI 1974 No 1269*) between the UK and the former Soviet Union was to be applied by the UK as if it were still in force between the UK and the former Soviet Republics until such time as new agreements took effect with particular countries. It later came to light that Armenia, Georgia, Kyrgyzstan, Lithuania and Moldova did not consider themselves bound by the UK/USSR convention and were not operating it in relation to UK residents. Accordingly, the UK ceased to apply it to residents of those countries from 1 April 2002 for corporation tax and from 6 April 2002 for income tax and capital gains tax (although new treaties are in force with Armenia, Lithuania, Georgia and Moldova). *SI 1986 No 224* is regarded as continuing in force between the UK and Tajikistan and Turkmenistan and also between the UK and Belarus until the coming into force of *SI 1995 No 2706* (HMRC SP 4/01).

(c) The convention published as *SI 1991 No 2876* is treated as remaining in force between the UK and, respectively, the Czech Republic and the Slovak Republic. (HMRC SP 5/93).

(d) The Agreement published as *SI 1981 No 1815* between the UK and Yugoslavia is regarded as in force between the UK and Bosnia-Herzegovina, Croatia and Serbia and Montenegro. (HMRC SP 3/07).

Double taxation treaties

Tax information exchange agreements

Country	SI Number
Agreements in force	
Anguilla	2010 No 2677
Antigua and Barbuda	2011 No 1075
Aruba	2011 No 2435
Bahamas	2010 No 2684
Belize	2011 No 1685
Bermuda	2008 No 1789
British Virgin Islands	2009 No 3013
Dominica	2011 No 1686
Gibraltar	2010 No 2680
Grenada	2011 No 1687
Guernsey	2009 No 3011
Isle of Man	2009 No 228
Jersey	2009 No 3012
Liberia	2011 No 2434
Liechtenstein	2010 No 2678
San Marino	2011 No 1688
St Christopher and Nevis	2011 No 1077
St Lucia	2011 No 1076
St Vincent and the Grenadines	2011 No 1078
Turks and Caicos Islands	2010 No 2679
Agreements signed but not in force	
Brazil	
Curaçao, Sint Maarten and BES Islands	2011 No 2433
Marshall Islands	
EU savings directive agreements	
Aruba	2005 No 1458
British Virgin Islands	2005 No 1457
Gibraltar	2006 No 1453
Guernsey	2005 No 1262
Isle of Man	2005 No 1263
Jersey	2005 No 1261
Montserrat	2005 No 1459
Netherlands Antilles	2005 No 1460

Agreements covering taxes on capital

Country	SI or SR & O Number
Estate duty agreements	
France	1963 No 1319
India	1956 No 998
Italy	1968 No 304
Pakistan	1957 No 1522
Capital transfer and inheritance tax agreements	
Irish Republic	1978 No 1107
Netherlands	1980 No 706
	1996 No 730
South Africa	1979 No 576
Sweden	1981 No 840
	1989 No 986
Switzerland	1994 No 3214
USA	1979 No 1454

Agreements covering shipping and air transport only

Country	SI or SR & O Number
Algeria (air transport only)	1984 No 362
Brazil	1968 No 572
—aircraft crew only	2011 No 2723
Cameroon (air transport only)	1982 No 1841
China (air transport only)	1981 No 1119
Congo Democratic Republic (formerly Zaire)	1977 No 1298
Ethiopia (air travel only)	1977 No 1297
Hong Kong SAR	
(air transport only)	1998 No 2566
(shipping only)	2000 No 3248
Iran (air transport only)	1960 No 2419
Lebanon	1964 No 278
Saudi Arabia	1994 No 767
USSR (see note (a))	1974 No 1269

Reciprocal agreements on social security

(see notes (b) and (c))

Country	SI Number
Barbados	1992 No 812
Bermuda	1969 No 1686
Bosnia-Herzegovinia	1958 No 1263
Canada	1995 No 2699
	1998 No 263
Croatia	1958 No 1698
Iceland (note (c))	1985 No 1202
	1992 No 3211
Isle of Man	1977 No 2150
	1989 No 483
	1989 No 2001
Israel	1957 No 1879
	1984 No 354
Jamaica	1997 No 871
Japan	2000 No 3063
Jersey and Guernsey	1994 No 2802
Korea (Republic of)	2000 No 1823
Macedonia	1958 No 1698
Mauritius	1981 No 1542
Montenegro	1958 No 1698
New Zealand	1964 No 495
	1983 No 1894
Norway (note (c))	1991 No 767
	1992 No 3212
Philippines	1989 No 2002
Serbia	1958 No 1698
Switzerland (note (c))	1969 No 384
Turkey	1961 No 584
USA	1984 No 1817
	1997 No 1778

Notes

(a) See note (b) on page 41.

(b) Only those agreements with countries which contain articles specifically relating to contribution (as distinct from benefit) matters are listed.

(c) Agreements with other EC member states have been superseded for most purposes by *EC Council Regulations 883/2004* and *987/2009* and are not listed. The *Regulations* are applied also to Switzerland and, from 1 June 2012, to Iceland, Liechtenstein and Norway. For social security purposes, the UK includes Gibraltar but excludes the Isle of Man and the Channel Islands.

Foreign exchange rates averages for tax year

Country	Method of quoting	Currency per £1			
		2012/13	2011/12	2010/11	2009/10
Afghanistan	Afghani	78.380992	69.855065	68.5431	not listed
Albania	Lek	172.781275	162.359977	162.221	not listed
Algeria	Dinar	124.78715	117.306367	114.760	115.670
Angola	Readj Kwanza	151.5323	150.405122	143.685	not listed
Antigua	E Caribbean Dollar	4.2866025	4.314367	4.1916	4.3023
Argentina	Peso	7.343248	6.707446	6.1477	6.0580
Armenia	Dram	643.669	602.531816	569.704	not listed
Aruba	Florin	2.84188	2.860271	2.7789	not listed
Australia	Dollar	1.544287	1.527388	1.6526	1.8829
Azerbaijan	New Manat	1.2456	1.257910	1.2438	not listed
Bahamas	Dollar	1.589812	1.595813	1.5534	not listed
Bahrain	Dinar	0.59856	0.623104	0.5853	0.6005
Bangladesh	Taka	129.431575	122.097979	108.732	110.103
Barbados	Dollar	3.175235	3.1958	3.1049	3.1853
Belarus	Rouble	13,327.6875	10,098.713469	4,667.51	not listed
Belize	Dollar	3.061117	3.153559	3.0273	not listed
Benin	CFA Franc	815.514775	758.896061	771.028	739.927
Bermuda	Dollar (US)	1.589812	1.595813	1.5534	not listed
Bhutan	Ngultrum	86.500239	76.204480	70.8063	not listed
Bolivia	Boliviano	10.969937	11.0613551	10.8805	11.1804
Bosnia-Herzegovina	Marka	2.431597	2.262785	2.2989	not listed
Botswana	Pula	12.544555	11.116155	10.5024	10.8900
Brazil	Real	3.2019	2.7055	2.6850	2.9799
Brunei	Dollar	1.977255	1.999428	2.0706	2.2677
Bulgaria	Lev	2.43159	2.262806	2.2989	2.2063
Burma (Myanmar)	Kyat	1,290.06751	10.242542	9.9512	10.2089
Burkina Faso	CFA Franc	815.514775	758.896061	771.028	739.927
Burundi	Franc	2,315.584	2,065.460816	1,912.31	1,959.83

Foreign exchange rates averages for tax year

Country	Method of quoting	Currency per £1			
		2012/13	2011/12	2010/11	2009/10
Cambodia	Riel	6,412.63325	6,475.170204	6,411.57	not listed
Cameroon Republic	CFA Franc	815.514775	758.896061	771.028	739.927
Canada	Dollar	1.588204	1.582388	1.5808	1.7398
Cape Verde Islands	Escudo	136.691475	125.241448	127.476	not listed
Cayman Islands	Dollar	1.301877	16.875577	1.2730	1.3067
Central African Republic	CFA Franc	815.514775	758.896061	771.028	739.927
Chad	CFA Franc	815.514775	758.896061	771.028	739.927
Chile	Peso	771.85795	771.868046	778.013	854.751
China	Renminbi Yuan	10.017312	10.233969	10.4195	10.8798
Colombia	Peso	73,260.12825	2,918.789591	2,919.66	3,183.33
Comoros	Franc	611.6362	569.173571	578.271	not listed
Congo (Brazzaville)	CFA Franc	815.514775	758.896061	771.028	739.927
Congo Dem Rep (Zaire)	Cong Franc	1,459.6485	1,452.243163	1,408.80	1,354.89
Costa Rica	Colon	795.054275	810.611653	797.682	906.539
Cote d'Ivoire	CFA Franc	815.514775	758.896061	771.028	739.927
Croatia	Kuna	9.3297425	8.641553	8.5941	not listed
Cuba	Peso	1.58765	1.597918	1.5524	1.5935
Czech Republic	Koruna	31.29844	28.608051	29.3266	29.3613
Denmark	Krone	9.262117	8.623805	8.7744	8.4083
Djibouti	Franc	279.107975	279.288836	272.593	not listed
Dominica	E Caribbean Dollar	4.286602	4.314367	4.1916	4.3023
Dominican Republic	Peso	62.354487	61.140210	57.3988	not listed
Ecuador	Dollar	1.589812	1.595813	1.5534	1.5962
Egypt	Egyptian pound	9.654277	9.556418	8.8873	8.8012
El Salvador	Colon	13.887712	13.977663	13.5802	13.9391
Equatorial Guinea	CFA Franc	815.514775	758.896061	771.028	739.927
Eritrea	Nakfa	23.813152	23.968518	23.2869	not listed
Ethiopia	Birr	28.445622	27.373510	23.7448	19.7973
European Union	Euro	1.243802	1.158234	1.1779	1.1298
Fiji	Dollar	2.853422	2.838495	2.9422	3.1723
French Polynesia	CFP franc	148.35845	138.058836	140.178	134.515

Foreign exchange rates averages for tax year

Country	Method of quoting	Currency per £1			
		2012/13	2011/12	2010/11	2009/10
Gabon	CFA Franc	815.514775	758.896061	771.028	739.927
Gambia	Dalasi	50.012227	46.145063	43.6734	42.4940
Georgia	Lari	49.854902	47.147438	46.9792	not listed
Ghana	Cedi	3.013477	2.534230	2.2560	2.3068
Grenada/Windward Isles	E. Caribbean dollar	4.286602	4.314367	4.1916	4.3023
Guatemala	Quetzal	12.477575	12.427604	12.3875	not listed
Guinea Bissau	CFA Franc	815.514775	758.896061	771.028	739.927
Guinea Republic	Franc	10,987.181715	11,045.720408	9,528.77	not listed
Guyana	Dollar	319.1083	323.391816	315.165	322.95
Haiti	Gourde	66.633315	64.538159	61.8747	not listed
Honduras	Lempira	30.81541	30.241383	29.3338	30.1084
Hong Kong	Dollar	12.33068	12.412126	12.0852	12.3810
Hungary	Forint	357.2737	328.864489	324.947	308.141
Iceland	Krona	179.505475	187.988285	185.726	200.920
India	Rupee	86.500239	76.204480	70.8063	75.5588
Indonesia	Rupiah	15,015.7875	14,013.842857	13,976.89	15,601.1
Iran	Rial	19,509.6825	17,459.891836	15,803.40	15,770.0
Iraq	Dinar	1,844.89425	1,863.107346	1,812.31	1,838.48
Israel	Shekel	6.162295	5.769878	5.7495	6.1280
Jamaica	Dollar	141.45215	137.063469	133.469	141.387
Japan	Yen	127.557341	126.098730	133.404	148.193
Jordan	Dinar	1.124432	1.132322	1.0992	1.1278
Kazakhstan	Tenge	237.301475	234.887938	228.3217	not listed
Kenya	Kenyan shilling	134.4561	142.959510	124.986	121.942
Korea (North)	Won	2.063802	2.077273	5.9759	not listed
Korea (South)	Won	1,786.164390	1,769.754230	1,789.59	1,924.48
Kuwait	Dinar	0.67081	0.441012	0.4424	0.4582
Kyrgyz Republic	Som	49.854902	47.147438	46.9792	not listed
Laos	Kip	12,647.16	12,758.136734	12,629.80	13,502.7
Latvia	Lats	0.866422	0.815826	0.8318	0.7975
Lebanon	Lebanese pound	2,388.616	2,407.453061	2,330.14	2,391.71
Lesotho	Loti	13.279955	11.804930	11.1799	not listed
Liberia	Dollar	1.589812	1.595813	1.5534	not listed
Libya	Libyan dinar	1.991437	1.939242	1.9555	1.9751
Lithuania	Litas	4.29271	3.994697	4.0586	3.8949

Foreign exchange rates averages for tax year

Country	Method of quoting	Currency per £1			
		2012/13	2011/12	2010/11	2009/10
Macao	Pataca	12.683102	12.802108	12.4302	not listed
Macedonia	Denar	76.625557	71.130687	72.3545	not listed
Madagascar	Malagasy Ariary	3,499.89	3,282.515102	3,235.71	not listed
Malawi	Kwacha	440.306325	255.308673	234.095	229.365
Malaysia	Ringgit	4.919212	4.881986	4.8847	5.5113
Maldive Islands	Rufiyaa	24.396255	24.037028	19.8715	not listed
Mali Republic	CFA Franc	815.514775	758.896061	771.028	739.927
Mauritania	Ouguiya	472.82065	452.906224	435.960	not listed
Mauritius	Rupee	48.321222	45.684714	47.4584	49.6959
Mexico	Peso	20.991612	20.160430	19.3674	20.8849
Moldova	Leu	19.35355	18.644859	19.0175	not listed
Mongolia	Tugrik	2,159.64525	2,054.568163	2,036.42	not listed
Montserrat	E Caribbean Dollar	4.286602	4.314367	4.1916	4.3023
Morocco	Dirham	13.772027	12.764963	13.1101	12.7327
Mozambique	Metical	45.448342	44.630057	53.4336	not listed
Nepal	Rupee	138.2563	121.368040	113.131	120.696
Netherlands Antilles	Antilles guilder				2.8523
New Caledonia	CFP Franc	148.35845	138.058836	140.178	134.515
New Zealand	Dollar	1.970724	1.981894	2.1253	2.3637
Nicaragua	Gold Cordoba	37.603287	36.206320	33.5288	32.8596
Niger Republic	CFA Franc	815.514775	758.896061	771.028	739.927
Nigeria	Naira	251.94395	250.632612	235.512	239.591
Norway	Krone	9.256758	8.964901	9.3501	9.6327
Oman (Sultanate of)	Rial	0.611292	0.615242	0.5958	0.6132
Pakistan	Rupee	149.7295	139.665653	132.5522	132.082
Panama	Balboa	1.58765	1.597918	1.5524	not listed
Papua New Guinea	Kina	3.26458	3.575102	4.1689	4.2584
Paraguay	Guarani	7,014.83425	6,668.881020	7,336.74	7,779.04
Peru	New sol	4.16687	4.366532	4.3585	4.6586
Philippines	Peso	66.694146	68.79605	69.2370	75.1918
Poland	Zloty	5.18775	4.834936	4.6846	4.7177
Qatar	Riyal	5.780567	5.818567	5.6514	5.7982
Romania	Leu	5.590047	4.937955	4.9797	4.7312
Russia	Rouble	49.854902	47.147438	46.9792	48.6544
Rwanda	Rwanda franc	979.919575	961.236734	914.592	908.223

Foreign exchange rates averages for tax year

Country	Method of quoting	Currency per £1			
		2012/13	2011/12	2010/11	2009/10
São Tomé & Principe	Dobra	29,991.6275	28,351.277551	28,529.41	not listed
Saudi Arabia	Riyal	5.962043	5.984640	5.8298	5.9728
Senegal	CFA Franc	815.514775	758.896061	771.028	739.927
Serbia	Dinar	142.497325	118.896142	122.468	not listed
Seychelles	Seychelles rupee	21.640117	20.373306	19.0717	19.6567
Sierra Leone	Leone	6,887.74925	6,990.352448	6,.301.37	5,723.55
Singapore	Dollar	1.978721	2.000944	2.0721	2.2719
Solomon Islands	Dollar	11.25496	11.822644	12.1765	12.7244
Somali Republic	Shilling	2,497.6395	2,511.687346	2,385.47	2,236.85
South Africa	Rand	13.288097	11.852196	11.1773	12.4676
Sri Lanka	Rupee	207.29165	178.794204	174.211	183.205
St Christopher & Nevis	E Caribbean Dollar	4.286602	4.314367	4.1916	4.3023
St Lucia	E Caribbean Dollar	4.286602	4.314367	4.1916	4.3023
St Vincent	E Caribbean Dollar	4.286602	4.314367	4.1916	4.3023
Sudan Republic	Pound	6.056327	4.285691	3.6864	3.7308
Surinam	Dollar	5.239172	5.273114	4.3988	4.3741
Swaziland	Lilangeni	13.279955	11.8049306	11.1799	12.3156
Sweden	Krona	10.7687	10.448853	10.9373	11.7215
Switzerland	Franc	1.498065	1.407255	1.5768	1.6961
Syria	Syrian pound	103.983882	80.319404	72.2270	73.1795
Taiwan	New Taiwan Dollar	46.947095	47.0277576	47.9890	51.7867
Tajikistan	Somoni	49.854902	47.147438	46.9792	not listed
Tanzania	Tanzanian shilling	2,514.73725	2,565.878367	2,290.20	2,118.02
Thailand	Baht	49.412148	48.795525	48.3928	53.7107
Togo Republic	CFA Franc	815.514775	758.896061	771.028	739.927
Tonga Islands	Pa anga	1.544287	1.527388	1.6526	3.1071
Trinidad &Tobago	Dollar	10.17442	10.232887	9.8753	10.0652
Tunisia	Dinar	2.50812	2.276393	2.2401	2.1345
Turkey	Turkish Lira	2.862235	2.752214	2.3646	2.4160
Turkmenistan	New Manat	4.518597	4.543610	30.3560	not listed
Uganda	New shilling	4,032.06325	4,055.644693	3,504.66	3,237.06
Ukraine	Hryvnia	12.860747	12.784306	12.3142	not listed
United Arab Emirates	Dirham	7.081095	5.869067	5.7021	5.8497
Uruguay	Peso uruguayo	32.491295	30.635430	31.0534	34.3153
USA	Dollar	1.589812	1.5958134	1.5534	1.5962
Uzbekistan	Sum	3,036.15975	2,792.517959	2,507.69	not listed

Foreign exchange rates averages for tax year

Country	Method of quoting	Currency per £1			
		2012/13	2011/12	2010/11	2009/10
Vanuatu	Vatu	150.209575	148.545367	153.126	not listed
Venezuela	Bolivar Fuerte	6.81797	6.862446	6.6673	3.4498 (1.4.09–10.1.10
Vietnam	Dong	33,125.295	33,256.906122	30,237.45	28,974.5
Wallis & Futuna Islands	CFP Franc	148.35845	138.058836	140.178	134.515
Western Samoa	Tala	3.65195	3.666714	3.8094	not listed
Yemen (Rep of)	Rial	341.167225	345.455408	340.988	329.603
Zambia	Kwacha	8,138.50675	7,907.839387	7,497.68	7,741.14
Zimbabwe	Dollar	600.613974	604.135510	587.473	not listed

Foreign exchange rates averages for calendar year

For general use Country	Method of quoting	Currency per £1 2012	2011	2010	2009
Afghanistan	Afghani	76.767648	69.078780	69.1915	not listed
Albania	Lek	171.529816	161.708470	160.437	not listed
Algeria	Dinar	123.093387	117.053862	114.004	113.373
Angola	Readj Kwanza	150.805061	150.193725	141.856	not listed
Antigua	E Caribbean Dollar	4.271626	4.328835	4.1700	4.2229
Argentina	Peso	7.181784	6.611286	6.0480	5.8426
Armenia	Dram	635.239489	595.023235	574.115	not listed
Aruba	Florin	2.831951	2.869862	2.7646	not listed
Australia	Dollar	1.530380	1.553232	1.6872	1.9923
Azerbaijan	New Manat	1.241604	1.266621	1.2405	not listed
Bahamas	Dollar	1.582875	1.603844	1.5457	not listed
Bahrain	Dinar	0.596475	0.624317	0.5822	0.5896
Bangladesh	Taka	129.561714	118.157254	107.448	108.191
Barbados	Dollar	3.164138	3.206519	3.0889	3.1280
Belarus	Rouble	13,228.889795	8,126.321960	4,601.43	not listed
Belize	Dollar	3.050991	3.165149	3.0117	not listed
Benin	CFA Franc	809.512836	755.748666	763.823	736.978
Bermuda	Dollar	1.582875	1.603844	1.5457	not listed
Bhutan	Ngultrum	84.532805	74.557648	70.7247	not listed
Bolivia	Boliviano	10.931695	11.126	10.8402	10.9794
Bosnia-Herzegovina	Marka	2.413702	2.2534	2.2774	not listed
Botswana	Pula	12.296653	10.915992	10.5076	11.0911
Brazil	Real	3.091557	2.67755	2.7216	3.1109
Brunei	Dollar	1.978051	2.013958	2.1075	2.2743
Bulgaria	Lev	2.413708	2.253421	2.2775	2.1974
Burma (Myanmar)	Kyat	998.850914	10.276898	9.8999	10.0277
Burkina Faso	CFA Franc	809.512836	755.748666	763.823	736.978
Burundi	Franc	2,278.453877	2,015.156274	1,900.760	1,929.10

Foreign exchange rates averages for calendar year

For general use Country	Method of quoting	Currency per £1 2012	2011	2010	2009
Cambodia	Riel	6,389.105714	6,475.575490	6,449.20	not listed
Cameroon Republic	CFA Franc	809.512836	755.748666	763.823	736.978
Canada	Dollar	1.583601	1.584378	1.5942	1.7801
Cape Verde Islands	Escudo	135.763795	124.081607	125.333	not listed
Cayman Islands	Dollar	1.297328	16.269574	1.2664	1.2851
Central African Republic	CFA Franc	809.512836	755.748666	763.823	736.978
Chad	CFA Franc	809.512836	755.748666	763.823	736.978
Chile	Peso	770.0784489	771.550411	788.607	870.827
China	Renminbi/Yuan	9.988053	10.374478	10.4587	10.7044
Colombia	Peso	60,320.529387	2,959.414509	2,932.07	3,358.97
Comoros	Franc	607.134714	566.812980	572.867	not listed
Congo (Brazzaville)	CFA Franc	809.512836	755.748666	763.823	736.978
Congo Dem Rep (Zaire)	Cong Franc	1,454.9075510204	1,458.637352	1,398.04	1,263.11
Costa Rica	Colon	795.48502040816	810.964078	812.658	898.802
Cote d'Ivoire	CFA Franc	809.512836	755.748666	763.823	736.978
Croatia	Kuna	9.276048	8.560872	8.4828	not listed
Cuba	Peso	1.582097	1.603278	1.5444	1.5673
Czech Republic	Koruna	31.050883	28.314162	29.4579	29.8025
Denmark	Krone	9.181059	8.576243	8.6860	8.3581
Djibouti	Franc	277.746816	280.387372	269.667	not listed
Dominica	E Caribbean Dollar	4.271626	4.328835	4.1700	4.2229
Dominican Republic	Peso	61.943573	60.816127	55.6198	not listed
Ecuador	Dollar	1.582875	1.603844	1.5457	1.5633
Egypt	Egyptian pound	9.598010	9.519580	8.6949	8.6820
El Salvador	Colon	13.839181	14.024547	13.5101	13.7107
Equatorial Guinea	CFA Franc	809.512836	755.748666	763.823	736.978
Eritrea	Nakfa	23.730136	24.048915	23.1668	not listed
Ethiopia	Birr	28.144177	27.1943392	22.2520	18.7056
European Union	Euro	1.233473	1.151701	1.1664	1.1235
Fiji	Dollar	2.834738	2.874145	2.9662	3.0833
French Polynesia	CFP franc	147.266612	137.471117	138.859	133.979

Foreign exchange rates averages for calendar year

For general use

Country	Method of quoting	Currency per £1 2012	2011	2010	2009
Gabon	CFA Franc	809.512836	755.748666	763.823	736.978
Gambia	Dalasi	49.346304	45.487305	42.8580	41.6103
Georgia	Lari	49.320938	47.057882	46.8976	not listed
Ghana	Cedi	2.9353	2.471605	2.2107	2.2426
Grenada/Windward Isles	E. Caribbean dollar	4.271626	4.328835	4.1700	4.2229
Guatemala	Quetzal	12.402746	12.498837	12.4608	not listed
Guinea Bissau	CFA Franc	809.512836	755.748666	763.823	736.978
Guinea Republic	Franc	11,031.342216	11,127.678431	8,621.46	not listed
Guyana	Dollar	318.159979	325.0505294	313.612	316.241
Haiti	Gourde	65.880948	64.599154	61.4082	not listed
Honduras	Lempira	30.551165	30.287207	29.1825	29.6097
Hong Kong	Dollar	12.279098	12.484348	12.0140	12.1317
Hungary	Forint	356.920591	321.140764	320.900	316.187
Iceland	Krona	181.907653	185.767450	188.908	193.524
India	Rupee	84.532805	74.557648	70.7247	75.6294
Indonesia	Rupiah	14,803.457142	14,037.286274	14,035.67	16,175.8
Iran	Rial	19,282.640816	16,977.892156	15,547.67	15,443.8
Iraq	Dinar	1,838.802040	1,872.536274	1,798.32	1,802.03
Israel	Shekel	6.108028	5.724734	5.7775	6.1341
Jamaica	Dollar	139.787857	137.1204117	134.233	137.646
Japan	Yen	126.15025	128.003692	136.104	146.366
Jordan	Dinar	1.120644	1.135860	1.0936	1.1077
Kazakhstan	Tenge	235.948204	235.107098	227.608	not listed
Kenya	Kenyan shilling	133.743897	142.140686	122.237	120.848
Korea (North)	Won	2.056610	6.119613	6.4555	not listed
Korea (South)	Won	1,785.194230	1,774.787692	1,789.25	1,993.87
Kuwait	Dinar	0.627044	0.443325	0.4432	0.4508
Kyrgyz Republic	Som	49.320938	47.057882	46.8976	not listed
Laos	Kip	12,601.877551	12,823.652941	12,730.19	13,295.8
Latvia	Lats	0.860487	0.814049	0.8252	0.7936
Lebanon	Pound	2,380.240816	2,413.901568	2,318.38	2,348.60
Lesotho	Loti	13.0064102	11.560037	11.3297	not listed
Liberia	Dollar	1.582875	1.603844	1.5457	not listed
Libya	Libyan Dinar	1.977814	1.946633	1.9500	1.9538
Lithuania	Litas	4.261118	3.978150	4.0206	3.8793

Foreign exchange rates averages for calendar year

For general use Country	Method of quoting	Currency per £1 2012	2011	2010	2009
Macao	Pataca	12.640185	12.854964	12.3571	not listed
Macedonia	Denar	76.009671	70.877366	71.6306	not listed
Madagascar	Malagasy Ariary	3,479.529183	3,246.625294	3,239.96	not listed
Malawi	Kwacha	395.980142	250.396784	232.259	221.896
Malaysia	Ringgit	4.889942	4.899313	4.9881	5.5051
Maldive Islands	Rufiyaa	24.315871	23.093664	19.7690	not listed
Mali Republic	CFA Franc	809.512836	755.748666	763.823	736.978
Mauritania	Ouguiya	469.061795	451.256274	426.049	not listed
Mauritius	Rupee	47.713481	46.046884	47.4705	49.8915
Mexico	Peso	20.875711	19.867946	19.5447	21.0920
Moldova	Leu	19.169014	18.811905	19.1203	not listed
Mongolia	Tugrik	2,149.365918	2,021.839215	2,099.56	not listed
Montserrat	E Caribbean Dollar	4.271626	4.328835	4.1700	4.2229
Morocco	Dirham	13.681197	12.740574	12.9956	12.6491
Mozambique	Metical	44.731187	46.630631	53.0502	not listed
Nepal	Rupee	135.203061	119.028039	112.992	121.294
New Caledonia	CFP Franc	147.266612	137.471117	138.859	133.979
New Zealand	Dollar	1.959825	2.029523	2.1475	2.4870
Nicaragua	Gold Cordoba	37.239314	35.904198	32.9591	31.9532
Niger Republic	CFA Franc	809.512836	755.748666	763.823	736.978
Nigeria	Naira	251.436428	249.169352	233.241	234.162
Norway	Krone	9.233155	8.977276	9.3440	9.8078
Oman (Sultanate of)	Rial	0.609144	0.617333	0.5926	0.6022
Pakistan	Rupee	147.702285	138.291588	131.523	127.926
Panama	Balboa	1.582097	1.603278	1.5444	not listed
Papua New Guinea	Kina	3.260636	3.792364	4.1784	4.2283
Paraguay	Guarani	7,021.556938	6,744.826274	7,356.67	7,783.09
Peru	New sol	4.177540	4.416507	4.3644	4.6983
Philippines	Peso	66.912084	69.410809	69.7964	74.5322
Poland	Zloty	5.169414	4.731154	4.6600	4.8775
Qatar	Riyal	5.760416	5.837937	5.6217	5.6946
Romania	Leu	5.512736	4.887498	4.9026	4.7645
Russia	Rouble	49.320938	47.0578823	46.8976	49.7386
Rwanda	Rwanda franc	971.315836	961.775333	900.073	891.257

Foreign exchange rates averages for calendar year

For general use Country	Method of quoting	Currency per £1 2012	2011	2010	2009
Saotome & Principe	Dobra	29,877.959183	28,235.141176	27,844.13	not listed
Saudi Arabia	Riyal	5.936051	6.014736	5.7997	5.8657
Senegal	CFA Franc	809.512836	755.748666	763.823	736.978
Serbia	Dinar	139.699734	117.515235	119.803	not listed
Seychelles	Seychelles rupee	21.708744	19.832025	18.6821	21.1657
Sierra Leone	Leone	6,872.885714	6,965.582156	6,134.06	5,314.64
Singapore	Dollar	1.980832	2.015259	2.1104	2.2711
Solomon Islands	Dollar	11.224248	12.114521	12.1738	12.4682
Somali Republic	Shilling	2,491.090204	2,510.116862	2,337.21	2,161.21
South Africa	Rand	13.006967	11.578746	11.3266	13.0021
Sri Lanka	Rupee	202.164448	177.075039	174.697	180.184
St Chrisopher & Nevis	E Caribbean Dollar	4.271626	4.328835	4.1700	4.2229
St Lucia	E Caribbean Dollar	4.271626	4.328835	4.1700	4.2229
St Vincent	E Caribbean Dollar	4.271626	4.328835	4.1700	4.2229
Sudan Republic	Pound	5.594983	4.230813	3.5933	3.6544
Surinam	Dollar	5.220865	5.205325	4.2395	4.3020
Swaziland	Lilangeni	13.006410	11.560037	11.3297	12.9656
Sweden	Krona	10.741259	10.395490	11.1487	11.9491
Switzerland	Franc	1.486984	1.421359	1.6133	1.6968
Syria	Syrian pound	100.277797	76.863907	71.4882	72.0249
Taiwan	New Taiwan Dollar	46.858536	47.0815961	48.7931	51.6003
Tajikistan	Somoni	49.320938	47.0578823	46.8976	not listed
Tanzania	Tanzanian shilling	2,509.602040	2,535.730980	2,220.88	2,071.20
Thailand	Baht	49.223330	48.820230	49.1000	53.6478
Togo Republic	CFA Franc	809.512836	755.748666	763.823	736.978
Tonga Islands	Pa anga	1.530380	1.553232	1.6872	3.1526
Trinidad &Tobago	Dollar	10.137330	10.261809	9.8046	9.8537
Tunisia	Dinar	2.476826	2.253631	2.2082	2.1093
Turkey	Turkish Lira	2.850042	2.677966	2.3258	2.4264
Turkmenistan	New Manat	4.500820	4.560825	40.7772	not listed
Uganda	New shilling	3,956.551836	4,042.469215	3,353.59	3,177.46
Ukraine	Hryvnia	12.792736	12.797878	12.2721	not listed
United Arab Emirates	Dirham	6.831167	5.888749	5.6727	5.7445
Uruguay	Peso uruguayo	32.104220	30.822629	30.8988	35.2328
USA	Dollar	1.582875	1.603844	1.5457	1.5633
Uzbekistan	Sum	2,986.947755	2,741.073725	2,446.83	not listed

Foreign exchange rates averages for calendar year

For general use Country	Method of quoting	Currency per £1 2012	2011	2010	2009
Vanuatu	Vatu	149.246306	149.979921	154.135	not listed
Venezuela	Bolivar Fuerte	6.794202	6.885468	6.4983	3.3620
Vietnam	Dong	33,021.285714	33,063.927450	29,549.79	28,019.6
Wallis & Futuna Islands	CFP Franc	147.266612	137.471117	138.859	133.979
Western Samoa	Tala	3.631644	3.720178	3.8429	not listed
Yemen (Rep of)	Rial	341.023040	345.071235	338.921	318.436
Zambia	Kwacha	8,132.805510	7,779.138823	7,400.46	7,870.74
Zimbabwe	Dollar	598.385187	606.220352	582.837	not listed

Foreign exchange rates at specified dates

For general use Country	Method of quoting	Currency per £1 31.3.13	31.12.12	31.3.12	31.12.11	31.3.11	31.12.10	31.3.10	31.12.09
Australia	Dollar	1.4626	1.5657	1.5423	1.5159	1.55	1.5274	1.6527	1.7956
Canada	Dollar	1.5489	1.6185	1.5969	1.5825	1.5593	1.5557	1.5390	1.6930
Denmark	Krone	8.8392	9.1989	8.9259	8.8978	8.4221	8.697	8.3459	8.3750
European Union	Euro	1.1857	1.233	1.1998	1.1972	1.1296	1.1671	1.1211	1.1255
Hong Kong	Dollar	11.826	12.5991	12.405	12.0701	12.4681	12.1708	11.7783	12.5217
Japan	Yen	142.058	140.549	131.487	119.572	132.853	126.982	141.739	150.335
Norway	Krone	8.8618	9.0463	9.1137	9.2748	8.8671	9.1003	9.0038	9.3287
South Africa	Rand	13.9881	13.7914	12.262	12.5469	10.8351	10.358	11.1401	11.8914
Sweden	Krona	9.9125	10.5746	10.6016	10.6539	10.1121	10.5256	10.9171	11.5302
Switzerland	Franc	1.4439	1.4879	1.4442	1.4532	1.4665	1.4593	1.5967	1.6693
USA	Dollar	1.5233	1.6255	1.5978	1.5541	1.603	1.5657	1.5169	1.6149

Note

The material on p 43–55 is reproduced from information provided by HMRC and is Crown copyright.

Government securities

Security		Interest dates
Annuities		
2½%	Undated (note (c))	5 Jan/Apr/Jul/Oct
2¾%	Undated (note (c))	5 Jan/Apr/Jul/Oct
Consolidated Stock		
2½%	Undated (note (c))	5 Jan/Apr/Jul/Oct
4%	Undated (note (c))	1 Feb/Aug
Conversion Stock		
3½%	Undated (note (c))	1 Apr/Oct
Exchequer Stock		
12%	2013/17 (note (c))	12 Jun/Dec

Security		Interest dates
Treasury Stock Index Linked		
0⅛%	2024	22 Mar/Sept
0⅛%	2029	22 Mar/Sept
0⅛%	2044	22 Mar/Sept
0¼%	2052	22 Mar/Sept
0⅜%	2062	22 Mar/Sept
0½%	2050	22 Mar/Sept
0⅝%	2040	22 Mar/Sept
0⅝%	2042	22 May/Nov
0¾%	2034	22 Mar/Sept
0¾%	2047	22 May/Nov
1⅛%	2037	22 May/Nov
1¼%	2017	22 May/Nov
1¼%	2027	22 May/Nov
1¼%	2032	22 May/Nov
1¼%	2055	22 May/Nov
1⅞%	2022	22 May/Nov
2%	2035	26 Jan/Jul
2¼%	2023	7 Mar/Sept
2½%	2013	16 Feb/Aug
2½%	2016	26 Jan/Jul
2½%	2020	16 Apr/Oct
2½%	2024	17 Jan/Jul
4⅛%	2030	22 Jan/Jul
Treasury Loan/Stock		
1%	2017	7 Mar/Sept
1¾%	2017	22 Jan/Jul
1¼%	2018	22 Jan/Jul
1¾%	2022	7 Mar/Sept
2%	2016	22 Jan/Jul
2¼%	2014	7 Mar/Sept
2½%	Undated (note (c))	1 Apr/Oct
2¾%	2015	22 Jan/Jul
3%	Undated (note (c))	5 Apr/Oct

Security		Interest dates
3¼%	2044	22 Jan/Jul
3½%	2068	22 Jan/Jul
3¾%	2019	7 Mar/Sept
3¾%	2020	7 Mar/Sept
3¾%	2021	7 Mar/Sept
3¾%	2052	22 Jan/Jul
4%	2016	7 Mar/Sept
4%	2022	7 Mar Sept
4%	2060	22 Jan/Jul
4¼%	2027	7 Jun/Dec
4¼%	2032	7 Jun/Dec
4¼%	2036	7 Mar/Sept
4¼%	2039	7 Mar/Sept
4¼%	2040	7 Jun/Dec
4¼%	2046	7 Jun/Dec
4¼%	2049	7 Jun/Dec
4¼%	2055	7 Jun/Dec
4½%	2019	7 Mar/Sept
4½%	2034	7 Mar/Sept
4½%	2042	7 Jun/Dec
4¾%	2015	7 Mar/Sept
4¾%	2020	7 Mar/Sept
4¾%	2030	7 Jun/Dec
4¾%	2038	7 Jun/Dec
5%	2014	7 Mar/Sept
5%	2018	7 Mar/Sep
5%	2025	7 Mar/Sept
6%	2028	7 Jun/Dec
8%	2013	27 Mar/Sept
8%	2015	7 Jun/Dec
8%	2021	7 Jun/Dec
8¾%	2017	25 Feb/Aug
War Loan		
3½%	Undated	1 Jun/Dec

Notes

(a) The government securities listed above are those in issue on 18 July 2013.

(b) Interest on all government securities is exempt from income tax if beneficially owned by persons who are not ordinarily resident in the UK. [*FA 1998, s 161; ITTOIA 2005, ss 713, 714*].

The securities are also excluded property for inheritance tax purposes if beneficially owned by persons who are not ordinarily resident in the UK. [*IHTA 1984, s 6(2)*].

(c) A restricted market applies to these securities because of the small amount of stock still in issue.

Income tax rates

Starting, basic, higher and additional rates

	Taxable income	Rate	Tax	Cumulative tax
2013/14	£		£	£
Basic rate	0–32,010	20%	6,402	6,402
Higher rate	32,011–150,000	40%	47,196	53,598
Additional rate	Over 150,000	45%		
2012/13	£		£	£
Basic rate	0–34,370	20%	6,874	6,874
Higher rate	34,371–150,000	40%	46,252	53,126
Additional rate	Over 150,000	50%		
2011/12	£		£	£
Basic rate	0–35,000	20%	7,000	7,000
Higher rate	35,001–150,000	40%	46,000	53,000
Additional rate	Over 150,000	50%		
2010/11	£		£	£
Basic rate	0–37,400	20%	7,480	7,480
Higher rate	37,401–150,000	40%	45,040	52,520
Additional rate	Over 150,000	50%		

	Taxable income	Rate	Tax	Cumulative tax
2009/10	£		£	£
Basic rate	0–37,400	20%	7,480	7,480
Higher rate	Over 37,400	40%		
2008/09	£		£	£
Basic rate	0–34,800	20%	6,960	6,960
Higher rate	Over 34,800	40%		
2007/08	£		£	£
Starting rate	0–2,230	10%	223	223
Basic rate	2,231–34,600	22%	7,121.40	7,344.40
Higher rate	Over 34,600	40%		

Trust rate (note (d))

	Rate
2013/14	45%
2010/11–2012/13	50%
2007/08–2009/10	40%

Construction industry sub-contractors' rates

	Rate
Registered rate	20%
Unregistered rate	30%

Notes

(a) For 2008/09 onwards, there is also a starting rate for savings band. For 2013/14 the band is £2,790; for 2012/13 it is £2,710; for 2011/12 it is £2,560; for 2009/10 and 2010/11 it is £2,440; for 2008/09 it is £2,320. Where an individual's non-savings income is less than the starting rate limit for savings, the savings income is taxable at the 10% starting rate for savings up to the limit. Where non-savings income exceeds the limit, the starting rate for savings does not apply. For 2007/08 the starting rate band applies to any income falling within the band, and the band is not withdrawn where income exceeds the limit.

(b) **Dividend income.** Where dividend income falls within the starting rate or the basic rate band (treating dividend income as the top slice of taxable income), the rate is set at 10% so that the liability is met by the 10% tax credit, where applicable. To the extent that taxable income exceeds the basic rate limit but not, for 2010/11 onwards, the higher rate limit, the rate is set at 32.5% (with a tax credit at 10%). Dividend income within the additional rate band is taxable at the rate of 37.5% for 2013/14 onwards, and at the rate of 42.5% for 2010/11 to 2012/13 (in both cases with a tax credit at 10%). The tax credit cannot be repaid where allowances are set against dividends, and tax credits may only be set against liability in respect of dividends brought into charge.

Discretionary and accumulation trusts pay tax on dividends at the rate of 37.5% (42.5% for 2010/11 to 2012/13; 32.5% for 2009/10 and earlier years). The non-repayable tax credit attaching to the dividend does not form part of the trustees' tax pool.

(c) **Interest income.** Interest income (i.e. bank and building society interest, interest distributions from authorised unit trusts, interest on gilts and other securities including qualifying corporate bonds and purchased life annuities) is treated as the second top slice of taxable income behind dividends. Where the income falls within the basic rate band, it is chargeable at 20% and to the extent that if falls within the higher rate band it is taxed at 40%. For 2010/11 onwards, interest income within the additional rate band is taxed at the rate of 45% for 2013/14 onwards, and at the rate of 50% for 2010/11 to 2012/13. For 2008/09 onwards, see note (a) above where the income falls within the starting rate for savings band. For 2007/08, income falling within the starting rate band is chargeable at the starting rate of 10%.

Tax deducted at source (at 20%) from interest income is repayable to the extent (if any) that it exceeds the liability on that income, computed as above.

(d) Trusts for vulnerable beneficiaries can be taxed (on election) as if the income arising were that of the beneficiary, taking into account personal allowances and the starting, basic, higher and additional rate bands.

Where any trust income consists of or includes income otherwise chargeable at the dividend trust rate or the trust rate ('special trust tax rate income'), so much of that income as does not exceed £1,000 is chargeable to income tax at the basic rate, savings rate or the ordinary dividend rate, depending on the nature of the income.

(e) **Personal representatives etc.** The starting, higher and additional rates do not apply to persons other than individuals (e.g. personal representatives). For 2008/09 onwards tax is chargeable at the ordinary dividend rate for dividends (covered by the tax credit where applicable) and at the basic rate for other income. For 2007/08, tax is chargeable at the savings rate for interest income, at the ordinary dividend rate and the basic rate.

(f) For 2014/15 the basic rate limit is £31,865.

Income tax allowances

	2013/14	2012/13	2011/12	2010/11	2009/10	2008/09	2007/08
	£	£	£	£	£	£	£
Personal allowance	9,440	8,105	7,475	6,475	6,475	6,035	5,225
Income limit (allowance reduced by ½ excess)	100,000	100,000	100,000	100,000	—	—	—
Persons born before 6.4.1948 and over 65 (note (a))							
Income limit (allowance reduced by ½ excess)	26,100	25,400	24,000	22,900	22,900	21,800	20,900
Personal allowance — person born before 6.4.1948 and after 5.4.1938	10,500	—	—	—	—	—	—
— effective maximum income for claim	28,220	—	—	—	—	—	—
Personal allowance age 65 to 74	—	10,500	9,940	9,490	9,490	9,030	7,550
— effective maximum income for claim	—	30,190	28,930	28,930	28,930	27,790	25,550
Personal allowance — person born before 6.4.1938	10,660	—	—	—	—	—	—
— effective maximum income for claim	28,540	—	—	—	—	—	—
Personal allowance age over 75	—	10,660	10,090	9,640	9,640	9,180	7,690
— effective maximum income for claim	—	30,510	29,230	29,230	29,230	28,090	25,830
Married couple's allowance — either partner born before 6.4.1935 and under 75 (note (b))	—	—	—	—	—	6,535	6,285
— reduced to minimum if income exceeds							
relevant partner under 65	—	—	—	—	—	29,790	28,590
relevant partner 65–74	—	—	—	—	—	35,780	33,240
Married couple's allowance — either partner born before 6.4.1935 and over 75 (note (b))	7,915	7,705	7,295	6,965	6,965	6,625	6,365
— reduced to minimum if income exceeds							
relevant partner under 65	35,850	34,890	32,990	31,490	31,490	29,970	28,750
relevant partner 65–74	37,970	39,680	37,920	37,520	37,520	35,960	33,400
relevant partner over 75	38,290	40,000	38,220	37,820	37,820	36,260	33,680
Married couple's allowance — minimum where income exceeds limit	3,040	2,960	2,800	2,670	2,670	2,540	2,440
Blind person's allowance	2,160	2,100	1,980	1,890	1,890	1,800	1,730

Notes

(a) For 2013/14 onwards, age-related allowances apply only to individuals born before 6 April 1948, and the higher level allowance applies only to those born before 6 April 1938. Previously, such allowances operated by reference to age thresholds; the allowances applying in the first tax year in which the relevant threshold was reached. The allowance is reduced by £1 for every £2 by which the adjusted net income (i.e. after deductions for allowable reliefs and pension contributions) exceeds the income limit. The age-related personal allowance is first reduced to the basic personal allowance and then any married couple's allowance is reduced (but not below the minimum amount).

(b) The married couple's allowance is available only where at least one of the spouses or civil partners reached the age of 65 before 6 April 2000. For 2009/10 at least one of the spouses or partners must reach the age of at least 75 during the year and so qualify for the over 75 allowance.

For marriages entered into before 5 December 2005, the allowance is given initially to the husband and the amount is determined by the level of his income. For marriages and civil partnerships entered into on or after that date, the allowance is initially given to whichever of the two individuals has the higher total income for the tax year and the amount is determined by the level of that individual's income. (If their total incomes are exactly the same, the partners may make a joint election to determine which of them receives the allowance.) A couple who married before 5 December 2005 may make a joint election for the rules for marriages on or after that date to apply.

The partner not initially entitled can elect in advance to be entitled to claim one-half of the minimum allowance. A couple may jointly elect for the full amount of the minimum allowance to be transferred between them (although the partner initially entitled can subsequently elect to be able to transfer back one-half of the basic allowance).

The allowance is given as a reduction in income tax liability restricted to the lower of 10% of the amount of the allowance and the claimant's total income tax liability.

(c) For 2014/15 the basic personal allowance is £10,000.

Income tax fixed rate employee expense allowances

	2008/09 onwards	2004/05–2007/08
	£	£
Agriculture — all workers	100	70
Aluminium (Note (b))		
Continual casting and process operators, de-dimplers, driers, drill punchers, dross unloaders, firemen, furnace operators and their helpers, leaders, mouldmen, pourers, remelt department labourers, roll flatteners	140	130
Cable hands, case-makers, labourers, mates, truck drivers and measurers, storekeepers	80	60
Apprentices	60	45
All other workers	120	100
Banks and building societies — uniformed doormen and messengers	60	45
Brass and copper — all workers	120	100
Building		
Joiners and carpenters	140	105
Cement workers and roofing felt and asphalt labourers	80	55
Labourers and navvies	60	45
All other workers	120	85
Building materials		
Stone masons	120	85
Tile makers and labourers	60	45
All other workers	80	55
Clothing		
Lacemakers, hosiery bleachers, dyers, scourers and knitters, and knitwear bleachers and dyers	60	45
All other workers	60	45
Constructional engineering (Note (b))		
Blacksmiths and their strikers, burners, caulkers, chippers, drillers, erectors, fitters, holders up, markers off, platers, riggers, riveters, rivet heaters, scaffolders, sheeters, template workers, turners and welders	140	115
Banksmen labourers, shophelpers, slewers and straighteners	80	60
Apprentices and storekeepers	60	45
All other workers	100	75
Electrical and electricity supply		
Those workers incurring laundry costs only	60	45
All other workers	120	90
Engineering (trades ancillary to)		
Pattern makers	140	120
Labourers, supervisory and unskilled workers	80	60
Apprentices and storekeepers	60	45
Motor mechanics in garage repair shops	120	100

	2008/09 onwards	2004/05–2007/08
	£	£
All other workers	120	100
Fire service		
Uniformed fire fighters and fire officers	80	60
Food — all workers	60	45
Forestry — all workers	100	70
Glass — all workers	80	60
Healthcare (staff in the NHS, private hospitals and nursing homes)		
Ambulance staff on active service	140	110
Nurses, midwives, chiropodists, dental nurses, occupation, speech and other therapists, orthoptists, phlebotomists, physiotherapists, radiographers	100	70
Plaster room orderlies, hospital porters, ward clerks, sterile supply workers, hospital domestics, hospital catering staff	100	60
Laboratory staff, pharmacists, pharmacy assistants	60	45
Uniformed ancillary staff, maintenance workers, ground staff, drivers, parking attendants and security guards, receptionists and other uniformed staff	60	45
Heating		
Pipe fitters and plumbers	120	100
Coverers, laggers, domestic glaziers, heating engineers and their mates	120	90
All gas workers and all other workers	100	70
Iron and steel		
Day labourers, general labourers, stockmen, timekeepers, warehouse staff and weighmen	80	60
Apprentices	60	45
All other workers	140	120
Iron mining		
Fillers, miners and underground workers	120	100
All other workers	100	75
Leather		
Curriers (wet workers), fellmongering workers and tanning operatives (wet)	80	55
All other workers	60	45
Particular engineering (Note (b))		
Pattern makers	140	120
All chainmakers—cleaners, galvanisers, tinners and wire drawers in the wire drawing industry—toolmakers in the lockmaking industry	120	100
Apprentices and storekeepers	60	45
All other workers	80	60

	2008/09 onwards	2004/05–2007/08
	£	£
Police force		
Uniformed police officers (ranks up to and including Chief Inspector) and community support officers (£110 for 2007/08 only)	140	55
Precious metals—all workers	100	70
Printing		
Letterpress section—electrical engineers (rotary presses), electrotypers, ink and roller markers, machine minders (rotary), maintenance engineers (rotary presses) and stereotypers	140	105
Benchhands (periodical and bookbinding section), compositors and readers (letterpress section), telecommunication and electronic section wireroom operators, warehousemen (paperbox making section)	60	45
All other workers	100	70
Prisons		
Uniformed prison officers	80	55
Public service		
Dock and inland waterways:		
Dockers, dredger drivers and hopper steerers	80	55
All other workers	60	45
Public transport:		
Garage hands (including cleaners)	80	55
Conductors and drivers	60	45
Quarrying — all workers	100	70
Railways		
All workers except craftsmen	100	70
For craftsmen see the appropriate category (eg engineers)		
Seamen		
Carpenters (passenger liners)	165	165
Carpenters (cargo vessels, tankers, coasters and ferries)	140	130
Shipyards		
Blacksmiths and their strikers, boilermakers, burners, carpenters, caulkers, drillers, furnacemen (platers), holders up, fitters, platers, plumbers, riveters, sheet iron workers, shipwrights, tubers and welders	140	115
Labourers	80	60
Apprentices and storekeepers	60	45
All other workers	100	75
Textiles and textile printing		
Carders, carding engineers, overlookers and technicians in spinning mills	120	85
All other workers	80	60
Vehicles		
Builders, railway vehicle repairers, and railway wagon lifters	140	105
Railway vehicle painters, letterers and builders' and repairers' assistants	80	60
All other workers	60	45
Wood and furniture		
Carpenters, cabinet makers, joiners, wood carvers and woodcutting machinists	140	115
Artificial limb makers (other than in wood), organ builders and packing-case makers	120	90
Coopers not providing own tools, labourers, polishers and upholsterers	60	45
All other workers	100	75

Notes

(a) The table above is reproduced from the HMRC Employment Income Manual, EIM 32712 and sets out the flat rate expenses agreed under *ITEPA 2003, s 367*. An employee may instead request a deduction under *ITEPA 2003, s 336* for the actual expenses incurred but should then retain evidence to demonstrate the expenditure.

(b) In the table above: (i) in the entry relating to aluminium, 'firemen' means persons engaged to light and maintain furnaces; (ii) 'constructional engineering' means engineering undertaken on a construction site, including buildings, shipyards, bridges, roads and other similar operations; and (iii) 'particular engineering' means engineering undertaken on a commercial basis in a factory or workshop for the purposes of producing components such as wire, springs, nails and locks.

(c) For flat rate expenses for uniformed airline pilots, co-pilots and other deck crew see HMRC Employment Income Manual EIM 50051.

Business use of own vehicle

Vehicle	Rate per mile
Car or goods vehicle	45p for the first 10,000 miles
	25p after that
Motor cycle	24p

Business use of home

Nos of hours worked per month	Allowable deduction per month	Allowable deduction for full tax year
	£	£
25 or more	10	120
51 or more	18	216
101 or more	26	312

Private use of business premises

Number of occupants	Add back per month	Add back for full tax year
	£	£
1	350	4,200
2	500	6,000
3 or more	650	7,800

Notes

(1) For the tax year 2013/14 and subsequent years, qualifying businesses can choose to use the above flat rate adjustments (deductions / add-backs) instead of normal trading income rules.

(2) Qualifying businesses are sole traders and partnerships. Partnerships where one of the partners is not an individual (eg corporate partner) and companies are excluded.

(3) With regard to vehicles there are rules:
- (a) To ensure, no deductions other than the above can be made,
- (b) Once the fixed rate deduction above are used in connection with a vehicle they must continue to be used in subsequent periods,
- (c) To prevent the use of fixed rate deductions where:
  - (i) Capital allowances have previously been claimed, or
  - (ii) The vehicle is a van or motor cycle and its cost deducted under the cash basis.
- (d) To ensure where a business has more than one vehicle, the total number of miles of business journeys added together is used in calculating the first 10,000 miles.
- (e) To define a business journey as a journey or an identifiable part of that journey that is wholly and exclusively for the purpose of the trade.

(4) Under business use of home the allowable deduction is the sum of the deductions for each month or part of a month at the rate applicable to the number of hours worked wholly and exclusively for the purpose of the business.

(5) Under private use of business premises, a business claims all expenses incurred mainly for the purpose of the trade less an add-back to reflect the non-business use of the premises. The level of add-back depends on the number of people occupying the premises as a home or staying at the premises otherwise than as part of the trade per month or part of a month.

(6) The adjustments for business / private use of premises are calculated per month or part of a month. For ease of reference an extra column has been included showing the equivalent yearly figures. These are only applicable where the accounting period covers a full tax year and the number of hours / occupants doesn't vary. Otherwise, the total adjustment is found by adding together the relevant monthly figures.

(7) The fixed rate deductions above can be used together with the cash basis (FA 2013, s 17) or in isolation. If used together there is some interaction on vehicles (see (3)(c)(ii) above).

(8) FA 2013, Sch 5 which inserts ITTOIA 2005, ss 94B–94I, HMRC Brief 14/2013.

Cap on tax relief [*FA 2013, Sch 3*]

For 2013–14 onwards a limit applies to the amount of income tax relief that may be claimed against general income by an individual in a tax year. The limit is the greater of £50,000 and 25% of the individual's adjusted total income for the tax year. The cap potentially applies to:

- Trade loss relief (*ITA 2007, ss 64 / 72 / 96*)
- Property loss relief (*ITA 2007, ss 120 / 125*)
- Employment loss relief (*ITA 2007, s 128; ITEPA 2003, s 555*)
- Share loss relief (except EIS & SEIS) (*ITA 2007, Pt 4, Ch 6*)
- Losses on deeply discounted securities (*ITTOIA 2005, ss 446 / 454*)
- Qualifying loan interest (*ITA 2007, Pt 8, Ch 1*)

Cash basis for small businesses [*FA 2013, Sch 4*]

For 2013/14 onwards, eligible small self-employed sole traders and partnerships can use the cash basis to calculate their taxable income. Eligibility is linked to turnover not exceeding the VAT registration threshold (£79,000 for 2013/14). Qualifying businesses also have the option to use fixed rates to calculate certain business expenses – see page 61.

Charitable giving

Gift Aid scheme [*ITA 2007, ss 413–430; FA 2007, s 60; FA 2012, s 50*]

Relief is available for qualifying donations to charity. The charity claims basic rate relief on the grossed up amount of the donation and the donor claims higher rate relief on the grossed up amount against income tax and capital gains tax by extension of the basic rate band. The donor may elect to treat any donation as made in the preceding tax year for higher rate relief purposes. The basic rate tax deemed to have been deducted by the donor at source is clawed back if he has insufficient liability (to income tax and capital gains tax) to match it. Following the reduction of the basic rate to 20% for 2008/09 onwards, a transitional relief supplement of 2% of grossed up qualifying donations is payable to charities for 2008/09 to 2010/11. The scheme also applies to gifts to Community Amateur Sports Clubs.

Before 6 April 2012, taxpayers could nominate a charity to receive all or part of any tax repayment due to them. The nomination is made on the taxpayer's self-assessment return, with an indication of whether Gift Aid should apply to the donation. This facility is withdrawn for repayments made after 5 April 2012.

Gifts in kind [*CAA 2001, s 63(2)–(4); ITTOIA 2005, ss 107–109; FA 2002, Sch 18 para 9(3)*]

Relief is available for gifts by traders, etc. to charities, community amateur sports clubs or educational establishments of goods produced or sold or of plant and machinery used in the donor's trade, etc.

Gifts of land, shares and securities etc. [*ITA 2007, ss 431–446; CTA 2010, ss 203–217*]

Relief is available where a person disposes of listed shares and securities, unit trust units, AIM shares etc. or of freehold or leasehold interests in land to a charity by way of gift or sale at an undervalue. The amount deductible in calculating net income is the market value of the shares etc. on the date of disposal plus incidental disposal costs less any consideration or value of benefits received by the donor or a connected person.

Payroll giving scheme [*ITEPA 2003, ss 713–715; FA 2000, s 38; FA 2003, s 146*]

An employee may make charitable donations of any amount by tax allowable deduction from earnings subject to PAYE. From 6 April 2004 to 31 December 2006, the first £10 donated by each employee every month was matched by the Government for six months.

Gifts of pre-eminent objects to the nation [*FA 2012, s 49, Sch 14*]

Under the cultural gift scheme from 1 April 2012, individuals who donate pre-eminent objects, or collections of objects, to the nation may qualify for an income tax reduction of 30% of the value of the objects. The taxpayer can spread the reduction forward across up to five years starting with the tax year in which the object is offered.

Child trust funds [*SI 2004 No 1450, Regs 24–38*]

The child trust fund scheme operates to provide savings funds for eligible children born after 31 August 2002 and before 3 January 2011. HMRC make an initial contribution in the form of a voucher, worth £250 (£500 for children in lower income families) for children born before 3 August 2010, and £50 (£100) for children born on or after that date but before 3 January 2011. The voucher is then used to open an account. Anyone may then pay money into the account up to a yearly limit of £3,720 (£3,600 before 6 April 2013) (£1,200 before 1 November 2011) and HMRC also make further contributions in certain cases. The account provider invests the funds in a limited range of qualifying investments. Normally no withdrawals are permitted before the fund matures when the child reaches 18. No tax is chargeable in respect of interest, dividends, distributions, alternative financial arrangement return or (from 1 January 2007) building society bonus on account investments. Income from account investments is not regarded as income for any income tax purposes. HMRC are consulting on the idea to transfer existing funds to Junior ISAs. See also page 18.

Community investment tax credit [*ITA 2007, ss 333–382; FA 2002, s 57, Sch 16; FA 2013, s 74, Sch 27*]

A tax relief worth up to 25% is available for qualifying investments in disadvantaged communities by individuals and companies via accredited intermediaries (Community Development Finance Institutions). The investment may be a loan or a subscription for shares or securities. The relief is given by way of tax reductions over a five-year period, the relief for each year being 5% of the invested amount (i.e. the average capital balance outstanding) but restricted, before 6 April 2013 if necessary, to the amount which reduced the investor's tax liability to nil.

The relief is amended from 6 April 2013, to provide for a limited carry forward of unused relief and to potentially restrict the amount of relief available to corporate investors in certain circumstances (state aid limits).

Employee share schemes

Approved share incentive plans (SIPs) *ITEPA 2003, ss 488–515, Sch 2; ITA 2007, ss 488–490*]

Under an approved SIP (open to all employees)

- a company may give an employee shares worth up to £3,000 per tax year (for which performance targets may be set)('free shares');
- an employee may purchase shares worth up to £1,500 per tax year (or 10% of annual salary if lower) by deductions from salary ('partnership shares'), these being allowable deductions for income tax and NICs; and
- the company may give an employee up to two free shares ('matching shares') for each partnership share purchased.

Shares are free of tax and NICs if held in the plan for five years. With some exceptions (e.g. on death, disability, retirement, redundancy or from 17 July 2013 certain cash takeovers), if shares are withdrawn within between three and five years, liability arises on the lower of their value on entering the plan and their value on leaving it. With similar exceptions, if shares are withdrawn within three years, liability is on their value on leaving the plan. Dividends which are reinvested in shares are tax-free (Before 6 April 2013, maximum of £1,500 per employee per tax year). No capital gains tax is payable on withdrawal of shares from the plan at any time; the shares withdrawn are treated as acquired by the employee at their market value at that time.

Employee shareholder employment status [*FA 2013, Sch 23*]

For shares received from 1 September 2013, subject to meeting certain conditions, no income tax (and NIC) is chargeable on the first £2,000 of share value received when an individual becomes an employee shareholder. Relief is given by deeming that the individual had paid £2,000 for the shares. No income tax or NIC arises on qualifying independent advice provided to individuals considering entering into a new employee shareholder agreement.

Enterprise management incentives [*ITEPA 2003, ss 527–541, Sch 5*]

Certain independent trading companies with gross assets not exceeding £30 million may grant options over shares then worth up to £250,000 (£120,000 for options granted before 16 June 2012; £100,000 for options granted before 6 April 2008) to an eligible employee without income tax or NIC consequences (except to the extent that the option is to acquire shares at less than their then market value). The total value of shares in respect of which unexercised qualifying options exist must not exceed £3 million. Any gain on sale of the shares is chargeable to capital gains tax, see page 18 for the interaction with entrepreneurs relief. An additional restriction, limiting the scheme to companies with fewer than 250 full-time equivalent employees, applies for options granted on or after 21 July 2008.

Approved profit sharing schemes [*ICTA 1988, ss 186, 187, Schs 9, 10; FA 2000, s 49*]

Before 1 January 2003, shares of value up to 10% of earnings (within PAYE but excluding benefits and after deducting superannuation contributions) for the year of assessment (or preceding year if greater) could be allocated to an individual in that year free of tax subject to a minimum of £3,000 and a maximum of £8,000. On disposal of the shares, income tax is chargeable on the following percentage of the initial market value when allocated (or sale proceeds if less).

Before 3rd anniversary of allocation	100%*
On or after 3rd anniversary	0%

* Reduced to 50%: employee leaves due to injury/disability/redundancy/reaching an age between 60–75 as specified by the scheme.

Approved SAYE option schemes [*ITEPA 2003, ss 516–520, Sch 3; FA 2003, Sch 21*]

No income tax charge arises on the receipt of the options or any increase in value of the shares between the date of grant of the option and its exercise provided certain conditions are met.

Maximum monthly contribution	£250
Minimum monthly contribution	£5
Maximum discount	20% of market value at time of grant

The seven year savings period of SAYE option schemes is withdrawn from 23 July 2013. Employees with SAYE contracts before this date are not affected.

Approved savings arrangement bonus rates

Date contract started	Monthly payment multiple		
	3-year contract	5-year contract	7-year contract
1.8.12–	0	0	0
23.9.11–31.7.12	0	0	1.6
12.8.11–22.9.11	0	0.9	3.5
27.2.11–11.8.11	0.1	1.7	4.8
12.9.10–26.2.11	0	0.9	3.2
14.5.10–11.9.10	0	1.8	4.9
29.5.09–13.5.10	0.3	2.2	5.2
17.2.09–28.5.09	0.6	2.6	5.6
27.12.08–16.2.09	1.5	4.8	9.3
1.9.08–26.12.08	2.4	7.0	12.7
4.4.08–31.8.08	1.6	5.1	9.8
1.9.07–3.4.08	2.4	7.2	13.3
1.9.06–31.8.07	1.8	5.5	10.3
1.9.05–31.8.06	1.4	4.4	8.4
1.9.04–31.8.05	1.9	6.1	11.5

Approved savings arrangement effective interest rates

Date contract started	3-year contract	5-year contract	7-year contract	Early withdrawal rate
1.8.12–	0%	0%	0%	0%
23.9.11–31.7.12	0%	0%	0.58%	0%
12.8.11–22.9.11	0%	0.59%	1.25%	0%
27.2.11–11.8.11	0.18%	1.1%	1.7%	0.12%
12.9.10–26.2.11	0%	0.59%	1.15%	0%
14.5.10–11.9.10	0%	1.16%	1.74%	0%
29.5.09–13.5.10	0.54%	1.42%	1.84%	0.36%
17.2.09–28.5.09	1.08%	1.67%	1.98%	0.5%
27.12.08–16.2.09	2.67%	3.04%	3.2%	2%
1.9.08–26.12.08	4.23%	4.36%	4.28%	3%
4.4.08–31.8.08	2.84%	3.22%	3.36%	2%
1.9.07–3.4.08	4.23%	4.48%	4.46%	3%
1.9.06–31.8.07	3.19%	3.46%	3.52%	2%
1.9.05–31.8.06	2.49%	2.79%	2.91%	1.5%
1.9.04–31.8.05	3.37%	3.82%	3.9%	2%

Approved CSOP (company share option plan schemes) [*ITEPA 2003, ss 521–526, Sch 4; FA 2003, Sch 21*]

No income tax charge arises

(a) when option granted provided the exercise price is not manifestly less than the market value of the shares at the date of the grant (i.e. not at a discount);

(b) when option exercised between 3 and 10 years after grant.

Options exercised within three years of the grant by reason of injury, disability, redundancy or retirement or from 17 July 2013, where there are certain cash takeovers of constituent companies do not lose their tax-exempt status.

Maximum value (at time of grant) of shares subject to options is £30,000.

Enterprise investment scheme [*ITA 2007, ss 156–257; ICTA 1988, ss 289–312*]

The EIS applies to investments in qualifying unquoted companies trading in the UK. Eligible shares must be held for 3 years from issue date or commencement of trade if later. Subject to this and other conditions relief is given by way of a tax reduction equal to 30% (20% for shares issued before 6 April 2011) of the amount invested.

Maximum investment	2012/13 onwards – £1,000,000
	2008/09 to 2011/12 – £500,000
	2006/07 to 2007/08 – £400,000
	2004/05 to 2005/06 – £200,000
Minimum investment	2012/13 onwards – no minimum
	2011/12 and earlier years – £500
Carry back to preceding year	For 2009/10 onwards, no restrictions (subject to annual maximum).
	For 2008/09 and earlier years, ½ amount invested between 6 April and 5 October (maximum £50,000 (£25,000 before 2006/07)).

Any loss on a disposal of EIS shares (net of income tax relief) may be relieved against income or capital gains. See also page 18.

Foster carers and shared lives carers [*ITTOIA 2005, ss 803–828; F(No 3)A 2010, s 1, Sch 1*]

In general, to the extent that local authority payments made to a foster carer or shared lives carer do no more than meet the actual costs of caring, the payments are not taxable. In other cases, if gross receipts from foster care or, for 2010/11 onwards, shared lives care do not exceed an 'individual limit' the carer is treated as having a nil profit and nil loss for the tax year concerned. Where gross receipts exceed the individual limit, the carer can choose to be either taxed on the excess or compute profit or loss using the normal business rules. The 'individual limit' is made up of a fixed amount of £10,000 per residence for a full tax year and an additional amount per placement per week, or part week, that the individual provides care. The amounts are £200 per week for a child under 11 and £250 per week for a child of 11 or over or an adult. Relief for shared lives care is not available if more than three adults are placed with the carer at any time. For 2010/11 only, shared lives carers can opt to use the previous non-statutory arrangements.

Individual savings accounts ('ISAs') [*ITTOIA 2005, ss 694–701; SI 1998 No 1870; SI 2001 No 908*]

Savers can subscribe to an ISA up to the following limits per tax year

	Overall limit	Cash limit	Junior ISA limit
2013/14	£11,520	£5,760	£3,720
2012/13	£11,280	£5,640	£3,600
2011/12	£10,680	£5,340	£3,600
2010/11	£10,200	£5,100	N/A
2009/10			
Age over 50	£10,200	£5,100	N/A
Under 50	£7,200	£3,600	N/A
2008/09	£7,200	£3,600	N/A
2005/06 – 2007/08	£7,000	£3,000	N/A

For 2009/10, the over 50 limits apply only from 6 October 2009.

In addition, before 2008/09, a limit of £4,000 applied to stocks and shares held in a mini-ISA. Savings are exempt from income tax and capital gains tax. Withdrawals may be made at any time without loss of tax relief. Shares acquired under an approved share incentive plan, profit sharing scheme or SAYE option scheme (see above) may be transferred to a stocks and shares component of an ISA within 90 days without tax consequences. See also page 19.

Insurance benefits in event of sickness etc [*ITTOIA 2005, ss 735–743*]

Certain insurance benefits paid in the event of accident, sickness, disability, infirmity or unemployment are exempt, including benefits payable during convalescence or rehabilitation or to top-up earned income reduced following such disabilities.

Interest received

The following interest is exempt.

(a) On damages for personal injury or death. [*ITTOIA 2005, s 751*].

(b) On government securities held by persons not ordinarily resident in the UK. [*ITTOIA 2005, ss 713–716*]. See page 56.

(c) On certain national savings income.

(d) On SAYE certified contractual savings schemes. (Bonuses are also exempt.) [*ITTOIA 2005, ss 702–707*].

(e) Repayment supplement and interest on overpaid tax (including income tax, capital gains tax, VAT and inheritance tax but not interest payable by HMRC in cases of official error under *VATA 1994, s78*). [*IHTA 1984, s235; ITTOIA 2005, ss 54, 749, 869*].

Landlord's energy-saving allowance [*ITTOIA 2005, ss 312–314; SI 2007 No 831*]

A deduction is available in computing the profits of a property business for capital expenditure incurred within any of the tax years 2004/05 to 2014/15 inclusive on the acquisition, and installation in a dwelling house, of a qualifying energy-saving item. The deduction is limited to a maximum of £1,500 per dwelling house (before 6 April 2007, £1,500 per building).

Qualifying items are cavity wall insulation, loft insulation, solid wall insulation, draught proofing and insulation for hot water systems, and (from 6 April 2007) floor insulation.

Maintenance payments [*ITA 2007, ss 453–456; ICTA 1988, s 347B*]

Payments are made gross and are not subject to tax in the hands of the recipient.

Where either party to the marriage was born before 6 April 1935, the payer obtains relief on qualifying maintenance payments (as defined) by means of a tax reduction on the lesser of the amount paid and the minimum married couple's allowance for the year (see page 58) at the rate of 10%.

Miscellaneous

The following income is exempt from income tax.

(a) **Adoption etc. allowances.** [*ITTOIA 2005, ss 744–747; F(No 3)A 2010, s 2*]. A similar exemption for allowances to special guardians and certain kinship carers applies for 2010/11 onwards.
(b) **Awards for bravery.** [*ITEPA 2003, s 638*].
(c) **Compensation for mis-sold pensions.** [*FA 1996, s 148;* HMRC ESC A99].
(d) **Compensation on unclaimed bank accounts of Holocaust victims.** [HMRC ESC A100; *FA 2006, s 64*].
(e) **Continuity of education allowances** (for 2012/13 onwards).
(f) **Damages and compensation for personal injury.** [*ITTOIA 2005, ss 731–734*].
(g) **Foreign service allowances.** [*ITEPA 2003, s 299*].
(h) **German and Austrian** pensions and annuities for victims of Nazi persecution. [*ITEPA 2003, s 642*].
(i) **Housing grants.** [*ITTOIA 2005, s 769*].
(j) **Members of Parliament.** Certain accommodation allowances and reimbursed costs paid to MPs. [*ITEPA 2003, ss 292–295; F(No 2)A 2010, Sch 4; FA 2011, s 37; FA 2013, s 10*].
(k) **Miners'** free coal or cash in lieu. [*ITEPA 2003, ss 306, 646*].
(l) **Non-resident competitors in certain sporting events.** Subject to conditions, the income arising to non-resident competitors from certain sporting events. For example, the 2013 Champions League Final, the London Anniversary Games and the Glasgow 2014 Commonwealth Games. [*FA 2012, s 13; FA 2013, ss 8–9*].
(m) **Sandwich courses.** Payments to an employee for periods of attendance provided (i) course lasts at least one academic year with an average of at least 20 weeks per year full-time attendance, and (ii) rate of payment does not exceed greater of £7,000 p.a. and rate of payment receivable in similar circumstances by way of public grant. (HMRC SP 4/86).
(n) **Scholarship** income and bursaries. [*ITTOIA 2005, s 766*]. See also page 4.
(o) **Universal credit.** Introduced October 2013 to replace various different income-related benefits and tax credits. [*FA 2013, s 13*].

See also benefits in kind on pages 2 to 5.

Personal equity plans ('PEPs')

Before 6 April 1999, subscriptions to PEPs could be made up to a maximum per year of £6,000 to a general plan and £3,000 to a single company plan. Dividend income is tax-free, and a 10% tax credit was payable until 5 April 2004 on dividends from UK equities. Interest on cash held is paid gross and is tax-free provided cash is eventually invested.

After 5 April 1999, no new subscriptions can be made to PEPs. Savers holding PEPs at that date can continue to hold them without affecting the amount which can be subscribed to an Individual Savings Account. Continuing PEPs are brought within the Individual Savings Account rules from 6 April 2008.

'Rent a room' relief [*ITTOIA 2005, ss 785–802*]

The *gross* rents on letting of rooms in a private residence are exempt up to £4,250. Where gross rents exceed the exempt amount, the taxpayer can elect to pay tax on the excess instead of on the full amount of gross rents less expenses under the normal rules.

Seed enterprise investment scheme [*ITA 2007 ss 257A–257HJ; FA 2012, Sch 6*]

The SEIS applies to investments made on or after 6 April 2012 in small qualifying companies carrying on or preparing to carry on a new business. Subject to conditions, relief is given by way of a tax reduction equal to 50% of the amount invested, up to a maximum investment of £100,000.

Gains on shares within the scope of the SEIS are exempt from capital gains tax. See also page 22.

Social security benefits

Certain social security benefits are not taxable. In October 2013, various income-related benefits and tax credits will be replaced by universal credit (UC). UC is exempt from income tax. See pages 97 and 98.

Termination payments [*ITEPA 2003, ss 401–416*]

Provided payment is not taxable under general employment earnings rules, termination payments (including non-contractual payments in lieu of notice and genuine non-statutory redundancy payments) fall to be taxed under *ITEPA 2003, ss 401–416* subject to the following exemptions.

(a) The first £30,000 of the payments.
(b) Payments where cessation arises from death, injury or disability.
(c) Payments in respect of foreign service where this comprised (i) three-quarters of the whole period of service, or (ii) the last 10 years, or (iii) where employment exceeded 20 years, one half of the whole, including 10 of the last 20 years. (Proportional relief applies in other cases.)
(d) Certain benefits under retirement schemes.

Venture capital trusts [*ITA 2007, ss 258–332; ITTOIA 2005, ss 709–712; FA 2012, s 40, Sch 8*]

An individual who *subscribes* for ordinary shares in a VCT obtains income tax relief at 30% (40% in 2004/05 and 2005/06) on an investment limit of £200,000 in any tax year. The shares must be held for at least five years. Any dividends received from a VCT are exempt from income tax to the extent that the shares *acquired* each year do not exceed the investment limit and provided the main purpose of acquiring the shares is not the avoidance of tax; tax credits are not repayable. See also page 22.

Income tax self-assessment

Payment of tax

1st interim payment. On or before 31 January in tax year

2nd interim payment. On or before 31 July following tax year

Interim payments are normally half the net income tax liability (including Class 4 NIC) of the previous year. Interim payments are not required if either the previous year's liability (net of tax at source) was less than £1,000 (£500 for 2008/09 and earlier years) or tax at source covered more than 80% of the gross liability. (Tax at source includes PAYE.) The taxpayer may make a claim to reduce (or dispense with) interim payments if the current year liability will be less than that of the previous year (or will be nil).

Final payment. Where necessary, 31 January following tax year except that

(a) where a person has given notice of chargeability to tax within six months of the tax year but was not given notice to deliver a return until after 31 October following the tax year, the due date is 3 months after the date of notice; and

(b) where a person's self-assessment is amended, the due date is deferred as regards any tax payable by virtue of the amendment until, if later, 30 days after the date of notice of amendment or closure notice following an enquiry (but not so as to defer the date from which interest on overdue tax runs).

The final payment (or repayment) is the total net liability for income tax and capital gains tax less any interim payments on account of income tax.

Surcharge. Where any income tax or capital gains tax for 2010/11 or earlier year is payable before 6 April 2010 and remains outstanding more than 28 days after the due date, a surcharge of 5% of the unpaid tax will be levied. A further 5% surcharge will be levied on any tax unpaid more than six months after the due date. Surcharges can be suspended where the taxpayer has agreed a time to pay arrangement with HMRC. Replaced by penalty for late payment of tax — see page 92.

Returns

For 2007/08 and subsequent years, the deadline for delivering the completed self-assessment return is determined as follows.

- If the return is an electronic return, it must be delivered to HMRC on or before **31 January** following the tax year to which it relates or, if later, within three months beginning with the date of HMRC's notice to deliver the return.
- If the return is a non-electronic return, it must be delivered to HMRC on or before **31 October** following the tax year to which it relates or, if later, within three months beginning with the date of HMRC's notice to deliver the return.

For earlier years, the deadline for delivering the completed return is as for electronic returns above.

For 2012/13 onwards HMRC have a statutory power to withdraw a notice to file a self-assessment tax return for an individual, partnership and or a trustee and to cancel any corresponding late filing penalties. [*FA 2013, Sch 51*].

See pages 87, 89 for penalties for late filing of returns.

Basis of assessment

Property income	All UK net property income arising in the current tax year, calculated as for trading profits and using ordinary accounting principles
Trading income	*Year 1* — Actual *Year 2* — 12 months ending with accounting date in Year 2 *or* (if period from commencement to accounting date in Year 2 is less than 12 months) the first 12 months *or* (if no accounting date in Year 1 or Year 2) actual *Year 3* — Current year basis (unless Year 3 is the first year in which there is an accounting date falling not less than 12 months after commencement, when assessment based on 12 months ending with the accounting date) *Intermediate years* — Current year basis *Closing year* — Period from end of basis period in the penultimate year to date of cessation (subject to transitional rules covering overlap profits for 1997/98) *Current year basis* normally means that assessment is based on the profits shown by the annual accounts ended within the current tax year
Savings/investment income	Income arising in the current tax year
Foreign income	As for UK property, trading or savings/investment income above See the table on page 66 for determining whether income is assessed on an arising or remittance basis
Other income	Income arising in the current tax year
Employment income	See the table on page 66 for determining whether earnings are assessed on a receipts or remittance basis
Income taxed at source	Dividends, interest, etc. receivable
Child benefit income	Potentially applies to those in receipt (directly or via a partner) of child benefit and adjusted net income of £50,000 or more. See note (a) page 103.

Foreign income

The table below shows whether foreign income is assessed on an arising or, where claimed, a remittance basis.

Resident	Domiciled	British subject	Trades, etc.	Pensions	Other income
No	N/A	N/A	Exempt	Exempt	Exempt
Yes	Yes	Yes	Arising	90% arising	Arising
Yes	No	Yes	Remittance	Remittance	Remittance
Yes	Yes	No	Arising	90% arising	Arising
Yes	No	No	Remittance	Remittance	Remittance

Employment income

The table below shows whether employment income is taxed on a receipts or, where claimed, a remittance basis.

Domiciled	Resident	UK employer	Foreign employer	Wholly UK income	Wholly overseas income (note (a))	Partly UK/partly overseas duties	
						UK duties	Overseas duties (note (a))
Yes	Yes	Immaterial	Immaterial	Receipts	Receipts	Receipts	Receipts
Yes	No	Immaterial	Immaterial	Receipts	Exempt	Receipts	Exempt
No	Yes	Yes	N/A	Receipts	Receipts	Receipts	Receipts
No	Yes	N/A	Yes	Receipts	Remittances	Receipts	Receipts
No	Yes	N/A	Yes	Receipts	Remittances	Receipts	Remittances
No	No	Yes	N/A	Receipts	Exempt	Receipts	Exempt
No	No	N/A	Yes	Receipts	Exempt	Receipts	Exempt

Notes

(a) Where such duties are performed by seafarers in the course of a qualifying period of 365 days or more, emoluments for those duties receive a 100% deduction. [*ITEPA 2003, s 378*].

(b) For 2008/09 onwards, an individual who claims to use the remittance basis for a tax year is not entitled to any income tax personal allowances or the capital gains tax annual exemption for that year. This does not apply if the individual's unremitted foreign income and gains for the year are less than £2,000. [*ITA 2007, s 809G*].

(c) For 2008/09 onwards, individuals aged over 18 who have been resident in the UK for more than seven years of the past ten years can claim the remittance basis for a tax year only if they pay a £30,000 tax charge in respect of the foreign income and gains they leave outside the UK. For 2012/13 onwards, the charge is £50,000 for those resident in the UK for 12 or more years. The charge does not apply if the individual's unremitted foreign income and gains for the year are less than £2,000. [*ITA 2007, s 809H*].

(d) The Government introduced a statutory definition of residence and abolished the concept of ordinary residence for tax purposes with effect from 6 April 2013. [FA 2013, s 218]. Before 6 April 2013 resident but not ordinary resident taxpayers could claim the remittance basis for duties performed abroad and other foreign income.

(e) Where an employee meets the requirements for a three year period of non-residence and are domiciled outside the UK they can claim the remittance basis for duties performed abroad. The test is met for a tax year X if the individual has been non-resident for three consecutive tax years and year X is any of the three years immediately following that period of non-residence.

Inheritance tax rates

Chargeable lifetime transfers

(a) Tax on gross transfers			Cumulative totals	
Cumulative transfers (gross)	Rate	Tax on band	Taxable transfers	Tax thereon
£	%	£	£	£
6.4.13 onwards				
0–325,000	Nil	Nil	325,000	Nil
Over 325,000	20%			
6.4.12–5.4.13				
0–325,000	Nil	Nil	325,000	Nil
Over 325,000	20%			
6.4.11–5.4.12				
0–325,000	Nil	Nil	325,000	Nil
Over 325,000	20%			
6.4.10–5.4.11				
0–325,000	Nil	Nil	325,000	Nil
Over 325,000	20%			
6.4.09–5.4.10				
0–325,000	Nil	Nil	325,000	Nil
Over 325,000	20%			
6.4.08–5.4.09				
0–312,000	Nil	Nil	312,000	Nil
Over 312,000	20%			
6.4.07–5.4.08				
0–300,000	Nil	Nil	300,000	Nil
Over 300,000	20%			
6.4.06–5.4.07				
0–285,000	Nil	Nil	285,000	Nil
Over 285,000	20%			
6.4.05–5.4.06				
0–275,000	Nil	Nil	275,000	Nil
Over 275,000	20%			
6.4.04–5.4.05				
0–263,000	Nil	Nil	263,000	Nil
Over 263,000	20%			

(b) Grossing-up of net lifetime transfers		Cumulative totals	
Net values	Tax payable thereon	Net values	Gross equivalent
£	%	£	£
6.4.13 onwards			
0–325,000	Nil	325,000	325,000
Over 325,000	Nil+ ¼ for each £1 over £325,000		
6.4.12–5.4.13			
0–325,000	Nil	325,000	325,000
Over 325,000	Nil+ ¼ for each £1 over £325,000		
6.4.11–5.4.12			
0–325,000	Nil	325,000	325,000
Over 325,000	Nil+ ¼ for each £1 over £325,000		
6.4.10–5.4.11			
0–325,000	Nil	325,000	325,000
Over 325,000	Nil+ ¼ for each £1 over £325,000		
6.4.09–5.4.10			
0–325,000	Nil	325,000	325,000
Over 325,000	Nil+ ¼ for each £1 over £325,000		
6.4.08–5.4.09			
0–312,000	Nil	312,000	312,000
Over 312,000	Nil+ ¼ for each £1 over £312,000		
6.4.07–5.4.08			
0–300,000	Nil	300,000	300,000
Over 300,000	Nil+ ¼ for each £1 over £300,000		
6.4.06–5.4.07			
0–285,000	Nil	285,000	285,000
Over 285,000	Nil+ ¼ for each £1 over £285,000		
6.4.05–5.4.06			
0–275,000	Nil	275,000	275,000
Over 275,000	Nil+ ¼ for each £1 over £275,000		
6.4.04–5.4.05			
0–263,000	Nil	263,000	263,000
Over 263,000	Nil+ ¼ for each £1 over £263,000		

Inheritance tax rates

Transfers on death

(a) Tax on transfers			Cumulative totals	
Cumulative transfers (gross) £	Rate %	Tax on band £	Taxable transfers £	Tax thereon £
6.4.13 onwards				
0–325,000	Nil	Nil	325,000	Nil
Over 325,000	40%			
6.4.12–5.4.13				
0–325,000	Nil	Nil	325,000	Nil
Over 325,000	40%			
6.4.11–5.4.12				
0–325,000	Nil	Nil	325,000	Nil
Over 325,000	40%			
6.4.10–5.4.11				
0–325,000	Nil	Nil	325,000	Nil
Over 325,000	40%			
6.4.09–5.4.10				
0–325,000	Nil	Nil	325,000	Nil
Over 325,000	40%			
6.4.08–5.4.09				
0–312,000	Nil	Nil	312,000	Nil
Over 312,000	40%			
6.4.07–5.4.08				
0–300,000	Nil	Nil	300,000	Nil
Over 300,000	40%			
6.4.06–5.4.07				
0–285,000	Nil	Nil	285,000	Nil
Over 285,000	40%			
6.4.05–5.4.06				
0–275,000	Nil	Nil	275,000	Nil
Over 275,000	40%			
6.4.04–5.4.05				
0–263,000	Nil	Nil	263,000	Nil
Over 263,000	40%			

(b) Grossing-up of net lifetime transfers do not bear their own tax		Cumulative totals	
Net values £	Tax payable thereon %	Net values £	Gross equivalent £
6.4.13 onwards			
0–325,000	Nil	325,000	325,000
Over 325,000	Nil+ 2/3 for each £1 over £325,000		
6.4.12–5.4.13			
0–325,000	Nil	325,000	325,000
Over 325,000	Nil+ 2/3 for each £1 over £325,000		
6.4.11–5.4.12			
0–325,000	Nil	325,000	325,000
Over 325,000	Nil+ 2/3 for each £1 over £325,000		
6.4.10–5.4.11			
0–325,000	Nil	325,000	325,000
Over 325,000	Nil+ 2/3 for each £1 over £325,000		
6.4.09–5.4.10			
0–325,000	Nil	325,000	325,000
Over 325,000	Nil+ 2/3 for each £1 over £325,000		
6.4.08–5.4.09			
0–312,000	Nil	312,000	312,000
Over 312,000	Nil+ 2/3 for each £1 over £312,000		
6.4.07–5.4.08			
0–300,000	Nil	300,000	300,000
Over 300,000	Nil+ 2/3 for each £1 over £300,000		
6.4.06–5.4.07			
0–285,000	Nil	285,000	285,000
Over 285,000	Nil+ 2/3 for each £1 over £285,000		
6.4.05–5.4.06			
0–275,000	Nil	275,000	275,000
Over 275,000	Nil+ 2/3 for each £1 over £275,000		
6.4.04–5.4.05			
0–263,000	Nil	263,000	263,000
Over 263,000	Nil+ 2/3 for each £1 over £263,000		

Notes

(a) Any nil-rate band which is unused on a person's death can be transferred to their surviving spouse or civil partner for the purposes of the charge to tax on the death of the survivor on or after 9 October 2007. [*IHTA 1984, ss 8A–8C*].

(b) For deaths on or after 6 April 2012, the rate of inheritance tax is 36% where 10% or more of the net estate (after deducting exemptions, reliefs and the nil-rate band) is left to charity. [*IHTA 1984, Sch 1A; FA 2012, s 209, Sch 33*].

(c) It is proposed to freeze the nil rate band at £325,000 until 2017/18.

	Delivery of account	Payment of tax	
Chargeable lifetime transfers	Within later of (a) 12 months from the end of the month in which the transfer is made; and (b) 3 months beginning with the date on which the person delivering the account first becomes liable for tax For chargeable transfers after 5 April 2007, no account need be delivered where: (i) the transfer is of cash or quoted shares or securities and the value of the transfer and other chargeable transfers made in the preceding seven years does not exceed the IHT threshold; or (ii) the value of the transfer and other chargeable transfers made in the preceding seven years does not exceed 80% of the IHT threshold and the value of the transfer does not exceed the net amount of the threshold available to the transferor at the time of the transfer.	6 April–30 September 1 October–5 April	30 April in following year Six months after end of month of transfer
PETs which prove to be chargeable	Within 12 months from the end of the month in which the transferor dies	6 months after the end of the month in which death occurs	
Gifts with reservation chargeable on death	Within 12 months from the end of the month in which death occurs	6 months after the end of the month in which death occurs	
Transfers on death	Within later of (a) 12 months from the end of the month in which death occurs; and (b) 3 months beginning with the date on which the personal representatives first act or the person liable first has reason to believe he is required to deliver an account *Excepted estates.* For deaths after 1 September 2006, no account need be delivered in respect of an estate falling into one of the following categories. (a) Where the deceased was never domiciled in the UK and the value of the UK estate is wholly attributable to cash or quoted shares or securities not exceeding £150,000. (b) Where the deceased died domiciled in the UK and (i) of the value of the estate, not more than £150,000 consisted of settled property and not more than £100,000 of overseas property; (ii) there were no chargeable transfers in the 7 years before death other than 'specified transfers' not exceeding £150,000; and (iii) the aggregate of the gross estate, specified transfers and 'specified exempt transfers' did not exceed the appropriate IHT threshold. (c) Where the deceased died domiciled in the UK and (i) the conditions in (b)(i) and (ii) above are satisfied; (ii) the aggregate of gross estate, specified transfers and specified exempt transfers did not exceed £1,000,000; and (iii) the aggregate in (ii) less any exempt spouse, civil partner or charity transfers and total estate liabilities did not exceed the appropriate IHT threshold. For deaths after 28 February 2011, it is also a condition that the transfers on death include exempt spouse, civil partner or charity transfers. Where the whole of a person's nil-rate band has been transferred to a spouse or civil partner (see note (a) on page 68) and the spouse or partner dies after 5 April 2010, for the purposes of (b) and (c) above, the normal appropriate IHT threshold is doubled (subject to further conditions). '*Specified transfers*'are transfers of cash, personal chattels or corporeal moveable property, quoted shares and securities, and interests in or over land. '*Specified exempt transfers*' are transfers in the seven years before death between spouses or civil partners, gifts to charities, political parties or housing associations, transfers to maintenance funds for historic buildings etc., or to employee trusts. For the purposes of (b)(ii)(iii) and (c)(ii) above, for deaths after 28 February 2011, transfers exempt as normal expenditure out of income exceeding £3,000 per tax year are treated as chargeable transfers.	6 months after end of the month in which death occurs or on delivery of account by personal representatives if earlier	
National heritage property	Within 6 months from the end of the month in which the charge arises on the ending of condition exemption	6 months after end of the month in which chargeable event occurs	

Inheritance tax exemptions

Exempt transfer	Limits and conditions		Reference
Lifetime only			
Potentially exempt transfers	Unless provided to the contrary (e.g. gifts with reservation) (a) transfers by individuals to other individuals; (b) transfers by individuals to certain trusts for the disabled; (c) transfers on or after 22 March 2006 by an individual to a bereaved minor's trust on the coming to an end of an immediate post-death interest; (d) transfers before 22 March 2006 by an individual to an accumulation and maintenance trust; (e) transfers by an individual into interest in possession trusts in which, for transfers on or after 22 March 2006, the beneficiary has a disabled person's interest; and (f) (in restricted circumstances following *FA 2006*) certain transfers on the termination or disposal of an individual's beneficial interest in possession in settled property are potentially exempt transfers. Such transfers made seven years or more before the death of the transferor are exempt transfers		*IHTA 1984, s 3A* *FA 2006, Sch 20 para 9*
Annual gifts	Transfers of value per fiscal year not exceeding Any shortfall in usage can be carried forward to the next year and added to the allowance for that year only	£3,000	*IHTA 1984, s 19*
Gifts in consideration of marriage	Parent of either party to marriage	£5,000	*IHTA 1984, s 22*
	Grandparent or remoter ancestor of either party to marriage; or by one party of marriage to the other	£2,500	
	Any other person	£1,000	
Normal expenditure out of income	Exempt if (a) transfer made out of post-tax income taking one year with another; and (b) transferor left with sufficient income to maintain usual standard of living		*IHTA 1984, s 21*
Small gifts	All gifts to the same person in the same year not exceeding	£250	*IHTA 1984, s 20*
Lifetime and on death			

Exempt transfer	Limits and conditions		Reference
Lifetime only			
Charities	Wholly exempt. Community Amateur Sports Clubs are treated as charities		*IHTA 1984, s 23*
National purposes	Property may be given or bequeathed to any of the bodies listed in the Schedule to the Act (British Museum, National Gallery, local authorities etc.)		*IHTA 1984, s 25, Sch 3*
Political parties	Wholly exempt		*IHTA 1984, s 24*
Shares to an employee trust by individuals	Exempt if trustees hold, within one year of transfer, over 50% of the ordinary shares trust by individuals and have voting control. Beneficiaries must include most of the employees		*IHTA 1984, s 28*
Spouse/civil partner	Wholly exempt unless spouse non-UK-domiciled when limit is (before 6.4.13 £55,000)	£325,000	*IHTA 1984, s 18*
	From 6.4.13 a non-UK-domiciled spouse / civil partner with a UK domiciled partner can elect for IHT purposes to be treated as UK domiciled. Where an election is made, the cap above does not apply although subsequent disposals would be liable to IHT (subject to their own nil rate band) irrespective of the location of the assets.		*FA 2013, s 177*
	The election can specify a date from which it applies, subject to the commencement date of 6 April 2013 and the ability to make a retrospective election for a maximum of seven years. Elections are irrevocable while the electing individual continues to remain resident in the UK. An election will cease to have effect if the electing person is resident outside the UK for more than four full consecutive tax years.		
	The ability to make an election includes an election:		
	(a) By an individual who has become UK domiciled to cover earlier periods when they were non-UK domiciled.		
	(b) By an individual whose marriage or civil partnership has dissolved to cover the period prior to dissolving.		
	(c) On death. Elections by the personal representatives must be made within two years of death or such longer period as an officer may allow.		
	See also note (a) on page 68.		

Agricultural property relief [*IHTA 1984, ss 115–124B*]

	Rates for disposals After 31.8.95
Vacant possession or right to obtain it within 12 months	100%
Entitled to 50% relief at 9 March 1981 and from that date beneficially entitled to interest but without vacant possession rights	100%
Agricultural land let on tenancy starting after 31 August 1995	100%
Other transfers	50%

The agricultural property must (inter alia) have been (i) *occupied* by the transferor for agricultural purposes throughout the 2 years before the transfer; or (ii) owned by him for the 7 years before the transfer and occupied (by him or another) for agricultural purposes throughout that period. With effect, broadly, from 22 April 2009, relief is extended to agricultural property within the European Economic Area.

Business property relief [*IHTA 1984, ss 103–114*]

	Rates for disposals After 5.4.96
Unincorporated business or interest in	100%
Shares in unquoted company	
— over 25% voting control	100%
— 25% or less	100%
Shares in quoted company giving control	50%
Shares in AIM or USM company	
— controlling interest	100%
— over 25% voting control	100%
— 25% or less	100%
Settled property comprising a life tenant's business or interest in a business	100%
Land, buildings, machinery or plant in a partnership or in a controlled company or in a settlement	50%

The property must (inter alia) (i) have been owned by the transferor for at least the 2 years immediately before the transfer; or (ii) have replaced other qualifying property and the qualifying properties together have been owned by the transferor for at least 2 out of the 5 years immediately before the transfer.

Transfers within seven years of death [*IHTA 1984, s 7, Sch 2 paras 1A, 2*]

Where a transferor dies within seven years of a lifetime transfer, IHT is recomputed at the death rates applying at the time of death but the tax rates (not the value of the lifetime transfer) are, subject to below, tapered as follows.

Years between transfer and death	Percentage of full tax rate
Not more than 3	100%
Over 3 but not more than 4	80%
Over 4 but not more than 5	60%
Over 5 but not more than 6	40%
Over 6 but not more than 7	20%

In the case of a chargeable lifetime transfer, the IHT payable cannot be reduced below that originally chargeable at half death rates.

Quick succession relief [*IHTA 1984, s 141*]

Where there is a later transfer of property within 5 years of an earlier transfer ('the first transfer') which increased the transferor's estate and the later transfer arises on death, the IHT payable on the later transfer is reduced by

$$\text{Percentage} \times \frac{(G - T)}{G} \times T$$

where

G = gross (chargeable) first transfer

T = IHT on first transfer

The percentages are as follow

Years between transfers	Percentage
One year or less	100%
Over 1 but not more than 2	80%
Over 2 but not more than 3	60%
Over 3 but not more than 4	40%
Over 4 but not more than 5	20%

Relief also applies where the later transfer is settled property in which the transferor had an interest in possession and the first transfer was the making of the settlement or was made after that time.

Interest on tax paid by companies

Corporation tax self assessment:

accounting periods ending after 30.6.99

Interest on unpaid tax

Interest on unpaid tax runs from the due date (generally nine months and one day after the end of the accounting period, see page 37) to the actual date of payment. It is deductible from profits.

Rates of interest		*Days*
6.9.05 – 5.9.06	6.5%	365
6.9.06 – 5.8.07	7.5%	334
6.8.07 – 5.1.08	8.5%	153
6.1.08 – 5.11.08	7.5%	305
6.11.08 – 5.12.08	6.5%	30
6.12.08 – 5.1.09	5.5%	31
6.1.09 – 26.1.09	4.5%	21
27.1.09 – 23.3.09	3.5%	28
24.3.09 – 28.9.09	2.5%	189
29.9.09 –	3%	

Interest on overpaid tax

Interest on overpaid tax runs from the later of

(a) the date on which the tax was paid, and
(b) the due date (generally nine months and one day after the end of the accounting period, see page 37)

to the date the repayment order is issued. The interest is taxable.

Rates of interest		*Days*
6.9.05 – 5.9.06	3%	365
6.9.06 – 5.8.07	4%	334
6.8.07 – 5.1.08	5%	153
6.1.08 – 5.11.08	4%	305
6.11.08 – 5.12.08	3%	30
6.12.08 – 5.1.09	2%	31
6.1.09 – 26.1.09	1%	21
27.1.09 – 28.9.09	0%	245
29.9.09	0.5%	

Interest on unpaid instalments

Interest on unpaid instalments for 'large companies' (see page 37) is paid from the due date to the earlier of

(a) the date of payment, and
(b) nine months after the end of the accounting period

(whereafter the normal interest rate provisions apply). The interest is deductible from profits.

Rates of interest		*Days*
20.4.00 – 18.2.01	7%	305
19.2.01 – 15.4.01	6.75%	56
16.4.01 – 20.5.01	6.5%	35
21.5.01 – 12.8.01	6.25%	84
13.8.01 – 30.9.01	6%	49
1.10.01 – 14.10.01	5.75%	14
15.10.01 – 18.11.01	5.5%	35
19.11.01 – 16.2.03	5%	455
17.2.03 – 20.7.03	4.75%	154
21.7.03 – 16.11.03	4.5%	119
17.11.03 – 15.2.04	4.75%	91
16.2.04 – 16.5.04	5%	91
17.5.04 – 20.6.04	5.25%	35
21.6.04 – 15.8.04	5.5%	56
16.8.04 – 14.8.05	5.75%	364
15.8.05 – 13.8.06	5.5%	364
14.8.06 – 19.11.06	5.75%	98
20.11.06 – 21.1.07	6%	63
22.1.07 – 20.5.07	6.25%	119
21.5.07 – 15.7.07	6.5%	56
16.7.07 – 16.12.07	6.75%	154
17.12.07 – 17.2.08	6.5%	63
18.2.08 – 24.4.08	6.25%	63
21.4.08 – 19.10.08	6%	182
20.10.08 – 16.11.08	5.5%	28
17.11.08 – 14.12.08	4%	28
15.12.08 – 18.1.09	3%	35
19.1.09 – 15.2.09	2.5%	28
16.2.09 – 15.3.09	2%	28
16.3.09 –	1.5%	

Interest on overpaid instalments and early payments

Interest on overpaid instalments for 'large companies' (see page 37) and on early payments by other companies is paid from the date the excess arises (but not earlier than the due date of the first instalment) to the earlier of

(a) the date of repayment, and
(b) nine months after the end of the accounting period

(whereafter the normal interest rate provisions apply). The interest is taxable.

Rates of interest		*Days*
19.2.01 – 15.4.01	5.5%	56
16.4.01 – 20.5.01	5.25%	35
21.5.01 – 12.8.01	5%	84
13.8.01 – 30.9.01	4.75%	49
1.10.01 – 14.10.01	4.50%	14
15.10.01 – 18.11.01	4.25%	35
19.11.01 – 16.2.03	3.75%	455
17.2.03 – 20.7.03	3.5%	154
21.7.03 – 16.11.03	3.25%	119
17.11.03 – 15.2.04	3.5%	91
16.2.04 – 16.5.04	3.75%	91
17.5.04 – 20.6.04	4%	35
21.6.04 – 15.8.04	4.25%	56
16.8.04 – 14.8.05	4.5%	364
15.8.05 – 13.8.06	4.25%	364
14.8.06 – 19.11.06	4.5%	98
20.11.06 – 21.1.07	4.75%	63
22.1.07 – 20.5.07	5%	119
21.5.07 – 15.7.07	5.25%	56
16.7.07 – 16.12.07	5.5%	154
17.12.07 – 17.2.08	5.25%	63
18.2.08 – 20.4.08	5%	63
21.4.08 – 19.10.08	4.75%	182
20.10.08 – 16.11.08	4.25%	28
17.11.08 – 14.12.08	2.75%	28
15.12.08 – 18.1.09	1.75%	35
19.1.09 – 15.2.09	1.25%	28
16.2.09 – 15.3.09	0.75%	28
16.3.09 – 20.9.09	0.25%	189
21.9.09 –	0.5%	

Interest on tax paid by companies

Corporation tax pay and file:

accounting periods ending before 1.7.99

Interest on unpaid tax

Interest on unpaid tax runs from the due date (generally nine months and one day after the end of the accounting period, see page 37) to the actual date of payment. It is not deductible from profits.

Rates of interest		*Days*
6.1.94 – 5.10.94	5.5%	273
6.10.94 – 5.3.95	6.25%	151
6.3.95 – 5.2.96	7%	337
6.2.96 – 5.8.97	6.25%	547
6.8.97 – 5.1.99	7.5%	518
6.1.99 – 5.3.99	6.5%	59
6.3.99 – 5.2.00	5.75%	337
6.2.00 – 5.5.01	6.75%	455
6.5.01 – 5.11.01	6%	184
6.11.01 – 5.8.03	5%	638
6.8.03 – 5.12.03	4.25%	122
6.12.03 – 5.9.04	5.25%	274
6.9.04 – 5.9.05	6%	365
6.9.05 – 5.9.06	5.25%	365
6.9.06 – 5.8.07	6%	334
6.8.07 – 5.1.08	6.75%	153
6.1.08 – 5.11.08	6%	305
6.11.08 – 5.12.08	5%	30
6.12.08 – 5.1.09	4.25%	31
6.1.09 – 26.1.09	3.5%	21
27.1.09 – 23.3.09	2.75%	28
24.3.09 – 28.9.09	1.75%	189
29.9.09 –	3%	

Interest on overpaid tax

Interest on overpaid tax runs from the later of

(a) the date on which the tax was paid, and
(b) the due date (generally nine months and one day after the end of the accounting period, see page 37

to the date the repayment order is issued. The interest is tax-free.

Rates of interest		*Days*
6.1.94 – 5.10.94	2.5%	273
6.10.94 – 5.3.95	3.25%	151
6.3.95 – 5.2.96	4%	337
6.2.96 – 5.8.97	3.25%	547
6.8.97 – 5.1.99	4%	518
6.1.99 – 5.3.99	3.25%	59
6.3.99 – 5.2.00	2.75%	337
6.2.00 – 5.5.01	3.5%	455
6.5.01 – 5.11.01	2.75%	184
6.11.01 – 5.8.03	2%	638
6.8.03 – 5.12.03	1.25%	122
6.12.03 – 5.9.04	2%	274
6.9.04 – 5.9.05	2.75%	365
6.9.05 – 5.9.06	2%	365
6.9.06 – 5.8.07	2.75%	334
6.8.07 – 5.1.08	3.5%	153
6.1.08 – 5.11.08	2.75%	305
6.11.08 – 5.12.08	2%	30
6.12.08 – 5.1.09	1.25%	31
6.1.09 – 26.1.09	0.5%	21
27.1.09 – 28.9.09	0%	245
29.9.09 –	0.5%	

Income tax on company payments

Interest on unpaid tax is chargeable on income tax payable by companies from the due date to the actual date of payment.

Interest on tax repaid carries interest from the material date (see page 75) until the repayment order is issued.

Rates of interest		*Days*
Payment due before 14.10.99		
6.11.01 – 5.8.03	5%	638
6.8.03 – 5.12.03	4.25%	122
6.12.03 – 5.9.04	5%	274
6.9.04 – 5.9.05	5.75%	365
6.9.05 – 5.9.06	5%	365
6.9.06 – 5.8.07	5.75%	334
6.8.07 – 5.1.08	6.5%	153
6.1.08 – 5.11.08	5.75%	305
6.11.08 – 5.12.08	5%	30
6.12.08 – 5.1.09	4.25%	31
6.1.09 – 26.1.09	3.5%	21
27.1.09 – 23.3.09	2.75%	28
24.3.09 – 28.9.09	2%	189
29.9.09 –	3%	
Payment due after 13.10.99		
6.9.04 – 5.9.05	7.5%	365
6.9.05 – 5.9.06	6.5%	365
6.9.06 – 5.8.07	7.5%	334
6.8.07 – 5.1.08	8.5%	153
6.1.08 – 5.11.08	7.5%	305
6.11.08 – 5.12.08	6.5%	30
6.12.08 – 5.1.09	5.5%	31
6.1.09 – 26.1.09	4.5%	21
27.1.09 – 23.3.09	3.5%	28
24.3.09 – 28.9.09	2.5%	189
29.9.09 –	3%	

Interest on tax and NIC paid by individuals

Income tax and capital gains tax (until 30.10.11), NICs Class 1, 1A and 4, (from 1.10.99) stamp duty and SDRT, and (from 26.9.05) SDLT

Interest on unpaid tax. Interest runs from the relevant date (see page 75) until the date of payment. Interest is payable gross and is not tax deductible. See page 75 for the harmonised interest regime which applies to income tax and capital gains tax with effect from 31 October 2011.

Rates of interest		*Days*
6.10.94 – 5.3.95	6.25%	151
6.3.95 – 5.2.96	7%	337
6.2.96 – 30.1.97	6.25%	360
31.1.97 – 5.8.97	8.5%	187
6.8.97 – 5.1.99	9.5%	518
6.1.99 – 5.3.99	8.5%	59
6.3.99 – 5.2.00	7.5%	337
6.2.00 – 5.5.01	8.5%	455
6.5.01 – 5.11.01	7.5%	184
6.11.01 – 5.8.03	6.5%	638
6.8.03 – 5.12.03	5.5%	122
6.12.03 – 5.9.04	6.5%	274
6.9.04 – 5.9.05	7.5%	365
6.9.05 – 5.9.06	6.5%	365
6.9.06 – 5.8.07	7.5%	334
6.8.07–5.1.08	8.5%	153
6.1.08 – 5.11.08	7.5%	305
6.11.08 – 5.12.08	6.5%	30
6.12.08 – 5.1.09	5.5%	31
6.1.09 – 26.1.09	4.5%	21
27.1.09 – 23.3.09	3.5%	56
24.3.09 – 28.9.09	2.5%	189
29.9.09	3%	

Interest on overpaid tax: repayment supplement

For 1996/97 onwards, interest runs from the date of payment (or, for income tax deducted at source, from 31 January following the year of assessment) to the date the repayment order is issued. See page 75 for the harmonised interest regime which applies to income tax and capital gains tax with effect from 31 October 2011.

Rates of interest		*Days*
6.10.94 – 5.3.95	6.25%	151
6.3.95 – 5.2.96	7%	337
6.2.96 – 30.1.97	6.25%	360
31.1.97 – 5.8.97	4%	187
6.8.97 – 5.1.99	4.75%	518
6.1.99 – 5.3.99	4%	59
6.3.99 – 5.2.00	3%	337
6.2.00 – 5.5.01	4%	455
6.5.01 – 5.11.01	3%	184
6.11.01 – 5.8.03	2.25%	638
6.8.03 – 5.12.03	1.5%	122
6.12.03 – 5.9.04	2.25%	274
6.9.04 – 5.9.05	3%	365
6.9.05 – 5.9.06	2.25%	365
6.9.06 – 5.8.07	3%	334
6.8.07 – 5.1.08	4%	153
6.1.08 – 5.11.08	3%	305
6.11.08 – 5.12.08	2.25%	30
6.12.08 – 5.1.09	1.5%	31
6.1.09 – 26.1.09	0.75%	21
27.1.09 – 28.9.09	0%	245
29.9.09 –	0.5%	

Inheritance tax

Unpaid tax

Interest is chargeable on unpaid inheritance tax from the due date for payment (see page 66) to the actual date of payment at the rates shown below. Interest is payable gross and is not deductible in computing income, profits or losses for tax purposes.

Rates of interest		*Days*
6.12.92 – 5.1.94	5%	396
6.1.94 – 5.10.94	4%	273
6.10.94 – 5.3.99	5%	1,612
6.3.99 – 5.2.00	4%	337
6.2.00 – 5.5.01	5%	455
6.5.01 – 5.11.01	4%	184
6.11.01 – 5.8.03	3%	638
6.8.03 – 5.12.03	2%	122
6.12.03 – 5.9.04	3%	274
6.9.04 – 5.9.05	4%	365
6.9.05 – 5.9.06	3%	365
6.9.06 – 5.8.07	4%	334
6.8.07 – 5.1.08	5%	153
6.1.08 – 5.11.08	4%	305
6.11.08 – 5.1.09	3%	61
6.1.09 – 26.1.09	2%	21
27.1.09 – 23.3.09	1%	56
24.3.09 – 28.9.09	0%	189
29.9.09 –	3%	

Interest on tax repaid

Any repayment of inheritance tax or interest paid carries interest from the date of payment to the date the repayment order is issued at the rates shown below. The interest is tax-free. Before 29.9.09, the rates of interest were the same as for unpaid tax.

Rates of interest		*Days*
29.9.09 –	0.5%	

Interest on tax and NIC

Relevant dates for unpaid tax

The relevant dates from which interest on unpaid tax and NIC runs are as follows.

(a) **IT, CGT, Class 4 NIC**
1996/97 and subsequent years and assessments raised after 5.4.98 (From 1997/98 and subsequent years for partnerships set up before 6.4.94)
Interim payments (see page 65) – due date for payment.
Any other case – 31 January after the year of assessment or, where taxpayer gave notice of chargeability before 5 October following the year of assessment and the return was not issued until after 31 October, three months after notice to deliver the return, if later.
In practice, where a return is submitted by 30 September for calculation by the Revenue of the tax due, interest runs from 30 days after notification of the liability to the taxpayer if after 31 December.
(b) **PAYE and Class 1 NIC.** See page 88.
(c) **Class 1A NIC.** 19 July after the end of the relevant tax year.
(d) **PAYE settlement agreement.** 19 October after the end of the relevant tax year. (e) **Class 1B NIC.** 19 October after the end of the relevant tax year.
(e) **Corporation tax** – see page 72.
(f) **Income tax on company payments.** 14 days after the end of the relevant return period.
(g) **SDLT.** 30 days after the effective date of the transaction.

Material dates for repayment supplements

The material dates from which interest repayment supplements run are as follows.

(a) **Corporation tax**
Accounting periods ending after 30.9.93 and before 1.7.99. Later of nine months after the end of the accounting period and the actual date of payment.
Accounting periods ending after 30.6.99. For instalment payments by 'large companies' and early payments by other companies, see page 72.
(b) **Tax credits and income tax on company payments.**
Accounting periods ending after 30.6.99. The day after the end of the accounting period in which the payments/franked investment income were received.
Accounting periods ending before 1.7.99. Nine months after the end of the accounting period in which the payments/franked investment income were received.
(c) **Close company loan repayment/release/write-off.** Later of the date tax was paid and nine months after the end of the accounting period in which the loan was repaid, released or written off.

Harmonised interest regime

FA 2009, ss 101–105, Schs 53–54A created a harmonised interest regime for all taxes and duties administered by HMRC. The new regime applies:

To	From	
Income tax & capital gains tax self-assessment	31 October 2011	SI 2011 No 701
Tax agent dishonest conduct penalty	1 April 2013	SI 2013 No 280
Corporation tax	Not expected to take effect before 2015	

The regime provides for 'late payment interest' and 'repayment interest' at differential rates, as under the existing rules. Where interest is already accruing immediately prior to 31 October 2011 on an income tax or capital gains tax self-assessment amount, it will accrue on and after that date under the new regime.

Late payment interest. A late payment of tax (or associated penalty) carries interest at the late payment interest rate from the date on which that amount becomes due and payable until the date on which payment is made. A special rule applies to determine the interest start date if:

(i) there is an amendment or correction to an assessment or self-assessment; or
(ii) HMRC make an assessment in place of, or in addition to, an assessment made by a taxpayer; or
(iii) HMRC make an assessment in place of an assessment that ought to have been made by a taxpayer.

In such a case, the late payment interest start date is what it would have been if:

- the original assessment or self-assessment had been complete and accurate and had been made on the date (if any) by which it was required to be made; and
- accordingly, the amount had been due and payable as a result of that original assessment or self-assessment.

Rates of interest		*Days*
31.10.11 –	3%	

Repayment interest. A repayment of tax (or associated penalty) carries interest at the repayment interest rate from the 'repayment interest start date' until the date on which the repayment is made. The '*repayment interest start date*' is arrived at as set out below.

- Where the repayment is of an amount which has been paid to HMRC, the repayment interest start date is the *later* of date A and date B, where:
  date A = the date on which the amount was paid to HMRC; and
  date B = the date on which payment of the amount to HMRC became due and payable to HMRC (where it was paid in connection with a liability to make a payment to HMRC).
- Where the repayment is of an amount which has not been paid to HMRC but is payable by them by virtue of a return having been filed or a claim having been made, the repayment interest start date is the *later* of date C and date D, where:
  date C = the date (if any) on which the return was required to be filed or the claim was required to be made; and
  date D = the date on which the return was in fact filed or the claim was in fact made.
- Where the repayment is the result of a loss relief claim affecting two or more years, the repayment interest start date is 31 January following the *later* year in relation to the claim, i.e. on a claim to carry back a loss, the tax year in which the loss arises.

Rates of interest		*Days*
31.10.11 –	0.5%	

Mileage allowances car, cycling and motor cycling allowances

Car mileage rates (note (a))

	Mileage allowance First 10,000	Over 10,000
2011/12 – onwards	45p	25p
2006/07 – 2010/11	40p	25p

Car passengers (note (b))

	Mileage allowance
2006/07 – onwards	5p

Cycling allowance (note (c))

	Mileage allowance
2006/07 – onwards	20p

Motorcycle allowance (note (c))

	Mileage allowance
2006/07 – onwards	24p

(a) The mileage allowances that can be paid free of tax and NICs to employees who use their own cars for business travel are statutory. Where employers pay less than the statutory rate, employees can claim tax relief on the difference. Employees cannot claim actual business motoring costs if these are above the statutory rates. [*ITEPA 2003, ss 229–232, 235, 236*].

(b) Tax and NIC free allowance for each fellow employee passenger carried. [*ITEPA 2003, ss 233, 234*].

(c) Employers can pay employees up to the mileage allowance tax free for using their own cycles/motorcycles for business travel. Employees can claim tax relief on the mileage allowance if their employer pays no cycle/motorcycle allowance (or on the balance up to the mileage allowance if the employer pays less than this rate). [*ITEPA 2003, ss 229–232, 235, 236*].

(d) The advisory fuel rates for company cars can be used to negotiate dispensations for mileage payments for business motoring in company cars and may be used for reimbursement by employees of fuel used for private motoring. The advisory rates will not be binding where the employer can demonstrate that the cost of business motoring is higher than the advisory rates or where a lower rate would cover the full cost of private fuel. HMRC will accept that, for one month from the date of change, employers may use either the previous or new current rates.

(e) The advisory fuel rates can also be used to reclaim VAT on fuel costs reimbursed for business travel by employees in company cars. The employer must obtain and keep a valid VAT invoice.

Advisory fuel rates for company cars (notes (d), (e))

	Fuel cost per mile Petrol	Diesel	LPG
1.6.13 onwards			
Up to 1,400 cc	15p	—	10p
Up to 1,600 cc	—	12p	—
1,401–2,000 cc	17p	—	12p
1,601–2,000 cc	—	14p	—
Over 2,000 cc	25p	18p	18p
1.3.13 – 31.5.13			
Up to 1,400 cc	15p	—	10p
Up to 1,600 cc	—	13p	—
1,401–2,000 cc	18p	—	12p
1,601–2,000 cc	—	15p	—
Over 2,000 cc	26p	18p	18p
1.12.12 – 28.2.13			
Up to 1,400 cc	15p	—	11p
Up to 1,600 cc	—	12p	—
1,401–2,000 cc	18p	—	13p
1,601–2,000 cc	—	15p	—
Over 2,000 cc	26p	18p	18p
1.9.12 – 30.11.12			
Up to 1,400 cc	15p	—	10p
Up to 1,600 cc	—	12p	—
1,401–2,000 cc	18p	—	13p
1,601–2,000 cc	—	15p	—
Over 2,000 cc	26p	18p	17p
1.6.12 – 31.8.12			
Up to 1,400 cc	15p	—	11p
Up to 1,600 cc	—	12p	—
1,401–2,000 cc	18p	—	13p
1,601–2,000 cc	—	15p	—
Over 2,000 cc	26p	18p	19p
1.3.12 – 31.5.12			
Up to 1,400 cc	15p	—	10p
Up to 1,600 cc	—	13p	—
1,401–2,000 cc	18p	—	12p
1,601–2,000 cc	—	15p	—
Over 2,000 cc	26p	19p	18p

Miscellaneous levies and taxes

Aggregates levy [*FA 2001 ss 16–49, Schs 4–10*]

Aggregates levy applies to any aggregate that is subjected to commercial exploitation unless specifically exempt or previously used for construction purposes. Aggregate is rock, gravel or sand, together with whatever substances are incorporated in the rock, gravel or sand or naturally occur mixed with it. The rate of tax (apportioned on amounts less than one tonne) is:

1.4.02 – 31.3.08	£1.60 per tonne
1.4.08 – 31.3.09	£1.95 per tonne
1.4.09 onwards	£2.00 per tonne

Annual tax on enveloped dwellings [*FA 2013, Part 3, ss 94-174 & Schs 33-35*]

Property value	**Annual charge**
Less than £2,000,000	NIL
£2,000,001 to £5,000,000	£15,000
£5,000,001 to £10,000,000	£35,000
£10,000,001 to £20,000,000	£70,000
£20,000,001 or more	£140,000

From 1 April 2013, an annual tax on enveloped dwellings (ATED) applies to certain non-natural persons (e.g. companies, collective investment schemes and partnerships with company members) holding a residential property valued at over £2 million. For 2013/14 a return is required by 1 October 2013 and the tax is due by 31 October 2013. For 2014/15 onwards, the return and the tax are due by 30 April during the year of assessment, e.g. 30 April 2014 for 2014/15. For properties purchased after the introduction of these rules, the return and tax are due 30 days after purchase. If the taxpayer is not chargeable (e.g. a disposal) for the full year a later repayment claim can be made. However, a charge to capital gains tax arises on any gain (since 6 April 2013) at 28% see page 19.

The property value above relates to the market value on the last valuation date. The first valuation date is 1 April 2012 and then reassessed every five years. A number of exemptions and reliefs exist including the property being used for various commercial purposes, for charities and for public / national bodies. There are also rules regarding situations where separate connected interests exist in a dwelling.

Penalties for any non-compliance are potentially charged under:

- Error in taxpayer's document – FA 2007, Sch 24 para 1 (page 91)
- Late filing of returns – FA 2009, Sch 55 (page 93)
- Failure to make payments on time – FA 2009, Sch 56 (page 92)
- Failure to keep and preserve records – FA 2013, Sch 33(7) (page 94)
- Failure to comply with HMRC investigatory powers – FA 2008, Sch 36 (page 92)

Bank levy [*FA 2011, s 73, Sch 19*]

Bank levy is a tax based upon the total chargeable equity and liabilities as reported in the relevant balance sheets of banks, banking and building society groups at the end of each chargeable period. The levy is collected through the corporation tax self-assessment system. The rates are as follows:

	Rate **(notes (a)(b))** **1.3.11 – 30.4.11**	**1.5.11 – 31.12.11**	**1.1.12 – 31.12.12**	**1.1.13 – 31.12.13**	**1.1.14 onwards**
Long term chargeable equity and liabilities	0.05%	0.0375%	0.044%	0.065%	0.071%
Short term chargeable liabilities	0.1%	0.075%	0.088%	0.130%	0.142%

Notes

(a) Where the chargeable period straddles any of the above periods, the chargeable equity and liabilities are apportioned between the periods on a time basis and the levy is charged accordingly.

(b) The first £20 billion of the chargeable equity and liabilities is exempt from the levy. The £20 billion is apportioned between the long-term equity and liabilities and the short-term liabilities.

Carbon price floor [*FA 2012 s 200; FA 2013, Sch 42*]

From 1 April 2013 the carbon price floor (CPF) applies to coal and other solid fossil fuels, gas and liquefied petroleum gas used in most forms of electricity generation in Great Britain. Under these rules such supplies are liable to the carbon price support (CPS) rates of climate change levy (CCL – see below). The CPS rates below may be reduced where there is use of certain carbon efficient technology. The government intend to introduce an exemption from CPF for Northern Ireland.

	2013/14	**2014/15**
Carbon price equivalent (per tonne of CO_2)	£4.94	£9.55
Supplies of commodity		
Natural gas (per kWh)	0.091p	0.175p
LPG (per kg)	1.46p	2.822p
Coals and other taxable solid fossil fuels (per gross gigajoule)	44.264p	85.489p
Gas oil; rebated bioblend (per litre)	1.365p	2.642p
Fuel oil; other heavy oil; rebated light oil (per litre)	1.568p	3.011p

From 1 April 2015 the rates will be equivalent to £18.08 per tonne of carbon dioxide with future indicative increasing rates already announced for 2016/17 & 2017/18.

Miscellaneous levies and taxes

Climate change levy [*FA 2000, s 30, Sch 6; FA 2006, ss 171, 172*]

Climate change levy (CCL) is a single stage tax chargeable on taxable supplies of taxable commodities. A supply is excluded from the levy if it is for domestic use or for use by a charity otherwise than in the course or furtherance of a business. The rates are as follows:

Taxable commodity	*Rate* (note (a)) 1.4.09 – 31.3.11	1.4.11 – 31.3.12	1.4.12 – 31.3.13	1.4.13 – 31.3.14
Electricity	0.47p per kWh	0.485p per kWh	0.509p per kWh	0.524p per kWh
Gas supplied by a gas utility or supplied in a gaseous state that is of a kind supplied by a gas utility	0.164p per kWh	0.169p per kWh	0.177p per kWh	0.182p per kWh
Gas (NI rate)	Exempt	0.059p per kWh	0.062p per kWh	0.064p per kWh (note (d))
Petroleum gas or other gaseous hydrocarbon supplied in a liquid state	1.05p per kg	1.083p per kg	1.137p per kg	1.172p per kg
Coal and lignite, coke and semi-coke of coal or lignite and petroleum coke	1.281p per kg	1.321p per kg	1.387p per kg	1.429p per kg

Notes

(a) This is the rate at which CCL is payable if the supply is not a reduced-rate supply.

(b) A 65% reduction in CCL (80% for supplies before 1 April 2011) applies for energy intensive industries that have entered into a negotiated energy efficiency CCL agreement. Energy intensive users are those that operate a Part A process listed in *Pollution Prevention and Control (England and Wales) Regulations 2000 (SI 2000/1973), Sch 1*. An 80% reduction applies for supplies of taxable commodities used in the recycling of steel and aluminium made on or after 1 April 2012. Previously such supplies were exempt.

(c) Increased rates will apply with effect from 1 April 2014: 0.541p per kWh for electricity; 0.188p per kWh for gas; 1.210p per kg for petroleum gas etc.; and 1.476p per kg for coal, coke etc.

(d) NI rate 0.064p per kWh on or before 31 October 2013 — main rate applies thereafter

Insurance premium tax [*FA 1994, ss 48–74, Schs 6A, 7, 7A*]

IPT is a tax on insurance premiums received under taxable insurance contracts. All types of insurance risk located in the UK are taxable unless they are specifically exempted by relating to one or more of (i) risks outside the UK; (ii) reinsurance; (iii) long-term business; (iv) commercial ships; (v) contracts relating to the Channel Tunnel; (vi) lifeboats and lifeboat equipment; (vii) commercial aircraft; (viii) international railway rolling stock; (ix) goods in foreign or international transit; (x) export finance related insurance; or (xi) contracts relating to motor vehicles for use by handicapped persons (Motability).

The rates of tax are as follows:

	Standard rate	*Higher rate* (note (a))
1.7.1999–3.1.2011	5% (Tax fraction 1/21)	17.5% (Tax fraction 7/47)
From 4.1.2011	6% (Tax fraction 3/53)	20% (Tax fraction 1/6)

Note

(a) The higher rate applies to insurance sales in three trading sectors where insurance is sold in relation to goods and services which are subject to VAT. These are (i) sales of motor cars, light vans or motorcycles; (ii) sales of electrical or mechanical domestic appliances; and (iii) sales of travel insurance.

Landfill tax [*FA 1996 ss 39–71, Sch 5*]

Landfill tax applies to all waste disposed of by way of landfill at a licensed landfill site unless the waste is specifically exempt. Exemption applies to (i) waste removed from inland waterways and harbours by dredging; (ii) waste arising from mining and quarrying operations; (iii) pet cemeteries; (iv) waste arising from the clearance of contaminated land (where the exemption certificate application was made before 1 December 2008); and (v) (before 1 September 2009) inactive waste which is used for the purposes of restoring to use a landfill site.

The rates of tax are as follows:

	Active waste per tonne	*Inactive waste per tonne*
1.4.13 – 31.3.14	£72	£2.50
1.4.12 – 31.3.13	£64	£2.50
1.4.11 – 31.3.12	£56	£2.50
1.4.10 – 31.3.11	£48	£2.50
1.4.09 – 31.3.10	£40	£2.50
1.4.08 – 31.3.09	£32	£2.50
1.4.07 – 31.3.08	£24	£2

The lower rate applies to those inactive wastes listed in the *Landfill Tax (Qualifying Material) Order 1996 (SI 1996 No 1528)* and the standard rate to all other taxable waste.

Notes

(a) From 1 April 2014 the rates will be £80 per tonne for active waste and £2.50 per tonne for inactive waste.

(b) Landfill site operators can claim a tax credit of 90% of any qualifying contributions made to approved environmental bodies, subject to a maximum percentage of the landfill tax liability during the contribution year.

Miscellaneous levies and taxes

Vehicle excise duty [*VERA 1994, Sch 1; FA 2009, ss 13, 14; FA 2011, ss 21, 22*]

VED ('car tax' or 'road tax') is a duty charged in respect of any mechanically-propelled vehicle which is used or kept on a public road in the UK. The duty is paid on a licence taken out by the person in whose name the vehicle is registered or by its keeper. Annual rates are as follows:

Band	CO_2 emissions g/km	1.4.11–31.3.12	1.4.12–31.3.13	1.4.13–31.3.14
Light passenger vehicles registered on or after 1 March 2001 (notes (a)(b))				
A	Up to 100	£0	£0	£0
B	101–110	£20	£20	£20
C	111–120	£30	£30	£30
D	121–130	£95	£100	£105
E	131–140	£115	£120	£125
F	141–150	£130	£135	£140
G	151–165	£165	£170	£175
H	166–175	£190	£195	£200
I	176–185	£210	£215	£220
J	186–200	£245	£250	£260
K (note (c))	201–225	£260	£270	£280
L	226–255	£445	£460	£475
M	Over 255	£460	£475	£490
First year rate (note (d))				
A	Up to 100	£0	£0	£0
B	101–110	£0	£0	£0
C	111–120	£0	£0	£0
D	121–130	£0	£0	£0
E	131–140	£115	£120	£125
F	141–150	£130	£135	£140
G	151–165	£165	£170	£175
H	166–175	£265	£275	£285
I	176–185	£315	£325	£335
J	186–200	£445	£460	£475
K	201–225	£580	£600	£620
L	226–255	£790	£815	£840
M	Over 255	£1,000	£1,030	£1,065
Light passenger vehicles registered before 1 March 2001				
Engine size below 1,550cc		£130	£135	£140
Over 1,549cc		£215	£220	£225
Motorcycles				
Engine size up to 150cc		£16	£16	£17
151–400cc		£35	£36	£37
401–600cc		£53	£55	£57
Over 600cc		£74	£76	£78
Light goods vehicles registered on or after 1 March 2001 (note (e))				
Standard rate		£210	£215	£220
Euro 4 & 5		£130	£135	£140

Notes

(a) Reduced rates apply to certain vehicles powered by alternative fuels.

(b) Duty can also be paid for a six-month licence. The charge is usually slightly more than half of the equivalent annual rate.

(c) Band K includes cars that have a CO_2 figure over 225g/km but were registered before 23 March 2006.

(d) First-year rates are payable for a vehicle's first licence taken out at first registration on or after 1 April 2010. The standard rate applies to subsequent licences.

(e) The reduced rate applies to Euro 4 vehicles registered between 1 March 2003 and 31 December 2006 inclusive and to Euro 5 vehicles registered between 1 January 2009 and 31 December 2010 inclusive. For light goods vehicles registered before 1 March 2001 the same rates apply as for light passenger vehicles registered before that date.

Motor cars car benefit

CO_2 emissions g/km 2008/09–2009/10	2010/11	2011/12	2012/13	2013/14	% of list price Petrol	Diesel (note (b))
N/A	75 (note (c))	75 (note (c))	75 (note (c))	75 (note (c))	5%	8%
120 (note (c))	120 (note (c))	120 (note (c))	99 (note (c))	94 (note (c))	10%	13%
N/A	N/A	N/A	100	95	11%	14%
N/A	N/A	N/A	105	100	12%	15%
N/A	N/A	N/A	110	105	13%	16%
N/A	N/A	N/A	115	110	14%	17%
135	130	125	120	115	15%	18%
140	135	130	125	120	16%	19%
145	140	135	130	125	17%	20%
150	145	140	135	130	18%	21%
155	150	145	140	135	19%	22%
160	155	150	145	140	20%	23%
165	160	155	150	145	21%	24%
170	165	160	155	150	22%	25%
175	170	165	160	155	23%	26%
180	175	170	165	160	24%	27%
185	180	175	170	165	25%	28%
190	185	180	175	170	26%	29%
195	190	185	180	175	27%	30%
200	195	190	185	180	28%	31%
205	200	195	190	185	29%	32%
210	205	200	195	190	30%	33%
215	210	205	200	195	31%	34%
220	215	210	205	200	32%	35%
225	220	215	210	205	33%	35%
230	225	220	215	210	34%	35%
235	230	225	220	215	35%	35%

Notes

(a) The cash equivalent of a car benefit is treated as earnings from employment of directors and 'P11D' employees i.e. employees with earnings, including benefits etc. to be entered on form P11D (including VAT), at the rate of £8,500 p.a. or more.

(b) The car benefit is linked to the car's CO_2 emissions. For all cars registered on or after 1 March 2001, the definitive CO_2 emissions figure for tax purposes is recorded on the vehicle registration document (V5). For cars first registered after 31 December 1997 and before 1 March 2001, the Vehicle Certification Agency supply CO_2 emissions and other relevant information on their website at carfueldata.direct.gov.uk/ and in their free booklet 'New Car Fuel Consumption & Emission Figures'. For cars registered after 31 December 1997 with no approved CO_2 emissions figure, the tax charge is 15% of the list price for engines up to 1,400 cc, 25% for engines of 1,401 to 2,000 cc and 35% for engines above 2,000 cc or cars without a cylinder capacity.
For cars registered after 31 December 1997
(i) for 2005/06, cars propelled solely by diesel, and meeting the European standard for cleaner cars, receive a discount of the diesel supplement (i.e. the normal petrol rates apply); for 2006/07 to 2010/11 the discount only applies to such cars registered before 1 January 2006 and it is withdrawn for 2011/12 onwards;
(ii) cars which are incapable of producing carbon dioxide engine emissions when driven are charged to tax on 0% of the list price for 2010/11 to 2014/15
(iii) for 2009/10 and earlier years electrically propelled cars are charged to tax on 9% of the list price;
(iv) for 2010/11 and earlier years cars capable of being propelled by electricity and petrol, cars propelled solely by road fuel gas (e.g. LPG), and bi-fuel cars all receive a special discount; and
(v) automatic cars made available to disabled drivers are taxable on the equivalent manual car, if less.
For 2008/09 to 2010/11, for cars registered on or after 1 January 2008 which are constructed to be capable of being propelled by bioethanol or E85 fuel, the percentage chargeable is reduced by 2%.

(c) Where a car's CO_2 emissions figure is not a multiple of 5, it is normally rounded down to the nearest 5. For the figures marked (c), the car's emissions only qualify if they are the exact figure or less; the rounding down rule above does not apply.

(d) For cars registered before 1 January 1998, the tax charge is 15% of the list price for engines up to 1,400 cc, 22% for engines of 1,401 to 2,000 cc and 32% for engines above 2,000 cc. Cars without a cylinder capacity are taxed on 32% of the car's price (or, for 2009/10 and earlier years, 15% for electric cars (0% for 2010/11 to 2014/15)).

(e) The 'list price' (subject, for 2010/11 and earlier years, to an overall limit of £80,000) is the price published by the manufacturer, importer or distributor (inclusive of delivery charges and taxes) at the time of registration. It includes any optional extras supplied with the car when first made available to the employee, together with any further accessory costing £100 or more, but does not include, for 2011/12 onwards, certain security enhancements for employees whose employment creates a threat to personal security. Where a car is converted to run on road fuel gas, the equipment is not regarded as an accessory. Where an employee makes a capital contribution to the initial cost of the car, the price of the car for the year of contribution and subsequent years is reduced by that contribution or £5,000 if less.

(f) The value of the benefit is reduced proportionately if the car is 'unavailable' for part of the year. It is unavailable before and after it is made available to the employee and on any day in a period of 30 consecutive days throughout which it is not available.

(g) The cash equivalent (after any reductions under (e) above) is reduced (or extinguished) by the amount of contributions which an employee is required to make for private use.

(h) Where a car is more than 15 years old at the end of the tax year and has a market value of at least £15,000, market value, if greater, is substituted for list price.

(i) Employers also pay Class 1A national insurance contributions on the scale charge.

[ITEPA 2003, ss 114–148; FA 2008, s 47; FA 2009, s 53, Sch 28; FA 2010, ss 58, 59; FA 2011, s 51; FA 2012, ss 14, 17; SI 2007 No 3068; SI 2010 No 695].

Motor cars Car fuel benefit

2005/06–2007/08 (note (b))

CO_2 emissions g/km	Petrol £	Diesel £
140	2,160	2,592
145	2,304	2,736
150	2,448	2,880
155	2,592	3,024
160	2,736	3,168
165	2,880	3,312
170	3,024	3,456
175	3,168	3,600
180	3,312	3,744
185	3,456	3,888
190	3,600	4,032
195	3,744	4,176
200	3,888	4,320
205	4,032	4,464
210	4,176	4,608
215	4,320	4,752
220	4,464	4,896
225	4,608	5,040
230	4,752	5,040
235	4,896	5,040
240	5,040	5,040

2008/09–2009/10 (note (b))

CO_2 emissions g/km	Petrol £	Diesel £
120	1,690	2,197
135	2,535	3,042
140	2,704	3,211
145	2,873	3,380
150	3,042	3,549
155	3,211	3,718
160	3,380	3,887
165	3,549	4,056
170	3,718	4,225
175	3,887	4,394
180	4,056	4,563
185	4,225	4,732
190	4,394	4,901
195	4,563	5,070
200	4,732	5,239
205	4,901	5,408
210	5,070	5,577
215	5,239	5,746
220	5,408	5,915
225	5,577	5,915
230	5,746	5,915
235	5,915	5,915

2010/11 (note (b))

CO_2 emissions g/km	Petrol £	Diesel £
75	900	1,440
120	1,800	2,340
130	2,700	3,240
135	2,880	3,420
140	3,060	3,600
145	3,240	3,780
150	3,420	3,960
155	3,600	4,140
160	3,780	4,320
165	3,960	4,500
170	4,140	4,680
175	4,320	4,860
180	4,500	5,040
185	4,680	5,220
190	4,860	5,400
195	5,040	5,580
200	5,220	5,760
205	5,400	5,940
210	5,580	6,120
215	5,760	6,300
220	5,940	6,300
225	6,120	6,300
230	6,300	6,300

2011/12 (note (b))

CO_2 emissions (g/km)	Petrol (£)	Diesel (£)
75	940	1,504
120	1,880	2,444
125	2,820	3,384
130	3,008	3,572
135	3,196	3,760
140	3,384	3,948
145	3,572	4,136
150	3,760	4,324
155	3,948	4,512
160	4,136	4,700
165	4,324	4,888
170	4,512	5,076
175	4,700	5,264
180	4,888	5,452
185	5,076	5,640
190	5,264	5,828
195	5,452	6,016
200	5,640	6,204
205	5,828	6,392
210	6,016	6,580
215	6,204	6,580
220	6,392	6,580
225	6,580	6,580

2012/13 (note (b))

CO_2 emissions (g/km)	Petrol (£)	Diesel (£)
75	1,010	1,616
99	2,020	2,626
100	2,222	2,828
105	2,424	3,030
110	2,626	3,232
115	2,828	3,434
120	3,030	3,636
125	3,232	3,838
130	3,434	4,040
135	3,636	4,242
140	3,838	4,444
145	4,040	4,646
150	4,242	4,848
155	4,444	5,050
160	4,646	5,252
165	4,848	5,454
170	5,050	5,656
175	5,252	5,858
180	5,454	6,060
185	5,656	6,262
190	5,858	6,464
195	6,060	6,666
200	6,262	6,868
205	6,464	7,070
210	6,666	7,070
215	6,868	7,070
220	7,070	7,070

2013/14 (note (b))

CO_2 emissions (g/km)	Petrol (£)	Diesel (£)
75	1,055	1,688
94	2,110	2,743
95	2,321	2,954
100	2,532	3,165
105	2,743	3,376
110	2,954	3,587
115	3,165	3,798
120	3,376	4,009
125	3,587	4,220
130	3,798	4,431
135	4,009	4,642
140	4,220	4,853
145	4,431	5,064
150	4,642	5,275
155	4,853	5,486
160	5,064	5,697
165	5,275	5,908
170	5,486	6,119
175	5,697	6,330
180	5,908	6,541
185	6,119	6,752
190	6,330	6,963
195	6,541	7,174
200	6,752	7,385
205	6,963	7,385
210	7,174	7,385
215	7,385	7,385

Notes

(a) The cash equivalent of the benefit of car fuel is taxable as earnings of directors and 'P11D' employees (i.e. employees with earnings, including benefits, etc. to be entered on form P11D, including VAT, at the rate of £8,500 p.a. or more) provided with free fuel for private use of company cars. [*ITEPA 2003, ss 149, 217*].

(b) The same percentage figure on page 80 used to calculate the car benefit charge for the company car, which is directly linked to the car's CO_2 emissions, is used to calculate the benefit charge for fuel provided for private motoring. The relevant percentage figure is multiplied by
£14,400 for 2005/06 to 2007/08,
£16,900 for 2008/09 to 2009/10,
£18,000 for 2010/11,
£18,800 for 2011/12,
£20,200 for 2012/13, and
£21,100 for 2013/14.

(c) The benefit is reduced to nil if the employee is required to, and does, make good all fuel provided for private use, including journeys between home and normal place of work. There is no taxable benefit where the employer only provides fuel for business travel. The charge is proportionately reduced where the employee stops receiving free fuel part way through the tax year, but where free fuel is subsequently provided in the same tax year, the full year's charge is payable. [*ITEPA 2003, ss 151, 152*].

(d) The benefit is proportionately reduced where a car is not available or is incapable of being used for part of a year (being at least 30 days). [*ITEPA 2003, s 152*].

(e) Fuel provided for private motoring of a director or 'P11D' employee but not for a company car and fuel provided for lower-paid employees (e.g. by paying garage bills or by use of credit tokens or vouchers) is taxable on the cost to the employer less any contributions from the employee.

(f) Employers pay Class 1A national insurance contributions on the amount of the benefit shown.

National insurance contributions Class 1

Class 1 (earnings related)		2013/14	
Lower earnings limit	— per week	£109	
	— per month	£473	
	— per year	£5,668	
Primary earnings threshold	— per week	£149	
	— per month	£646	
	— per year	£7,755	
Secondary earnings threshold	— per week	£148	
	— per month	£641	
	— per year	£7,696	
Upper accruals point	— per week	£770	
	— per month	£3,337	
	— per year	£40,040	
Upper earnings limit	— per week	£797	
	— per month	£3,454	
	— per year	£41,450	
Not contracted out			
Employee (note (a))		First £149 pw	Nil
		From £149 pw to £797 pw	12%
		Balance above £797 pw	2%
Employer (note (c))		First £148 pw	Nil
		Balance above £148 pw	13.8%
Contracted out — salary related schemes			
Employee (note (a))		First £149 pw	Nil
		From £149 pw to £770 pw	10.6%
		From £770 pw to £797 pw	12%
		Balance above £797 pw	2%
— rebate (note (b))		From £109 pw to £149 pw	1.4%
Employer (note (c))		First £148 pw	Nil
		From £148 pw to £770 pw	10.4%
		Balance above £770 pw	13.8%
— rebate		From £109 pw to £148 pw	3.4%
Women at reduced rate			
Employee (note (a))		First £149 pw	Nil
		From £149 pw to £797 pw	5.85%
		Balance above £797 pw	2%

Notes

(a) For 2013/14, NICs are not payable on earnings up to and including the primary earnings threshold. Employees' rates are nil for employees of pensionable age although normal employers' contributions are still payable. For 2013/14, pensionable age for a man is 65. For women born before 6 April 1950 pensionable age is 60. Sliding scales apply for women born after 5 April 1950 and men born after 5 November 1963. These initially seek to increase the pensionable age of women to 65 and then increase the pensionable age for men and women to 66, 67 & 68.

(b) Where insufficient employee contributions are paid to cover the rebate, it is offset against employers' contributions to the extent of the shortfall.

(c) For 2013/14, NICs are not payable on earnings up to and including the secondary earnings threshold.

(d) See page 74 for interest on Class 1 NIC.

(e) An NIC 'holiday' is available for new businesses in Northern Ireland, Scotland, Wales and six English regions. Under the scheme, an employer does not have to pay the first £5,000 of its employer NICs for each of its first ten employees hired in its first year of business. The scheme applies to businesses starting up in the period from 22 June 2010 to 5 September 2013, but only to NICs in respect of earnings paid on or after 6 September 2010 (and before 6 September 2013).

National insurance contributions Class 1

Class 1 (earnings related)		2012/13		2011/12	
Lower earnings limit	— per week	£107		£102	
	— per month	£464		£442	
	— per year	£5,564		£5,304	
Primary earnings threshold	— per week	£146		£139	
	— per month	£634		£602	
	— per year	£7,605		£7,225	
Secondary earnings threshold	— per week	£144		£136	
	— per month	£624		£589	
	— per year	£7,488		£7,072	
Upper accruals point	— per week	£770		£770	
	— per month	£3,337		£3,337	
	— per year	£40,040		£40,040	
Upper earnings limit	— per week	£817		£817	
	— per month	£3,540		£3,540	
	— per year	£42,475		£42,475	
Not contracted out					
Employee (note (a))		First £146 pw	Nil	First £139 pw	Nil
		From £146 pw to £817 pw	12%	From £139 pw to £817 pw	12%
		Balance above £817 pw	2%	Balance above £817 pw	2%
Employer (note (c))		First £144 pw	Nil	First £136 pw	Nil
		Balance above £144 pw	13.8%	Balance above £136 pw	13.8%
Contracted out					
Employee (note (a))		First £146 pw	Nil	First £139 pw	Nil
		From £146 pw to £770 pw	10.6%	From £139 pw to £770 pw	10.4%
		From £770 pw to £817 pw	12%	From £770 pw to £817 pw	12%
		Balance above £817 pw	2%	Balance above £817 pw	2%
— rebate (note (b))		From £107 pw to £146 pw	1.4%	From £102 pw to £139 pw	1.6%
Employer — salary related schemes (note (c))		First £144 pw	Nil	First £136 pw	Nil
		From £144 pw to £770 pw	10.4%	From £136 pw to £770 pw	10.1%
		Balance above £770 pw	13.8%	Balance above £770 pw	13.8%
— rebate		From £107 pw to £144 pw	3.4%	From £102 pw to £136 pw	3.7%
Employer — money purchase scheme (notes (c), (d))		N/A		First £136 pw	Nil
				From £136 pw to £770 pw	12.4%
				Balance above £770 pw	13.8%
— rebate				From £102 pw to £136 pw	1.4%
Women at reduced rate					
Employee (note (a))		First £146 pw	Nil	First £139 pw	Nil
		From £146 pw to £817 pw	5.85%	From £139 pw to £817 pw	5.85%
		Balance above £817 pw	2%	Balance above £817 pw	2%

Notes

(a) For 2011/12 and 2012/13, NICs are not payable on earnings up to and including the primary earnings threshold. Employees' rates are nil for employees of pensionable age although normal employers' contributions are still payable.

(b) Where insufficient employee contributions are paid to cover the rebate, it is offset against employers' contributions to the extent of the shortfall.

(c) For 2011/12 and 2012/13, NICs are not payable on earnings up to and including the secondary earnings threshold.

(d) Contracting out is abolished for money purchase schemes with effect from 6 April 2012.

(e) See page 74 for interest on Class 1 NIC.

(f) An NIC 'holiday' is available for new businesses in Northern Ireland, Scotland, Wales and six English regions. Under the scheme, an employer does not have to pay the first £5,000 of its employer NICs for each of its first ten employees hired in its first year of business. The scheme applies to businesses starting up in the period from 22 June 2010 to 5 September 2013, but only to NICs in respect of earnings paid on or after 6 September 2010 (and before 6 September 2013).

National insurance contributions Class 1

Class 1 (earnings related)		2010/11		2009/10	
Lower earnings limit	— per week	£97		£95	
	— per month	£421		£412	
	— per year	£5,044		£4,940	
Primary/secondary earnings threshold	— per week	£110		£110	
	— per month	£476		£476	
	— per year	£5,715		£5,715	
Upper accruals point	— per week	£770		£770	
	— per month	£3,337		£3,337	
	— per year	£40,040		£40,040	
Upper earnings limit	— per week	£844		£844	
	— per month	£3,656			
	— per year	£43,875		£43,875	
Not contracted out					
Employee (note (a))		First £110 pw	Nil	First £110 pw	Nil
		From £110 pw to £844 pw	11%	From £110 pw to £844 pw	11%
		Balance above £844 pw	1%	Balance above £844 pw	1%
Employer (note (c))		First £110 pw	Nil	First £110 pw	Nil
		Balance above £110 pw	12.8%	Balance above £110 pw	12.8%
Contracted out					
Employee (note (a))		First £110 pw	Nil	First £110 pw	Nil
		From £110 pw to £770 pw	9.4%	From £110 pw to £770 pw	9.4%
		From £770 pw to £844 pw	11%	From £770 pw to £844 pw	11%
		Balance above £844 pw	1%	Balance above £844 pw	1%
— rebate (note (b))		From £97 pw to £110 pw	1.6%	From £95 pw to £110 pw	1.6%
Employer — salary related schemes (note (c))		First £110 pw	Nil	First £110 pw	Nil
		From £110 pw to £770 pw	9.1%	From £110 pw to £770 pw	9.1%
		Balance above £770 pw	12.8%	Balance above £770 pw	12.8%
— rebate		From £97 pw to £110 pw	3.7%	From £95 pw to £110 pw	3.7%
Employer — money purchase scheme (note (c))		First £110 pw	Nil	First £110 pw	Nil
		From £110 pw to £770 pw	11.4%	From £110 pw to £770 pw	11.4%
		Balance above £770 pw	12.8%	Balance above £770 pw	12.8%
— rebate		From £97 pw to £110 pw	1.4%	From £95 pw to £110 pw	1.4%
Women at reduced rate					
Employee (note (a))		First £110 pw	Nil	First £110 pw	Nil
		From £110 pw to £844 pw	4.85%	From £110 pw to £844 pw	4.85%
		Balance above £844 pw	1%	Balance above £844 pw	1%

Notes

(a) For 2009/10 and 2010/11, NICs are not payable on earnings up to and including the primary earnings threshold. Employees' rates are nil for employees of pensionable age although normal employers' contributions are still payable.

(b) Where insufficient employee contributions are paid to cover the rebate, it is offset against employers' contributions to the extent of the shortfall.

(c) For 2009/10 and 2010/11, NICs are not payable on earnings up to and including the secondary earnings threshold.

(d) See page 74 for interest on Class 1 NIC.

(e) An NIC 'holiday' is available for new businesses in Northern Ireland, Scotland, Wales and six English regions. Under the scheme, an employer does not have to pay the first £5,000 of its employer NICs for each of its first ten employees hired in its first year of business. The scheme applies to businesses starting up in the period from 22 June 2010 to 5 September 2013, but only to NICs in respect of earnings paid on or after 6 September 2010 (and before 6 September 2013).

National insurance contributions Class 1

Class 1 (earnings related)		2008/09		2007/08	
Lower earnings limit	— per week	£90		£87	
	— per month	£390		£377	
	— per year	£4,680		£4,542	
Primary (employees) earnings threshold	— per week	£105		£100	
	— per month	£453		£435	
	— per year	£5,435		£5,225	
Secondary (employers) earnings threshold	— per week	£105		£100	
	— per month	£453		£435	
	— per year	£5,435		£5,225	
Upper earnings limit	— per week	£770		£670	
	— per month	£3,337		£2,904	
	— per year	£40,040		£34,840	
Not contracted out					
Employee (note (a))		First £105 pw	Nil	First £100 pw	Nil
		From £105 pw to £770 pw	11%	From £100 pw to £670 pw	11%
		Balance above £770 pw	1%	Balance above £670 pw	1%
Employer (note (c))		First £105 pw	Nil	First £100 pw	Nil
		Balance above £105 pw	12.8%	Balance above £100 pw	12.8%
Contracted out					
Employee (note (a))		First £105 pw	Nil	First £100 pw	Nil
		From £105 pw to £770	9.4%	From £100 pw to £670 pw	9.4%
		Balance above £770 pw	1%	Balance above £670 pw	1%
— rebate (note (b))		From £90 pw to £105 pw	1.6%	From £87 pw to £100 pw	1.6%
Employer — salary related schemes (note (c))		First £105 pw	Nil	First £100 pw	Nil
		From £105 pw to £770	9.1%	Balance up to £670 pw	9.1%
		Balance above £770 pw	12.8%	Balance over £670 pw	12.8%
— rebate		From £90 pw to £105 pw	3.7%	From £87 pw to £100 pw	3.7%
Employer — money purchase scheme (note (c))		First £105 pw	Nil	First £100 pw	Nil
		From £105 pw to £770	11.4%	Balance up to £670 pw	11.4%
		Balance above £770 pw	12.8%	Balance over £670 pw	12.8%
— rebate		From £90 pw to £105 pw	1.4%	From £87 pw to £100 pw	1.4%
Women at reduced rate					
Employee (note (a))		First £105 pw	Nil	First £100 pw	Nil
		From £105 pw to £770	4.85%	From £100 pw to £670 pw	4.85%
		Balance above £770 pw	1%	Balance above £670 pw	1%

Notes

(a) For 2007/08 and 2008/09, NICs are not payable on earnings up to and including the primary earnings threshold. Employees' rates are nil for men over 65 and women over 60 although normal employers' contributions are still payable.

(b) Where insufficient employee contributions are paid to cover the rebate, it is offset against employers' contributions to the extent of the shortfall.

(c) For 2007/08 and 2008/09, NICs are not payable on earnings up to and including the secondary earnings threshold.

(d) See page 74 for interest on Class 1 NIC.

National insurance contributions Classes 1A, 1B, 2, 3 and 4

	2013/14	2012/13	2011/12	2010/11	2009/10	2008/09	2007/08
Class 1A (note (a))	13.8%	13.8%	13.8%	12.8%	12.8%	12.8%	12.8%
Class 1B (PSAs) (note (b))	13.8%	13.8%	13.8%	12.8%	12.8%	12.8%	12.8%
Class 2 (self-employed, flat rate)							
Small earnings exemption—per year	£5,725	£5,595	£5,315	£5,075	£5,075	£4,825	£4,635
Contributions —per week	£2.70	£2.65	£2.50	£2.40	£2.40	£2.30	£2.20
Share fishermen	£3.35	£3.30	£3.15	£3.05	£3.05	£2.95	£2.85
Volunteer development workers	£5.45	£5.35	£5.10	£4.85	£4.75	£4.50	£4.35
Class 3 (voluntary contributions)							
Contributions —per week	£13.55	£13.25	£12.60	£12.05	£12.05	£8.10	£7.80
Class 4 (self-employed, profits related) (note (c))							
Lower annual limit	£7,755	£7,605	£7,225	£5,715	£5,715	£5,435	£5,225
Upper annual limit	£41,450	£42,475	£42,475	£43,875	£43,875	£40,040	£34,840
Percentage rate between lower and upper annual limits	9%	9%	9%	8%	8%	8%	8%
Percentage rate above upper annual limit	2%	2%	2%	1%	1%	1%	1%
Maximum contributions (note (d))							
Class 1 or Class 1/Class 2	£4,121.28	£4,267.56	£4,312.08	£4,279.22	£4,279.22	£3,876.95	£3,323.10
Class 4 limiting amount	£3,175.65	£3,278.75	£3,305.00	£3,180.00	£3,180.00	£2,890.30	£2,485.80

Notes

(a) **Class 1A contributions.** Class 1A contributions are payable by employers on the provision of cars and private fuel to employees and most other benefits in kind provided by employers. Employees' contributions are not payable. The income tax rules are used to determine the chargeable amount (see pages 76 to 78). Contributions are payable by 19 July following the tax year to which they relate. If private fuel is provided for use in an employee's own car, Class 1A contributions do not apply but there may be a liability for both employer's and employee's Class 1 contributions depending upon how the fuel is provided.

For the provisions relating to interest on unpaid and overpaid Class 1A contributions, see page 74.

(b) **Class 1B contributions.** Class 1B contributions are payable by employers by reference to the value of any items included in a PAYE settlement agreement (PSA) which would otherwise be earnings for Class 1 or Class 1A, including the amount of tax paid. Employees' contributions are not payable. Income tax and Class 1B contributions on a PSA are payable by 19 October following the end of the tax year to which the PSA applies.

(c) **Class 4 contributions.** The provisions relating to interest on unpaid tax and interest on overpaid tax also apply to Class 4 contributions. See page 74.

Where Class 4 contributions are due, the same penalties for failure to make a return within the required period or making an incorrect return apply as for income tax purposes. See pages 86, 89.

(d) **Maximum contributions.** Where an earner is employed in more than one employment (whether employed earners' employments or self-employments) liability for Class 1 or Class 1 and Class 2 contributions cannot exceed a maximum figure. Similarly, where Class 4 contributions are payable in addition to Class 1 and/or Class 2 contributions, liability for Class 4 contributions cannot exceed a limiting amount.

Subject to below, the Class 1/Class 2 maximum is the equivalent of 53 primary Class 1 contributions at the maximum standard rate. The Class 4 maximum is such amount as, when added to the Class 1/Class 2 contributions payable (after applying the maximum if appropriate), equals the limiting amount shown above (this being the maximum Class 4 contributions payable at 9%/8% plus 53 Class 2 contributions).

Because of the open-ended Class 1 and Class 4 contributions at 2%/1%, each person has, in effect, their own 'personalised maximum'. Further adjustments to the figures quoted in the table above are required for any contributions payable at the 2% or 1% rate on earnings over the upper earnings limit and profits over the upper annual limit.

PAYE thresholds

2013/14	£182 per week	£787 per month

Payment by quarterly instalments

Employers whose average monthly liability for PAYE and NIC is less than £1,500 can choose to pay quarterly instead. Payments are due 14 days after the end of the relevant quarter (extended to 17 days where payment is made by electronic means).

PAYE codes

Code suffix	*Meaning*
L	Basic personal allowance
P	Full personal allowance for those born between 6.4.1938 and 5.4.1948
Y	Full personal allowance for those born before 6.4.1938
T	Either there are other items HMRC need to review in the code or taxpayer has asked for none of the codes listed above to be used
K	Total allowances in the code are less than total deductions
D0	Tax to be deducted at higher rate
D1	Tax to be deducted at additional rate
BR	Tax to be deducted at basic rate; no allowances given
NT	No tax to be deducted
0T	No allowances available; tax to be deducted at appropriate rate

Paying HMRC

Under RTI the allocation of tax payments can have a significant impact on any late payment penalties. For PAYE payments via BACS, online/telephone banking or CHAPS made early or late, it is possible to add four digits to the 13 character accounts office reference number to inform HMRC where to allocate. The digits represent the tax year ending on the 5 April and the month / quarter. E.g. adding 1403 allocates a payment to the month or quarter ending 5 July 2013; adding 1412 allocates to the month/quarter ending 5 April 2014. For payments via direct debit or bill pay there are separate boxes to allocate payments.

For 2013/14 onwards, all PAYE payments should be made to HMRC's Cumbernauld bank account. As at 19 July 2013 the details for this account are:

Sort code: 08 32 10

Account number: 12001039

Account name HMRC: Cumbernauld Reference: Taxpayer's 13 character accounts office reference + 4 digits (if early/late)

Penalties—Real Time Information

Failure to submit RTI returns. For 2013/14, the penalty rules below for failure to submit forms P14, P35, P38 & P38A continue to apply. These rules apply to returns not submitted by the due date i.e. 19 May 2014. Therefore for 2013/14 only, there will be no penalties for late filing of monthly in-year RTI returns provided the final return is made by 19 May 2014. There is also a temporary relaxation of reporting arrangements for small businesses for a transitional period. The transitional period is currently set to October 2013 but HMRC plan to extend until April 2014. www.hmrc.gov.uk/payerti/reporting/when-to-report.htm#4.

For 2014/15 onwards, new rules will apply for the failure to make a return for a tax month i.e., the introduction of in-year penalties. Regulations are to be announced although it is expected:

First failure – no penalty
Second and subsequent failures – penalty (calculation to be announced although expected to reflect number of employees / number of previous defaults)
Failure continues for more than three months – 5% of tax due.

Failure to pay tax on time. For 2013/14 the existing rules under *FA 2009, Sch 56* continue to apply see page 92. The existing rules will be modified slightly to suit RTI from 6.4.14.

Error in taxpayer's document. For 2013/14 onwards penalties under *FA 2007, Sch 24* (see page 91) can be applied to all documents submitted under RTI e.g., the monthly / weekly in-year returns and the final RTI submission.

Penalties—P14, P35, P38 and P38A

Failure to submit returns. For returns not submitted by due date (i.e. 19 May following the tax year)

(a) an automatic penalty of the 'monthly amount' for each month (or part month) the failure continues, up to 12 months; and
(b) for failure beyond 12 months, a penalty of up to the amount of the PAYE or NIC payable which was unpaid after 19 April following the tax year.

The '*monthly amount*' is £100 for every 50 employees or subcontractors (or part thereof).

Penalties—P9D and P11D

Failure to submit returns. For returns not submitted by 6 July following the tax year

(a) a penalty of up to £300 per form;
(b) if failure continues after penalty under (a) imposed, continuing penalty of up to £60 per form per day.

Penalties—security

From 6 April 2012, HMRC can ask for financial security where there is a risk of non-payment of PAYE. Security can be requested from the employer and or various other persons, e.g. a director. A person who fails to comply with the notice to give security or further security is liable on summary conviction to a fine not exceeding level 5 on the standard scale (*ITEPA 2003, s 684(4A)*).

RTI guidance

HMRC have issued a four page index with links to all the RTI PAYE pages on their website which is useful to find guidance on specific issues. www.hmrc.gov.uk/rti/guidelist.pdf.

Gross pay for PAYE and NIC purposes (HMRC Guide CWG2 (2013))

The following payments should be entered as pay on the deduction working sheet (as opposed to being returned at the year end on forms P9D or P11D or included in a PAYE settlement agreement).

Childcare vouchers not meeting the qualifying conditions (NIC only).

Christmas boxes in cash.

Clothing or uniforms—(i) Payments to employees for non-durable items such as tights or stockings (PAYE only); and (ii) other payments to employees to purchase clothing or uniforms whether this can be worn at any time or (for PAYE only) only at work.

Council tax paid on employee's living accommodation except where the value does not have to be included on forms P9D or P11D (NICs only).

Credit cards, charge cards, etc.—employees' use of an employer's card for expenditure, *other than* goods or services bought on the employer's behalf, on readily convertible assets (see below), and (for NICs) where no reimbursement made.

Credit card reward payments for detecting/withdrawing lost/stolen cards made by employer or (for PAYE purposes only) a third party.

Damages or similar payments made to an employee injured at work if there is a contractual liability to make it.

Directors' remuneration, salary, bonuses, fees etc. including any advance or anticipatory payments paid, voted or credited.

Employment income provided through third parties when taxable under "**disguised remuneration**" rules in Part 7A ITEPA 2003.

Employment Tribunal awards under an order for re-instatement or re-engagement or for continuation of employment, or a protective award.

Guarantee payments under *Employment Rights Act 1996*.

Honoraria

Incentive awards made by cash or vouchers exchangeable for cash including (for NICs) those made by third parties.

Inducement payments such as 'golden hellos' to recruit or retain employees.

Loans written off (NICs only.)

Long service awards in cash or cash vouchers or readily convertible assets (see below).

Lost time payments but not including those made by a third party or by the employer on behalf of a third party.

Maternity suspension payments made under the *Employment Rights Act 1996*.

Meal allowances and vouchers comprising (i) cash payments for meals; and (ii) vouchers redeemable for food and drink or cash alternative (but not vouchers redeemable for food and drink only except for NICs on any excess value over 15p per working day).

Medical suspension payments made under the *Employment Rights Act 1996*.

Mortgage payments (for NICs only) on a contract between the employee and mortgagee.

Payments in kind (other than readily convertible assets for which see below) which can be turned into cash *by surrender*, e.g. premium bonds.

Payments made to an employee whilst he or she pursues a claim for *damages against a third party* for loss of earnings following an accident and where the employee is not required to repay the employer.

Pensions (PAYE only)

Personal bills paid for goods and services supplied to employees and directors, club memberships, etc. where the payments are made or reimbursed direct to the employee, and (for NICs only) where made direct to the provider or via an overdrawn director's loan account into which director's earnings normally paid.

Personal incidental expenses (other than benefits in kind) exceeding the prescribed limit or failing the qualifying conditions (the whole amount is liable to tax and NICs).

Prize money paid in cash to employees for competitions the employer runs in connection with its business and which are not open to the public.

Readily convertible assets i.e. assets which (i) are capable of being sold on a recognised investment exchange, the London Bullion market or the New York Stock Exchange (other than shares under an approved scheme); (ii) are a right over a money debt; (iii) are subject to a fiscal warehousing regime; (iv) give rise to a right to enable an employee to obtain money; (v) are subject to trading arrangements; or (vi) are already owned by the employee and whose value is enhanced by the employer.

Relocation payments that are non-qualifying.

Round sum allowances unless otherwise agreed with HMRC.

Sickness, maternity and other absence from work payments.

Statutory adoption pay (SAP), **statutory maternity pay** (SMP), **statutory paternity pay** (SPP) and **statutory sick pay** (SSP)

Subscriptions or fees to professional bodies:
(i) Paid directly by the employer but not allowable under ITEPA 2003, ss 343–344 (NIC only)
(ii) Reimbursed by the employer: (a) Allowable under ITEPA 2003, ss 343–344 (PAYE only) (b) Not allowable under ITEPA 2003, ss 343–344 (PAYE & NIC).

Suggestion scheme awards to employees (see *ITEPA 2003, s 321* for exemption).

Telephone bills — NICs on full amount of rental and on private calls where telephone used for business and private calls, the employee is the subscriber and the employer pays for the calls and/or rental. See also *Personal bills* above where the telephone is used exclusively for private calls.

Termination payments — (i) payments made under the terms and conditions of employment (such as compensation for loss of office, accrued pay and pay in lieu of notice); (ii) payments for a restrictive covenant; (iii) redundancy payments and payments made as damages (PAYE only) subject to a £30,000 relief under certain circumstances; (iv) certain payments made to unapproved retirement benefits schemes (NICs only).

Tips and service charges where a scheme is operated by the employer (if separate organised arrangements exist, for example, employees are paid out of a tronc, then the troncmaster is responsible for operating PAYE but not for NICs).

Training payments (for course fees, books, etc.) unless the training is work-related or is encouraged or required by the employer in connection with the employee's work.

Travelling time payments.

Trivial commutations from registered pension schemes (PAYE only)

Vouchers which can be redeemed or exchanged for (i) goods and cash or cash alone; (ii) goods alone or transport services (NICs only) or (iii) readily convertible assets.

Wages, salaries, fees, overtime, bonuses, commission, etc.

PAYE settlement agreements (PSAs) *[ITEPA 2003, ss 703–707; SI 2003 No 2682 Pt 6; HMRC SP 5/96]*

PSAs cover arrangements under which employers can settle, in a single payment, the tax and Class 1B NICs (see page 87) liability on certain benefits in kind and expense payments. Expenses payments and benefits can be included in a PSA if they are minor or payable on an irregular basis or in circumstances where it is impracticable to apply PAYE or apportion the value of particular benefits which have been shared by employees.

The scope of the PSA must be finalised by 6 July, and any tax paid by 19 October, following the tax year to which the PSA applies.

Personal service companies etc. *[ITEPA 2003, ss 48–61]*

Where a worker who would otherwise have been an employee provides his services through an intermediary such as a service company, it must operate PAYE and pay NICs. For this purpose, the income from the worker's relevant engagements in the year, less the amounts provided to the worker as salary/benefits in kind and less allowable expenses, are deemed to have been paid to the worker as salary on 5 April. Allowable expenses include normal deductible employment expenses, employer's NICs and pension contributions and 5% of income from relevant engagements. From 6 April 2013 the provisions are extended to office holders.

Managed service companies *[ITEPA 2003, ss 61A–61J; FA 2007, s 25, Sch 3]*

Where a worker provides his services through an intermediary which is a managed service company (as defined), all payments received by him from the company on or after 6 April 2007 which are not otherwise employment income are deemed to be employment income. The company must operate PAYE and, from 6 August 2007, pay NICs on each such payment. PAYE and NIC debts which cannot be recovered from a managed service company will be collectible from certain other persons, primarily the company's director or the person who provided the company to the worker.

The personal service companies provisions above are disapplied where the managed service companies rules apply.

Student loan repayments *[SI 2009 No 470]*

Student loan repayments of employees are collected through the PAYE system. The employer must calculate and deduct student loan repayments due each pay period, based on the employee's earnings for that period. The deduction is 9% of earnings in excess of the threshold in the table below. If total earnings for a tax year do not exceed the yearly threshold, the employee can claim a refund of any repayments deducted in that tax year. Repayments must also be made by reference to other income (from self-employment, savings and investments etc.) through the self-assessment system where total income exceeds the yearly threshold.

Year	*Percentage*	*Threshold*		
		Per week	Per month	Per year
2013/14	9%	£314.71	£1,363.75	£16,365.00
2012/13	9%	£303.75	£1,316.25	£15,795.00
2005/06 to 2011/12	9%	£288.46	£1,250.00	£15,000.00

National minimum wage

Age	*Hourly rate*			
	1.10.10–30.9.11	**1.10.11–30.9.12**	**1.10.12–30.9.13**	**1.10.13 onwards**
Under 18	£3.64	£3.68	£3.68	£3.72
18–20	£4.92	£4.98	£4.98	£5.03
21 or over	£5.93	£6.08	£6.19	£6.31
Apprentice rate	£2.50	£2.60	£2.65	£2.68

Offence	Penalty
Error in taxpayer's document [*FA 2007, Sch 24 para 1*] Careless or deliberate error in document amounting to or leading to understatement of liability, overstatement or loss or false or inflated claim to repayment of tax. Applies to (a) IT, CIS, CGT, CT and VAT returns, statements, declarations, claims etc. relating to tax years, accounting periods and VAT periods beginning on or after 1 April 2008. No penalty can be charged in respect of any period for which a return is required before 1 April 2009; (b) further taxes, including to IHT where the date of death is on or after 1 April 2009 or, in other cases, where the tax liability arises on or after 1 April 2010; (c) SDLT where the liability arises on or after 1 April 2010; (d) RTI PAYE for 2013/14 onwards in respect of any penalty assessed after 17 July 2013.	Deliberate and concealed action or omission: 100% of potential lost revenue. Deliberate but not concealed action or omission: 70% of potential lost revenue. Careless action or omission: 30% of potential lost revenue. *Reductions.* A statutory reduction in the amount of the penalty is made for disclosure of an inaccuracy. The table below sets out the minimum percentage a penalty may be reduced to where a disclosure is voluntary (unprompted) or prompted by HMRC action. HMRC can also reduce a penalty in special circumstances. The table below sets out the minimum percentage a penalty may be reduced to where disclosure is voluntary (unprompted) or prompted by HMRC action. HMRC can also reduce a penalty in special circumstances. *Max penalty* / *Voluntary disclosure* / *Prompted disclosure* Deliberate & concealed: 100% / 30% / 50% Deliberate not concealed: 70% / 20% / 35% Careless: 30% / 0% / 15% *Offshore evasion.* See page 93 for the increase in the amount of the penalty where the error involves an offshore matter.
Error in taxpayer's document attributable to another person [*FA 2007, Sch 24 para 1A*] Deliberately supplying false information to, or deliberately withholding information from, a person giving a document within the above provisions to HMRC resulting in document containing an inaccuracy amounting to or leading to understatement of liability, overstatement of loss or false or inflated claim to repayment of tax. Applies to tax years, accounting periods and VAT periods beginning on or after 1 April 2009 where the filing date is on or after 1 April 2010; to repayment claims for a tax period made on or after 1 April 2010; to inheritance tax accounts where the date of death is on or after 1 April 2009; and in any other case where the tax liability arises on or after 1 April 2010.	100% of potential lost revenue, subject to the same reductions as above for disclosure or in special circumstances.
Failure to notify HMRC of error in assessment [*FA 2007, Sch 24 para 2*] Failure to take reasonable steps to notify HMRC of an under-assessment to IT, CT, CGT or VAT for a tax year, accounting period or VAT period beginning on or after 1 April 2008 within the 30 days beginning with the date of the assessment. Also applies to further taxes including IHT and SDLT for tax periods beginning on or after 1 April 2009 where the filing date is on or after 1 April 2010.	30% of potential lost revenue, subject to the same reductions as above for disclosure or in special circumstances.
Failure to comply with notification obligations and VAT offences [*FA 2008, Sch 41*] Failure to comply with any of the following obligations: • to notify chargeability to IT or CGT within six months of tax year • to notify chargeability to CT within one year of accounting period • to notify liability to register for VAT • to notify acquisition of goods from another member state (for VAT purposes) Issue of invoice showing VAT by person not authorised to do so. Penalty applies to obligations arising on or after 1 April 2010 and to invoices issued on or after that date. Applies also to similar obligations in relation to insurance premium tax, aggregates levy, climate change levy, landfill tax, air passenger duty and certain other types of duty.	Deliberate and concealed failure: 100% of potential lost revenue. Deliberate but unconcealed failure: 70% of potential lost revenue. Any other case: 30% of potential lost revenue. *Reductions.* A statutory reduction in the amount of the penalty is made for disclosure of a failure. For an unprompted disclosure, a 100% penalty may be reduced to no less than 30%, a 70% penalty to no less than 20% and a 30% penalty to any percentage, including 0%, unless HMRC do not become aware of the failure until twelve months after the time tax first became unpaid because of the failure, in which case the penalty may be reduced to no less than 10%. For a prompted disclosure, a 100% penalty may be reduced to no less than 50%, a 70% penalty to no less than 35% and a 30% penalty to no less than 10% (20% where HMRC do not become aware of the failure until twelve months after the time tax first became unpaid because of the failure). HMRC can also reduce a penalty in special circumstances. *Offshore evasion.* See page 93 for the increase in the amount of the penalty where the failure to comply with an obligation involves an offshore matter.

Offence	Penalty
Failure to comply with HMRC investigatory powers [*FA 2008, Sch 36 paras 39, 40*] Failure to comply with an information notice within *FA 2008, Sch 36 Pt 1* or deliberately obstructing an HMRC officer in the course of an inspection of premises under *FA 2008, Sch 36 Pt 2* which has been approved by the First-tier Tribunal. Applies to (a) IT, CT, CGT, VAT and certain foreign taxes with effect from 1 April 2009; (b) further taxes, including IHT and SDLT, from 1 April 2010; (c) ATED (see page 77) from 17 July 2013.	(i) initial penalty of £300. (ii) if failure/obstruction continues, a further penalty up to £60 per day. (iii) if failure/obstruction continues after penalty under (i) imposed, a tax-related amount determined by the Upper Tribunal.
HMRC investigatory powers: inaccurate information etc [*FA 2008, Sch 36 para 40A*] Providing inaccurate information or document carelessly or deliberately or failing to take reasonable steps to notify HMRC of an inaccuracy discovered later. One penalty for each inaccuracy. Applies with effect from 21 July 2009.	Up to £3,000
Tax agents: dishonest conduct [*FA 2012, Sch 38 para 26; SI 2013 No 279*] HMRC also have the power to publish the names and details of tax agents who incur penalties under these rules over £5,000. From 1 April 2013.	Up to £50,000 (minimum £5,000) although HMRC have the discretion to apply a special reduction to a £5,000 penalty to reflect the quality of the disclosure and compliance with any access notice.
Tax agents: failure to comply with file access notice [*FA 2012, Sch 38 paras 22, 23*] From 1 April 2013.	(i) initial penalty of £300. (ii) if failure continues, a further penalty up to £60 per day.
Failure to make payments on time [*FA 2009 Sch 56*] Applies for 2010/11 onwards to income tax and Class 1 NICs collected through in-year PAYE and to Class 1A and Class 1B NICs and student loan deductions. These rules will be amended slightly from 6 April 2014 to accommodate the introduction of RTI. Applies for 2011/12 onwards to income tax and capital gains tax payable under self assessment for 2010/11 onwards. To be extended over a number of years to other taxes.	*In-year payments.* The first failure in a tax year does not count as a default. If there are one, two or three defaults during a tax year, penalty of 1% of total amount of defaults. If four, five or six defaults during a tax year, penalty of 2%; if seven, eight or nine defaults, penalty of 3%; if ten or more defaults in one tax year penalty 4%. If tax remains unpaid six months after penalty date a penalty of 5% of the unpaid amount applies; a further 5% penalty applies if tax is still unpaid after a further six months. *IT, CGT, Class 1A, 1B NICs.* A 5% penalty applies if full amount not paid within 30 days of due date. If amount remains unpaid six months after due date a penalty of 5% applies; a further 5% penalty applies if amount is still unpaid after a further six months.

Offence	Penalty
Late filing of returns [*FA 2009, Sch 55*] Failure to make a return or deliver a specified document on or before the filing date. Applies to (1) income tax (and CGT) returns and documents for 2010/11 onwards with effect from 6 April 2011; (2) pension scheme returns for periods ending after 31 March 2011; (3) construction industry scheme returns for which the filing date is on or after 19 October 2011; (4) PAYE for the tax year 2014/15 onwards in connection with failure to make returns with a filing date after 6 April 2014. See page 88. To be extended over a number of years to other taxes.	(i) initial penalty of £100. (ii) if failure continues two months after penalty date a further penalty of £200 (CIS only). (iii) if failure continues three months after penalty date and HMRC give notice, a further penalty of £10 per day for each day failure continues in 90-day period beginning with date specified in notice. Penalty does not apply to CIS returns. (iv) if failure continues six months after penalty date, a further penalty of the greater of 5% of the tax liability and £300. (v) for returns other than CIS returns, if failure continues 12 months after penalty date and the withholding of information is deliberate and concealed a further penalty of the greater of 100% of the tax liability and £300; if the withholding is deliberate and not concealed, the greater of 70% of the liability and £300; or otherwise, greater of 5% of the liability and £300. (vi) for CIS returns, if failure continues 12 months after penalty date and the withholding of information is deliberate and concealed a further penalty of the greater of 100% of the tax liability and £3,000; if the withholding is deliberate and not concealed, the greater of 70% of the liability and £1,500; or otherwise, greater of 5% of the liability and £300. Where the information required in the return relates only to persons registered for gross payment, and the withholding of information is deliberate and concealed the penalty is £3,000; if the withholding is deliberate but not concealed the penalty is £1,500. For the first CIS return made by a contractor (together with any returns with an earlier filing date), the total fixed penalties cannot exceed £3,000 and any tax-geared penalty which would otherwise be the greater of £300 and 5% of the tax due is instead 5% of the tax. *Reductions*. A statutory reduction in the amount of the penalty is made for disclosure of a failure. For an unprompted disclosure, a 100% penalty may be reduced to no less than 30% and a 70% penalty to no less than 20%. For a prompted disclosure, a 100% penalty may be reduced to no less than 50% and a 70% penalty to no less than 35%. HMRC can also reduce a penalty in special circumstances. *Offshore evasion*. See below.
Offshore evasion [*FA 2010, Sch 10*] For documents, returns and assessments relating to periods beginning after 5 April 2011, penalties in respect of income tax or CGT under *FA 2007, Sch 24 para 1*, *FA 2008, Sch 41 para 1* and *FA 2009, Sch 55* are increased where the error or failure is linked to an offshore matter relating to a territory within category 2 or 3. No increase is made in relation to category 1 territories. From 24 July 2013 the categories are: **1:** Anguilla; Aruba; Australia; Belgium; Bulgaria; Canada; Cayman Islands; Cyprus; Czech Republic; Denmark (excluding Faroe Islands and Greenland); Estonia; Finland; France; Germany; Greece; Guernsey; Hungary; Ireland; Isle of Man; Italy; Japan; Latvia; Liechtenstein; Lithuania; Malta; Montserrat; Netherlands (excluding Bonaire, Sint Eustatius and Saba); New Zealand (excluding Tokelau); Norway; Poland; Portugal; Romania; Slovakia; Slovenia; South Korea; Spain; Sweden; Switzerland; USA (excluding overseas territories and possessions). **2:** All territories (except the UK) not within categories 1 or 3. **3:** Albania; Algeria; Andorra; Bonaire, Sint Eustatius and Saba; Brazil; Cameroon; Cape Verde; Colombia; Republic of the Congo; Cook Islands; Costa Rica; Curaçao; Cuba; Democratic People's Republic of Korea; Dominican Republic; Ecuador; El Salvador; Gabon; Guatemala; Honduras; Iran; Iraq; Jamaica; Kyrgyzstan; Lebanon; Macau; Marshall Islands; Federated States of Micronesia; Monaco; Nauru; Nicaragua; Niue; Palau; Panama; Paraguay; Peru; Seychelles; Sint Maarten; Suriname; Syria; Tokelau; Tonga; Trinidad and Tobago; UAE; Uruguay.	*Category 2 territories*. The amount of the penalty, and the statutory limits for reductions for disclosure are increased by 50%. *Category 3 territories*. The amount of the penalty, and the statutory limits for reductions for disclosure are increased by 100%.

Offence	Penalty
(a) The table of Designated Territories was amended by SI 2013/1618 from 24 July 2013 to re-categories 14 countries as follows: From category 2 to category 1 – Liechtenstein and Switzerland. From category 3 to category 2 – Antigua & Barbuda, Armenia, Bahrain, Barbados, Belize, Dominica, Grenada, Mauritius, San Marino, Saint Kitts & Nevis, Saint Lucia and Saint Vincent & the Grenadines.	
Failure to notify chargeability to tax [*TMA 1970, s 7; FA 1998, Sch 18 para 2*]	
(a) Failure to notify chargeability to IT or CGT within six months of tax year	Up to tax liability still outstanding after 31 January following tax year
(b) Failure to notify chargeability to CT within one year of accounting period.	Up to amount of CT unpaid one year after end of accounting period
Replaced by penalty under *FA 2008, Sch 41* for obligations arising after 31 March 2010 (see page 91)	
Failure to maintain records [*TMA 1970, s 12B*]	
Failure to keep and preserve appropriate records supporting personal and trustees' returns or partnership returns	Up to £3,000
Failure to keep and preserve records supporting ATED return (see page 77) [*FA 2013, Sch 33*].	
Failure to render return [*TMA 1970, ss 93, 93A; FA 1998, Sch 18 paras 17, 18*]	
(a) Income tax and capital gains tax Replaced by penalty under FA 2009, Sch 55 for returns for 2010/11 onwards (see page 93)	(i) Automatic penalty of £100 (or tax due if less); (ii) For each day failure continues, a further penalty of up to £60 per day as directed by the tribunal or Commissioners on application by HMRC; (iii) If failure continues after six months from filing date and no penalty imposed under (ii), a further automatic penalty of £100 (or tax due if less); (iv) If failure continues after one year from filing date, a further penalty of up to the amount of tax due
(b) Corporation tax	(i) £100 if up to 3 months late (£500 if previous two returns also delivered late); (ii) £200 if over 3 months late (£1,000 if previous two returns also late);
Failure continuing at later of final day for delivery of return and 18 months after return period	Further penalty of 10% of tax unpaid 18 months after return period (20% of tax unpaid at that date if return not made within 2 years of return period)
Failure to remedy error [*FA 1998, Sch 18 para 20*] Failure to remedy an error discovered on an incorrect corporation tax return without unreasonable delay. Replaced by penalty under *FA 2007, Sch 24* for returns for accounting periods beginning after 31 March 2008 (see page 91)	Up to amount of tax underpaid by reason of incorrectness for the accounting period to which the return relates
Negligence or fraud (a) Negligently or fraudulently making or submitting an incorrect return, accounts, claim for allowances or relief, etc. [*TMA 1970, ss 95, 95A; FA 1998, Sch 18 para 89*]. (Replaced by penalty under *FA 2007, Sch 24* for returns etc for 2008/09 onwards (accounting periods beginning after 31 March 2008 for CT). See page 91.)	Up to amount of tax underpaid by reason of incorrectness for (i) (IT and CGT purposes) the tax year in which the return, etc. delivered, the following tax year and any preceding tax year; (ii) (CT purposes) the accounting period(s) to which the return, etc. relates
(b) Negligently or fraudulently making an incorrect statement in connection with a claim to reduce payments on account [*TMA 1970, s 59A*]	Up to the amount (or additional amount) payable on account if a correct statement had been made
Failure to produce documents [*TMA 1970, s 97AA; FA 1998, Sch 18 para 29*] Failure to produce documents, etc. for the purposes of an enquiry where notice given before 1 April 2009 under *TMA 1970, s 19A* or under *FA 1998, Sch 18 para 27*. Replaced by penalty under *FA 2008, Sch 36* (see page 92)	(i) Initial penalty of £50; (ii) If failure continues after penalty under (i) imposed, additional penalty up to £30 per day if determined by HMRC, or £150 per day if determined by the tribunal or Commissioners
Failure to notify within charge to corporation tax [*TMA 1970, s 98; FA 2004, s 55*] Failure to notify within three months after the beginning of the first accounting period and any subsequent accounting period not following on immediately from the end of a previous accounting period. Repealed for obligations arising after 31 March 2010	(i) Initial penalty of £300; (ii) If failure continues after penalty in (i) imposed, additional penalty up to £60 per day

Penalties income tax, capital gains tax and corporation tax

Offence	Penalty
Other returns, etc. [*TMA 1970, ss 98, 98A*]	
Failure to comply with a notice to deliver any return or other document, to furnish any particulars, to produce any document or record, to make anything available for inspection or give any certificate under the provisions listed in *TMA 1970, s 98*	(i) up to £300 (£3,000 in certain specified cases) (ii) if failure continues after penalty under (i) imposed, continuing penalty of up to £60 (£600) per day
Negligently or fraudulently delivering any return, incorrect information, etc. within those provisions. (Replaced by penalty under *FA 2007, Sch 24*. See page 91.)	Up to £3,000
Failure to submit PAYE returns (P14, P35, P38 and P38A) or returns of sub-contractors in the construction industry	See under PAYE (page 88) which provisions also apply to returns of sub-contractors
Sub-contractors in the Construction Industry Scheme	
Failure by contractor to check validity of registration card (pre-6 April 2007 scheme) [*ICTA 1988, s 566(2B)–(2E)*]	Up to £3,000
Fraudulent attempt by sub-contractor to obtain or misuse a sub-contractor's certificate (pre-6 April 2007 scheme) [*ICTA 1988, s 561(10), (11)*]	Up to £3,000
Making false statements etc. for the purpose of becoming registered for gross payment (post-5 April 2007 scheme) [*FA 2004, s 72*]	Up to £3,000
Assisting in the preparation of incorrect returns, accounts and other documents [*TMA 1970, s 99*] Repealed from 1 April 2013 and replaced by penalty under *FA 2012, Sch 38*. See page 92.	Up to £3,000
Certificates of non-liability to income tax [*TMA 1970, s 99A*] Fraudulently or negligently giving such a certificate in connection with receiving bank or building society interest gross or failing to comply with an undertaking in the certificate	Up to £3,000
Refusal to allow deduction of income tax at source [*TMA 1970, s 106*]	£50
Obstructing an officer inspecting any property to ascertain its market value [*TMA 1970, s 111*] Replaced by penalty under *FA 2008, Sch 36 paras 39, 40* with effect from 1 April 2009 (see page 92)	Up to £50
Falsification of documents [*TMA 1970, s 20BB*] Intentionally falsifying, concealing or destroying documents	On summary conviction, a penalty not exceeding the statutory maximum (currently £5,000). On conviction on indictment, imprisonment for up to 2 years or a fine or both
Witnesses before Commissioners [*SI 1994 No 1812*] Neglect or refusal to appear before Commissioners or refusal to be sworn or answer questions. Repealed with effect from 1 April 2009	Up to £1,000
Advance pricing agreements [*TIOPA 2010, s 227; FA 1999, s 86*] Fraudulently or negligently making a false or misleading statement in the preparation of, or application to enter into, any advance pricing agreement	Up to £10,000
Fraudulent evasion of income tax [*TMA 1970, s 106A; FA 2000, s 144*]	On summary conviction, imprisonment for up to 6 months or a fine not exceeding the statutory maximum (currently £5,000). On conviction on indictment, imprisonment for up to 7 years or a fine or both

Offence	Penalty
Failure to deliver inheritance tax account [*IHTA 1984, s 245*] Failure to deliver an account within 12 months of death	(i) An initial penalty of £100 (or tax payable if less); (ii) A further penalty up to £60 for each day on which the failure continues (where failure is declared by court, tribunal or Special Commissioners); (iii) If failure continues after six months after the date on which account is due, and proceedings under (ii) not commenced, a further penalty of £100 (or tax payable if less); (iv) If failure continues one year after end of the period in which account is due, and tax is payable, a penalty up to £3,000
Failure to notify instrument varying disposition on death [*IHTA 1984, s 245A(1A)(1B)*] Failure to notify HMRC within six months after the date of the instrument (where additional tax is payable)	(i) An initial penalty up to £100; (ii) A further penalty up to £60 for each day on which the failure continues (where failure is declared by court, tribunal or Special Commissioners); (iii) If failure continues one year after end of the period in which notification is due, a penalty up to £3,000
Negligence or fraud (IHT) [*IHTA 1984, s 247*]	
Taxpayer negligently or fraudulently delivering, furnishing or producing incorrect account, information or document. Replaced by penalty under *FA 2007, Sch 24* where the date of death is on or after 1 April 2009 or, in other cases, where the tax liability arises on or after 1 April 2010 (see page 91)	Up to amount of tax underpaid by reason of incorrectness
Person other than taxpayer negligently or fraudulently furnishing or producing incorrect information or document	Up to £3,000
Assisting in or inducing the delivery, furnishing or production of any account, information or document knowing it to be incorrect. Repealed from 1 April 2013.	Up to £3,000
Failure to deliver SDLT return [*FA 2003, Sch 10 paras 3, 4*] Failure to deliver return within 30 days after the effective date of the land transaction	(i) £100 if return delivered within three months of filing date, otherwise £200; (ii) If return not delivered within 12 months after filing date, a penalty up to the tax chargeable
Failure to comply with notice to deliver SDLT return [*FA 2003, Sch 10 para 5*] Failure to comply within period specified in notice	Up to £60 for each day on which the failure continues after notification of penalty decision by tribunal or General or Special Commissioners
Negligence or fraud (SDLT) [*FA 2003, Sch 10 para 8, Sch 11 para 3*]	
Purchaser negligently or fraudulently delivering an incorrect return or failing to remedy an error without unreasonable delay. Replaced by penalty under *FA 2007, Sch 24* for liabilities arising on or after 1 April 2010 (see page 91)	Up to amount of tax understated
Purchaser negligently or fraudulently giving a self-certificate or failing to remedy an error in respect of such certificate without unreasonable delay. Repealed for transactions with an effective date on or after 12 March 2008	Up to amount of tax chargeable
Failure to keep and preserve records [*FA 2003, Sch 10 para 11, Sch 11 para 6*] Failure to keep and preserve such records as may be needed to enable delivery of correct return or certificate for required period	Up to £3,000 unless information is provided by other documentary evidence

Pensions

Registered pension schemes [*FA 2004, ss 149–284, Schs 28–36; FA 2013, ss 47-49*]]

Individual contributions. An individual may make unlimited contributions but tax relief is only available on contributions up to the higher of 100% of relevant earnings and £3,600 gross (provided the scheme operates tax relief at source). There is no provision for the carry-back or carry-forward of contributions to tax years other than the year of payment.

Special annual allowance charge. This charge applies with effect from 22 April 2009 to 5 April 2011 to individuals with incomes of £130,000 or more. Broadly, the effect of the charge is to restrict tax relief on pension savings above the individual's special annual allowance to basic rate by taxing the excess relief. An individual's special annual allowance is the higher of their regular pension savings and £20,000 (£30,000 where money purchase scheme contributions have been paid less regularly than quarterly).

Employer contributions are deductible for tax purposes, with exceptionally large contributions being spread over a period of up to 4 years. The contributions are not treated as taxable income of the employee (from 6 April 2013 this relief does not extend to payments for the benefit of family members).

'Tax-free' lump sum. The maximum 'tax-free' lump sum that can be paid out is 25% of the fund, subject to an overriding maximum of 25% of the lifetime allowance. There is transitional protection of lump sum rights accrued before 6 April 2006.

Lifetime allowance. Each individual has a lifetime allowance as follows.

2013/14	£1,500,000	2011/12	£1,800,000	2009/10	£1,750,000
2012/13	£1,500,000	2010/11	£1,800,000	2008/09	£1,650,000

For 2014/15 the life time allowance is £1,250,000. If benefits are withdrawn in excess of the allowance, tax is charged on the excess at 55% if taken as a lump sum and at 25% if used to buy a pension. Any tax due may be deducted from the individual's benefits.

Annual allowance. Each individual has an annual allowance for maximum 'pension inputs' (i.e. contributions paid to money purchase schemes and/or increases in accrued benefits under final salary schemes) as follows.

2013/14	£50,000	2011/12	£50,000	2009/10	£245,000
2012/13	£50,000	2010/11	£255,000	2008/09	£235,000

For 2014/15 the annual allowance is £40,000. If pension inputs exceed the annual allowance, the excess is chargeable at the individual's marginal tax rate (40% for 2010/11 and earlier years). The individual is liable for the tax subject, for 2011/12 onwards, to an election for the scheme to pay the charge if it exceeds £2,000 (in which event scheme benefits are proportionately reduced). For 2011/12 onwards, an individual can carry forward unused annual allowance for up to three tax years. Unused allowances for 2008/09 to 2010/11 can be carried forward to 2011/12, but only on the assumption that for each of those years the annual allowance was £50,000.

Minimum pension age. The minimum pension age is 55 (50 before 6 April 2010) with earlier retirement permitted on ill-health grounds. Those with existing contractual rights to draw a pension earlier will have those rights protected and there is special protection for members of pre-6 April 2006 approved schemes with early retirement ages. The available lifetime allowance for these protected groups will, however, be reduced.

Maximum benefit age. There is no maximum age at which benefits must be taken with effect from 6 April 2011. Previously, benefits had to be taken at latest at age 77 (75 for those reaching that age before 22 June 2010). A member of a money purchase scheme could take a pension from the age of 77 (75) by way of income withdrawal ('alternatively secured pension'). The maximum alternatively secured pension is 70% of a comparable annuity and, after 5 April 2007, the minimum is 55% of a comparable annuity.

Retail price index

CROSS REFERENCE. Capital gains tax—indexation

Year	Jan	Feb	Mar	Apr	May	Jun	Jul	Aug	Sep	Oct	Nov	Dec
1982	78.7	78.8	79.44	81.04	81.62	81.85	81.88	81.90	81.85	82.26	82.66	82.51
1983	82.61	82.97	83.12	84.28	84.64	84.84	85.30	85.68	86.06	86.36	86.67	86.89
1984	86.84	87.20	87.48	88.64	88.97	89.20	89.10	89.94	90.11	90.67	90.95	90.87
1985	91.20	91.94	92.80	94.78	95.21	95.41	95.23	95.49	95.44	95.59	95.92	96.05
1986	96.25	96.60	96.73	97.67	97.85	97.79	97.52	97.82	98.30	98.45	99.29	99.62
1987	100.0	100.4	100.6	101.8	101.9	101.9	101.8	102.1	102.4	102.9	103.4	103.3
1988	103.3	103.7	104.1	105.8	106.2	106.6	106.7	107.9	108.4	109.5	110.0	110.3
1989	111.0	111.8	112.3	114.3	115.0	115.4	115.5	115.8	116.6	117.5	118.5	118.8
1990	119.5	120.2	121.4	125.1	126.2	126.7	126.8	128.1	129.3	130.3	130.0	129.9
1991	130.2	130.9	131.4	133.1	133.5	134.1	133.8	134.1	134.6	135.1	135.6	135.7
1992	135.6	136.3	136.7	138.8	139.3	139.3	138.8	138.9	139.4	139.9	139.7	139.2
1993	137.9	138.8	139.3	140.6	141.1	141.0	140.7	141.3	141.9	141.8	141.6	141.9
1994	141.3	142.1	142.5	144.2	144.7	144.7	144.0	144.7	145.0	145.2	145.3	146.0
1995	146.0	146.9	147.5	149.0	149.6	149.8	149.1	149.9	150.6	149.8	149.8	150.7
1996	150.2	150.9	151.5	152.6	152.9	153.0	152.4	153.1	153.8	153.8	153.9	154.4
1997	154.4	155.0	155.4	156.3	156.9	157.5	157.5	158.5	159.3	159.5	159.6	160.0
1998	159.5	160.3	160.8	162.6	163.5	163.4	163.0	163.7	164.4	164.5	164.4	164.4
1999	163.4	163.7	164.1	165.2	165.6	165.6	165.1	165.5	166.2	166.5	166.7	167.3
2000	166.6	167.5	168.4	170.1	170.7	171.1	170.5	170.5	171.7	171.6	172.1	172.2
2001	171.1	172.0	172.2	173.1	174.2	174.4	173.3	174.0	174.6	174.3	173.6	173.4
2002	173.3	173.8	174.5	175.7	176.2	176.2	175.9	176.4	177.6	177.9	178.2	178.5
2003	178.4	179.3	179.9	181.2	181.5	181.3	181.3	181.6	182.5	182.6	182.7	183.5
2004	183.1	183.8	184.6	185.7	186.5	186.8	186.8	187.4	188.1	188.6	189.0	189.9
2005	188.9	189.6	190.5	191.6	192.0	192.2	192.2	192.6	193.1	193.3	193.6	194.1
2006	193.4	194.2	195.0	196.5	197.7	198.5	198.5	199.2	200.1	200.4	201.1	202.7
2007	201.6	203.1	204.4	205.4	206.2	207.3	206.1	207.3	208.0	208.9	209.7	210.9
2008	209.8	211.4	212.1	214.0	215.1	216.8	216.5	217.2	218.4	217.7	216.0	212.9
2009	210.1	211.4	211.3	211.5	212.8	213.4	213.4	214.4	215.3	216.0	216.6	218.0
2010	217.9	219.2	220.7	222.8	223.6	224.1	223.6	224.5	225.3	225.8	226.8	228.4
2011	229.0	231.3	232.5	234.4	235.2	235.2	234.7	236.1	237.9	238.0	238.5	239.4
2012	238.0	239.9	240.8	242.5	242.4	241.8	242.1	243.0	244.2	245.6	245.6	246.8
2013	245.8	247.6	248.7	249.5								

Notes

(a) The index was re-referenced in January 1987 from 394.5 to 100.
(b) The figures above which relate to months before January 1987 have been recomputed from the new base.

Social security taxable benefits

Weekly rates from weeks commencing	8.4.13	9.4.12	11.4.11	12.4.10	6.4.09	7.4.08	9.4.07
Retirement pensions (note (a))	£	£	£	£	£	£	£
Category A or B	110.15	107.45	102.15	97.65	95.25	90.70	87.30
Category B (lower)	66.00	64.40	61.20	58.50	57.05	54.35	52.30
Category C or D (non-contributory)	66.00	64.40	61.20	58.50	57.05	54.35	52.30
Category C (lower)	39.45	38.50	36.60	35.00	34.15	32.50	31.30
Increase for adult dependant (note (b))	63.20	61.85	58.80	57.05	57.05	54.35	52.30
Age addition—over 80	0.25	0.25	0.25	0.25	0.25	0.25	0.25
Bereavement benefit (note (a))							
Widowed parent's allowance	108.30	105.95	100.70	97.65	95.25	90.70	87.30
Bereavement allowance (standard rate) (note (c))	108.30	105.95	100.70	97.65	95.25	90.70	87.30
Carer's allowance (previously invalid care allowance)(note (a))							
Basic	59.75	58.45	55.55	53.90	53.10	50.55	48.65
Increase for adult dependant (note (b))	35.15	34.40	32.70	31.70	31.70	30.20	29.05
Employment and support allowance (notes (f)(g))							
Under 25	56.80	56.25	53.45	51.85	50.95	47.95	—
25 or over	71.70	71.00	67.50	65.45	64.30	60.50	—
Incapacity benefit (note (f))							
Long term (after 52 weeks)	101.35	99.15	94.25	91.40	89.80	84.50	81.35
—increase for adult dependant	58.85	57.60	54.75	53.10	53.10	50.55	48.65
Increase of long term benefit for age							
—higher rate (under 35)	10.70	11.70	13.80	15.00	15.65	17.75	17.10
—lower rate (35 to under 45)	6.00	5.90	5.60	5.80	6.55	8.90	8.55
Short term (over pension age)							
—higher rate (from week 29 to 52) (note (f))	101.35	99.15	94.25	91.40	89.80	84.50	81.35
—increase for adult dependant	56.65	55.45	52.70	51.10	51.10	48.65	46.80
Short term (under pension age)							
—higher rate (from week 29 to 52)	90.50	88.55	84.15	81.60	80.15	75.40	72.55
—increase for adult dependant	45.85	44.85	42.65	41.35	41.35	39.40	37.90
Industrial death benefit (deaths before 11.4.88 only) (note (a))							
Widow's pension (higher permanent rate)	110.15	107.45	102.15	97.65	95.25	90.70	87.30
Widow's pension (lower permanent rate)	33.05	32.24	30.65	29.30	28.58	27.21	26.19
Widower's pension	110.15	107.45	102.15	97.65	95.25	90.70	87.30
Statutory adoption pay (note (d))							
Rate (note (j))	136.78	135.45	128.73	124.88	123.06	117.18	112.75
Earnings threshold	109.00	107.00	102.00	97.00	95.00	90.00	87.00

Social security taxable benefits

Weekly rates from weeks commencing	8.4.13	9.4.12	11.4.11	12.4.10	6.4.09	7.4.08	9.4.07
Statutory maternity pay (note (d))	£	£	£	£	£	£	£
Higher rate— 9/10ths of average weekly earnings	Varies	Varies	Varies	Varies	Varies	Varies	Varies
Standard rate	136.78	135.45	128.73	124.88	123.06	117.18	112.75
Earnings threshold	109.00	107.00	102.00	97.00	95.00	90.00	87.00
Statutory paternity pay							
Standard rate (note (j))	136.78	135.45	128.73	124.88	123.06	117.18	112.75
Earnings threshold	109.00	107.00	102.00	97.00	95.00	90.00	87.00
Statutory sick pay (note (d))							
Standard rate	87.60	85.85	81.60	79.15	79.15	75.40	72.55
Earnings threshold	109.00	107.00	102.00	97.00	95.00	90.00	87.00
Invalidity allowances when paid with retirement pensions (note (f))							
Higher rate (under 40 when first taken ill)	20.70	20.25	19.25	18.65	18.65	17.75	17.10
Middle rate (40–49 when first taken ill)	13.30	13.00	12.40	12.00	12.00	11.40	11.00
Lower rate (50 to pension age when first taken ill)	6.65	6.50	6.20	6.00	6.00	5.70	5.50
Jobseekers allowance (note (e))							
Single —under 18 (usual rate)	56.80	56.25	53.45	51.85	50.95	47.95	35.65
—18–24	56.80	56.25	53.45	51.85	50.95	47.95	46.85
—25 or over	71.70	71.00	67.50	65.45	64.30	60.50	59.15
Couple —both under 18	56.80	56.25	53.45	51.85	50.95	47.95	35.65
—both under 18, one disabled	56.80	56.25	53.45	51.85	50.95	47.95	46.85
—both under 18, with child responsibility	85.80	84.95	80.75	78.30	76.90	72.35	70.70
—one under 18, one 18–24	56.80	56.25	53.45	51.85	50.95	47.95	46.85
—one under 18, one over 25	71.70	71.00	67.50	65.45	64.30	60.50	59.15
—both over 18	112.55	111.45	105.95	102.75	100.95	94.95	92.80

Notes

(a) Any increase for a child dependant paid with retirement pension, bereavement benefit, carer's allowance, incapacity benefit and higher rate industrial death benefit is non-taxable.

(b) Adult dependency increases to state pension and carer's allowance are paid after 5 April 2010 only to claimants receiving the increase at that date. The increase is to be withdrawn completely with effect from 6 April 2020.

(c) Reduced rates apply if the claimant/widow aged below 55 at the time of spouse's/husband's death.

(d) Rates for statutory sick pay, statutory maternity pay, statutory paternity pay and statutory adoption pay apply from 6 April each year.

(e) Jobseekers allowance applies to claimants who are required to be both available for and actively seeking employment. Where the amount of a jobseekers allowance paid exceeds the figure shown above, the excess is not taxable.

(f) Employment and support allowance replaces incapacity benefit for new claimants on or after 27 October 2008. Existing claimants continue to receive incapacity benefit. Incapacity benefit itself replaced invalidity allowance from April 1995: invalidity allowances still payable are for a transitional period.

(g) Only contributory employment and support allowance is taxable. Income related allowance is not taxable.

(h) Incapacity benefit is taxable except for benefits paid in the first 28 weeks of incapacity and benefits paid to persons already receiving invalidity benefit on 13 April 1995 so long as they remain incapable of work.

(i) The short-term, higher rate of incapacity benefit for over pension age is not a taxable benefit for those eligible to receive the benefit before 13 April 1995.

(j) 9/10ths of average weekly earnings, if less.

Social security taxable benefits

Total benefit if received for full tax year (52 weeks)	2013/14	2012/13	2011/12	2010/11	2009/10	2008/09	2007/08
Retirement pensions	£	£	£	£	£	£	£
Category A or B	5,727	5,587	5,311	5,077	4,953	4,716	4,539
Category B (lower)	3,432	3,348	3,182	3,042	2,966	2,826	2,719
Category C or D (non-contributory)	3,432	3,348	3,182	3,042	2,966	2,826	2,719
Category C (lower)	2,051	2,002	1,903	1,820	1,775	1,690	1,627
Increase for adult dependant	3,286	3,216	3,057	2,966	2,966	2,826	2,719
Age addition—over 80 (each)	13	13	13	13	13	13	13
Bereavement benefit							
Widowed parent's (mother's) allowance	5,631	5,509	5,236	5,077	4,953	4,716	4,539
Bereavement allowance (widow's pension)	5,631	5,509	5,236	5,077	4,953	4,716	4,539
Carer's allowance (previously invalid care allowance)							
Basic	3,107	3,039	2,888	2,802	2,761	2,628	2,529
Increase for adult dependant	1,827	1,788	1,700	1,648	1,648	1,570	1,510
Incapacity benefit							
Long term (after 52 weeks)	5,270	5,155	4,901	4,752	4,669	4,394	4,230
—increase for adult dependant	3,060	2,995	2,847	2,761	2,761	2,628	2,529
Increase of long term benefit for age							
—higher rate (under 35)	556	608	717	780	814	923	889
—lower rate (35 to under 45)	312	306	291	301	340	462	444
Industrial death benefit (deaths before 11.4.88 only)							
Widow's pension (higher permanent rate)	5,727	5,587	5,311	5,077	4,953	4,716	4,539
Widow's pension (lower permanent rate)	1,718	1,676	1,593	1,523	1,486	1,414	1,361
Widower's pension	5,727	5,587	5,311	5,077	4,953	4,716	4,539
Invalidity allowances when paid with retirement pensions							
Higher rate	1,076	1,053	1,001	969	969	923	889
Middle rate	691	676	644	624	624	592	572
Lower rate	345	338	322	312	312	296	286

Notes

(a) See notes on previous page.

(b) All figures are exclusive of additional benefits in respect of graduated pension, additional pension, etc. which vary with the individual. Certain benefits may be subject to reduction or withdrawal occasioned by earnings of the individual or of an adult dependant. See note (d) below for the basis of assessment.

(c) Retirement pension may be deferred. For periods of deferral after 5 April 2005, subject to conditions, either the benefit finally payable is increased or a taxable lump sum is payable. Increased benefit is calculated by adding 0.2% of the pension otherwise payable for each full week of deferral, subject to a minimum deferral of 5 weeks. The lump sum is equal to the pension that would have been payable in the deferral period plus interest at a rate at least 2% above the Bank of England base rate, subject to a minimum deferral of 12 months. For deferral periods before 6 April 2005, benefit finally payable is increased by 1/7th% for each full week of deferral, subject to a minimum deferral of 7 weeks and a maximum of 5 years (and there is no lump sum option).

(d) Benefits are assessed on the 'accruals' basis rather than on a receipts basis. HMRC consider that where a person is entitled to receive 53 weekly payments within a single tax year, the taxable amount is 53 times the weekly amount, rather than the amount shown in the above table. This applies also where the benefit is paid four-weekly and 14 payments are made in the tax year.

Social security non-taxable benefits

Weekly rates from weeks commencing		8.4.13	9.4.12
Attendance allowance		£	£
Higher rate (day and night)		79.15	77.45
Lower rate (day or night)		53.00	51.85
Child benefit (see note (a))			
Eldest child		20.30	20.30
Each subsequent child		13.40	13.40
Child dependency addition			
Paid with retirement pension, bereavement benefit, carer's allowance, incapacity benefit, severe disablement allowance and higher rate industrial death benefit		11.35	11.35
Council tax benefit (income related)		Varies	Varies
Disability living allowance/personal independence payment			
Care component	higher rate	79.15	77.45
	middle rate	53.00	51.85
	lower rate	21.00	20.55
Mobility component	higher rate	55.25	54.05
	lower rate	21.00	20.55
Guardian's allowance		15.90	15.55
Housing benefit (income related)		Varies	Varies
Incapacity benefit (short-term)			
Over pension age—lower rate (first 28 weeks)		97.25	95.15
—increase for adult dependant		56.65	55.45
Under pension age—lower rate (first 28 weeks)		76.45	74.80
—increase for adult dependant		45.85	44.85
Income support (income related)		Varies	Varies
Non-taxable in hands of those not available for employment and not involved in a trade dispute			

Weekly rates from weeks commencing		8.4.13	9.4.12
		£	£
Industrial injuries disablement benefit			
18 and over (or under 18 with dependants)	Disablement %		
	100%	161.60	158.10
	90%	145.44	142.29
	80%	129.28	126.48
	70%	113.12	110.67
	60%	96.96	94.86
	50%	80.80	79.05
	40%	64.64	63.24
	30%	48.48	47.43
	20%	32.32	31.62
under 18 rate (before 5 December 2012)	100%	—	96.90
	90%	—	87.21
	80%	—	77.52
	70%	—	67.83
	60%	—	58.14
	50%	—	48.45
	40%	—	38.76
	30%	—	29.07
	20%	—	19.38
Unemployability supplement		99.90	97.75
— increase for early incapacity:			
higher rate		20.70	20.25
middle rate		13.30	13.00
lower rate		6.65	6.50
Constant attendance allowance			
— exceptional rate		129.40	126.60
— intermediate rate		97.05	94.95
— normal maximum rate		64.70	63.30
— part-time rate		32.35	31.65
Exceptionally severe disablement allowance		64.70	63.30

Weekly rates from weeks commencing		8.4.13	9.4.12
		£	£
Maternity allowance (where SMP not available)			
Standard rate		136.78	135.45
MA threshold		30.00	30.00
Pneumoconiosis, byssinosis and miscellaneous diseases schemes and the workmen's compensation (supplementation) (before 5 December 2012)			
Total disablement allowance		—	158.10
Partial disablement allowance		—	58.45
Unemployment supplement, constant attendance allowance and exceptionally severe disablement allowance — as for industrial injuries disablement pension			
Severe disablement allowance			
Basic rate		71.80	69.00
Age-related addition	under 40	10.70	11.70
—(age when disabled)	under 50	6.00	5.90
	under 60	6.00	5.90
Increase for adult dependant		35.35	34.60

Notes

(a) Where an individual or their partner is in receipt of child benefit a high income child benefit charge can arise from 7 January 2013. The charge is applied to the higher earner. A taxpayer, with adjusted net income between £50,000 and £60,000 is subject to an income tax charge of 1% of the amount of child benefit for every £100 of income that exceeds £50,000. For a taxpayer with income above £60,000, the charge equals the amount of child benefit received. Alternatively, a taxpayer with expected income over £60,000 can elect not to receive any child benefit. The election has effect for weeks beginning after it is made and can be revoked at any time up to two years after the end of the tax year to which it relates, in order for child benefit to be paid for the period (ITEPA 2003, ss 681B-H; Social Security Administration Act 1992, section 13A). There is a separate form to authorise an agent to act in respect of the high income child benefit charge (CH995).

(b) Universal credit is being introduced to replace:

- Income support
- Child tax credits
- Working tax credits
- Housing benefit
- Income-based jobseeker's allowance
- Income-based employment and support allowance
- Budgeting loans and crisis loans

Universal credit will not replace child benefit.
It is anticipated that new claimants will start making claims for universal credits from October 2013 while existing benefits and credits are gradually phased out by 2017.

(c) From April 2013 a benefits cap exists to potentially limit the amount of benefit available to those of working age. See www.gov.uk/benefit-cap

Tax Credits	2013/14	2012/13
Child tax credit per annum		£
Family element	545	545
Child element	2,720	2,690
Disabled child additional element	3,015	2,950
Enhanced disabled child additional element	1,220	1,190
Working tax credit per annum/weekly equivalents		
Basic element	1,920	1,920
Additional couple's and lone parent element	1,970	1,950
30 hour element	790	790
Disabled worker element	2,855	2,790
Enhanced disabled adult element	1,220	1,190
Childcare element (weekly)		
— maximum eligible cost	300	300
— maximum eligible cost for 1 child	175	175
— percent of eligible costs covered	70%	70%
Common features		
Income threshold	6,420	6,420
Withdrawal rate	41%	41%
Income threshold for those entitled to child tax credit only	15,910	15,860
Income rise disregard	5,000	10,000
Income fall disregard	2,500	2,500
Pension credit (weekly amounts)		
Standard minimum guarantee		
— claimant with partner	222.05	217.90
— other claimants	145.40	142.70
Additional amounts for severely disabled		
— single	59.50	58.20
— couple (one qualifies)	59.50	58.20
— couple (both qualify)	119.00	116.40
Additional amount for carers	33.30	32.60
Capital disregarded	10,000	10,000

Stamp taxes

Stamp duty land tax

Land transactions (notes (a)(g)(f))	**Consideration***					**Rate**
Dates	3.9.08–31.12.09	1.1.10–5.4.11	6.4.11–21.3.12	22.3.12—5.4.13	6.4.13–	
Residential property	Up to £175,000	Up to £125,000	Up to £125,000	Up to £125,000	Up to £125,000	Nil
	£175,001–£250,000	£125,001–£250,000	£125,001–£250,000	£125,001–£250,000	£125,001–£250,000	1%
	£250,001–£500,000	£250,001–£500,000	£250,001–£500,000	£250,001–£500,000	£250,001–£500,000	3%
	£500,001 or more	£500,001 or more	£500,001–£1,000,000	£500,001–£1,000,000	£500,001–£1,000,000	4%
	—	—	£1,000,001 or more	£1,000,001–£2,000,000	£1,000,001–£2,000,000	5%
	—	—	—	£2,000,001 or more	£2,000,001 or more	7%
Non-natural persons	—	—	—	£2,000,001 or more	£2,000,001 or more	15%
Non-residential or mixed property	Up to £150,000	Up to £150,000	Up to £150,000	Up to £150,000	Up to £150,000	Nil
	£150,001–£250,000	£150,001–£250,000	£150,001–£250,000	£150,001–£250,000	£150,001–£250,000	1%
	£250,001–£500,000	£250,001–£500,000	£250,001–£500,000	£250,001–£500,000	£250,001–£500,000	3%
	£500,001 or more	£500,001 or more	£500,001 or more	£500,001 or more	£500,001 or more	4%
Disadvantaged areas	(notes (g)(d))				**Disadvantaged areas relief withdrawn from 6.4.13**	
	3.9.08–31.12.09	**1.1.10–5.4.11**	**6.4.11–21.3.12**	**22.3.12–5.4.13**		
Residential property	Up to £150,000	Up to £150,000	Up to £150,000	Up to £150,000		Nil
	£150,001–£250,000	£150,001–£250,000	£150,001–£250,000	£150,001–£250,000		1%
	£250,001–£500,000	£250,001–£500,000	£250,001–£500,000	£250,001–£500,000		3%
	£500,001 or more	£500,001 or more	£500,001–£1,000,000	£500,001–£1,000,000		4%
	—	—	£1,000,001 or more	£1,000,001–£2,000,000		5%
	—	—	—	£2,000,001 or more		7%

* Rates apply to the full consideration, not only to that in excess of the previous band.

Premiums (note (d))

Lease rentals (notes (g)(h))	**On net present value of rent over term of lease (applying a discount rate of 3.5%)**					
	3.9.08–31.12.09	**1.1.10–5.4.11**	**6.4.11–21.3.12**	**22.3.12–5.4.13**	**6.4.13–**	
Residential property	Up to £175,000	Up to £125,000	Up to £125,000	Up to £125,000	Up to £125,000	Nil
	£175,001 or more	£125,001 or more	£125,001 or more	£125,001 or more	£125,001 or more	1%
Non-residential or mixed property	Up to £150,000	Up to £150,000	Up to £150,000	Up to £150,000	Up to £150,000	Nil
	£150,001 or more	£150,001 or more	£150,001 or more	£150,001 or more	£150,001 or more	1%

* Rates apply to the amount of npv in the slice, not the whole value (but see note (d)).

Stamp taxes

Stamp duty (notes (h), (i), (j) & (k))

Shares, etc.

Shares converted into depositary receipts or put into

duty free clearance systems	1.5%
Purchase of own shares by company	0.5%
Transfers of stock or marketable securities	0.5%
Takeovers, mergers, demergers, schemes of reconstruction and amalgamation (except where no real change of ownership)	0.5%

Stamp duty reserve tax

Agreements to transfer chargeable securities for money or money's worth (e.g. renounceable letters of allotment)	0.5%
Chargeable securities converted into depository receipts or put into clearance services (note (l))	1.5%
Dealings in units of unit trusts and shares in OEICs	0.5%

Notes

(a) **SDLT exemptions and reliefs.** No SDLT is chargeable on:
- (i) gifts inter vivos;
- (ii) transfers to beneficiaries under a will or an intestacy;
- (iii) certain transfers on divorce or dissolution of a civil partnership;
- (iv) transfers to charities for use for charitable purposes;
- (v) transfers to bodies established for national purposes or (where the effective date is on or after 17 July 2012) certain National Health Service bodies;
- (vi) land transfers within groups of companies;
- (vii) land transferred for shares on company reconstructions and acquisitions;
- (viii) transfers of intellectual property;
- (ix) certain transfers to registered providers of social housing;
- (x) certain leases granted by registered providers of social housing;
- (xi) A further exemption applies between 1.10.07 and 30.9.12 for the first sale of certificated zero-carbon homes and flats. No SDLT is chargeable where the consideration does not exceed £500,000. Where the consideration is more than £500,000, the SDLT liability is reduced by £15,000;
- (xii) With effect from 19 July 2011 a further relief applies where more than one residential property is purchased from the same vendor. SDLT will be charged on the mean consideration for each property, subject to a minimum rate of 1%.

(b) Interest on unpaid SDLT runs from 30 days after the effective date of the transaction, or the date of a disqualifying event, until the tax is paid. In the case of a deferred payment, interest runs from the date payment is due until the tax is paid. Interest is added to repayments of overpaid SDLT and runs from the date the tax was paid or an amount was lodged with HMRC to the date the order for repayment is issued. For rates of interest see page 74.

(c) The 15% rate applies where residential property is acquired by certain non-natural persons (e.g. a company, collective investment scheme or partnership of which a company or such a scheme is a member) and relief cannot be claimed under the exclusions in FA 2012 (for property developers and or certain corporate trustees) or FA 2013, Sch 40 (for various commercial businesses). The exclusions only apply where the relevant qualifying conditions are meet throughout the three years following purchase. If the conditions are not met, additional SDLT becomes payable.

(d) For areas designated as disadvantaged areas see *SI 2001 No 3747*. Disadvantaged areas relief is withdrawn for transactions with an effective date on or after 6 April 2013. No claims can be made after 5 May 2014.

(e) **First-time buyers.** For purchases of residential property where the effective date is on or after 25 March 2010 and before 25 March 2012 and the purchaser is a first-time buyer intending to occupy the property as his only or main home, the 0% rate applies where the consideration does not exceed £250,000.

(f) For transactions with an effective date on or after 3 September 2008 and before 21 December 2009, the £175,000 threshold does not apply to the grant of a lease for fewer than 21 years or to the assignment of a lease which has fewer than 21 years to run (the previous £125,000 threshold (or 150,000 for disadvantaged areas) continuing to apply).

(g) For residential properties in the period 3 September 2008 to 21 April 2009, where the npv of the rentals exceeds £175,000, the 1% rate applies to the slice of the npv that exceeds £125,000.

(h) Stamp duty applies only to shares and marketable securities and to the transfer of an interest in a partnership holding stock or marketable securities.

(i) For instruments executed on or after 13 March 2008, stamp duty is not chargeable where the amount or value of the consideration is £1,000 or under.

(j) **Stamp duty exemptions and reliefs.** No stamp duty is chargeable on:
- (i) gifts inter vivos;
- (ii) transfers to charities for use for charitable purposes;
- (iii) transfers to bodies established for national purposes;

It is proposed to introduce legislation to abolish stamp duty on shares quoted on growth markets e.g. the Alternative Investment Market and the ISDX Growth Market and stamp duty reserve tax charge on unit trusts and open-ended investment companies.

(k) Following the Tribunal decision in *HSBC Holdings plc and Bank of New York Mellon Corporation v HMRC* FTT, [2012] UKFTT 163 (TC), the 1.5% stamp duty reserve tax charge is no longer applicable to issues of UK shares and securities to clearance services or depositary receipt issuers anywhere in the world. The charge continues to apply to transfers of such shares or securities to clearance services or depositary receipt issuers. See HMRC Notice, 27 April 2012.

Time limits claims and elections

	Provision	Time limit
General		
TMA 1970, s 43(1)	Under self-assessment for individuals etc., unless otherwise prescribed	With effect from 1 April 2010 (2012 for taxpayers outside self-assessment), 4 years after end of tax year. Previously, on or before 5th anniversary of 31 January following tax year
FA 1998, Sch 18 para 55	For companies, unless otherwise prescribed	With effect from 1 April 2010, 4 years after end of accounting period. Previously, 6 years after end of accounting period
	Listed below are the more important *prescribed* time limits. Unless otherwise stated, time limits run from the end of the chargeable period	
Income tax		
ITTOIA 2005, s 239	**Barristers** — election for increased adjustment under transitional spreading provisions	1 year after 31 January following tax year
ITA 2007, s 202	**Enterprise investment scheme relief**	5th anniversary of 31 January following tax year in which shares issued
ITEPA 2003, Sch 5 para 44	**Enterprise management incentives**—notification of grant of options to HMRC	92 days after grant of option
ITTOIA 2005, ss 222, 225	**Farming**—averaging of profits	1 year after 31 January following second tax year to which claim relates
ITA 2007, s 426	**Gift aid**—election to treat donations as made in the previous tax year	On or before date the donor delivers his tax return for the previous tax year but no later than 31 January following the end of that tax year
	Losses set off against other income	
ITA 2007, s 124	(a) Property business losses	1 year after 31 January following tax year of loss
ITA 2007, s 64	(b) Trading losses	1 year after 31 January following tax year of loss
ITA 2007, s 72	(c) Trading losses in any of the first 4 tax years	1 year after 31 January following tax year of loss
ITA 2007, s 132	(d) Losses on disposal of shares in unlisted trading companies	1 year after 31 January following tax year of loss
ITA 2007, s 96	**Post-cessation expenditure**—set off against income	1 year after 31 January following tax year of payment
ITTOIA 2005, s 257	**Post-cessation receipts** received within, broadly, 6 years of date of discontinuance to be treated as received on that date	1 year after 31 January following tax year of receipt
ITTOIA 2005, s 818	**Qualifying care receipts**—election to tax on the alternative method of calculating profits	1 year after 31 January following tax year
ITTOIA 2005, ss 799, 800	**Rent a room relief**—(a) relief not to apply; (b) relief to apply to gross income in excess of limit; or (c) withdrawal of claim under (a) or (b)	1 year after 31 January following tax year
ITA 2007, s 357EA	**Seed enterprise investment scheme relief**	5th anniversary of 31 January following tax year in which shares issued
ITTOIA 2005, s 185	**Trading stock**—work in progress on discontinuance valued at cost	1 year after 31 January following tax year of cessation;
Income tax and corporation tax		
CTA 2009, s 122 *ITTOIA 2005, s 124*	**Herd basis**	2 years after first accounting period in which herd kept (CT) or 1 year after 31 January following first year of assessment for which herd kept in basis year (IT)
CTA 2009, s 178(6) *ITTOIA 2005, s 194(6)*	**Know-how** used in trade—sale not to be treated as goodwill	2 years from date of disposal
CTA 2009, ss 914(5), 917(4); *ITTOIA 2005, ss 590(6), 591(3)*	**Patents**—capital sums to be treated (a) by UK residents as charged in period received, or (b) by non-residents as spread over 6 years	1 year after 31 January following tax year of receipt (IT); 2 years after accounting period of receipt (CT)
CTA 2009, s 268(6); *ITTOIA 2005, s 326(6)*	**Rents etc** Furnished holiday lettings—averaging provisions	1 year after 31 January following tax year (IT) 2 years after accounting period (CT)
CTA 2009, s 1275(5); *ITTOIA 2005, s 842(5)*	**Unremittable overseas income** to be excluded from liability to tax	1 year after 31 January following tax year in which income arises (IT); 2 years after accounting period in which income arises (CT)

Time limits claims and elections

	Provision	Time limit
Corporation tax		
	Controlled foreign companies	
ICTA 1988, Sch 24 para 9	(a) Losses in pre-apportionment accounting periods to be taken into account in computing chargeable profit	20 months
ICTA 1988, s 751A	(b) Reduction in profits for activities of EEA business establishment	Filing date for the return
FA 2000, Sch 15 para 68	**Corporate venturing**—relief for losses on disposal of shares against income	2 years
FA 1989, s 43(5)	**Directors' remuneration**—adjustment for remuneration paid after computations made and within 9 months of accounts (accounting periods ending before 1 April 2009 only)	2 years
FA 1998, Sch 18 para 83W	**Film tax relief**—claims to be made, amended or withdrawn in the company tax return	1 year from filing date for the return
FA 1998, Sch 18 para 74	**Group relief**	The latest of: (i) 1 year from the filing date of the claimant company's return for the accounting period for which the claim is made; (ii) 30 days after the end of an enquiry into the return; (iii) if HMRC amend the return after an enquiry, 30 days after the issue of notice of assessment;(iv) if an appeal is made against the amendment, 30 days after the determination of the appeal; (or such later date as HMRC allow). (NB filing date is generally 1 year after end of accounting period)
	Intangible assets	
CTA 2009, s 730(3)	(a) Election to replace accounts depreciation with fixed WDA of 4%	2 years
CTA 2009, s 816(2)	(b) Election to exclude certain expenditure on computer software	2 years
	Losses set off against other income	
CTA 2010, s 37(7)	(a) Trading losses	2 years
CTA 2010, s 70(4)	(b) Losses by an investment company on disposal of shares in unlisted trading companies	2 years
CTA 2009, s 458(2)	(c) Non-trading deficit on loan relationships	2 years
CTA 2010, s 357G(3)	**Patent box**	1 year from filing date for the return for the first accounting period for which the election is to apply
FA 1998, Sch 18 paras 83E, 83LE	**Research and development**—tax relief claims to be made, amended or withdrawn in the company tax return	1 year from filing date for the return
Capital allowances	(NB: A 'chargeable period' for capital allowances purposes is an accounting period of a company or a period of account of an individual.)	
CAA 2001, s 382	**Agricultural buildings**—balancing adjustment where acquisition by another person or building destroyed before 21 March 2007	1 year after 31 January following tax year (IT) 2 years (CT)
CAA 2001, s 3(2),(3)(b); FA 1998, Sch 18 para 82	**Companies**—claims for capital allowances (including variations and withdrawals)	1st anniversary of filing date for claimant company's tax return but deferred in cases of HMRC enquiry (NB: filing date is generally 1 year after accounting period)
	Connected persons	
CAA 2001, s 266	(a) Successions to trades between connected persons: machinery or plant treated as transferred at tax written down value	2 years from date of succession
CAA 2001, s 570(5)	(b) Sales between persons under common control treated as being at tax written down value	2 years from date of sale
CAA 2001, s 177(5)	**Equipment leasing**—fixtures treated as belonging to lessor	1 year after 31 January following tax year in which ends lessor's chargeable period in which expenditure incurred (IT); 2 years after that chargeable period (CT)
CAA 2001, s 260(6)	**Excess capital allowances**—set-off against other income of companies	2 years

Time limits claims and elections

	Provision	Time limit
	Industrial buildings	
CAA 2001, s 291(4)	Grant of long lease to be treated as a sale to lessee	2 years after lease takes effect
	Plant and machinery	
CAA 2001, s 183(2)	Fixture on land subsequently let to be treated as belonging to lessee	2 years after lease takes effect
	Oilfields	
CAA 2001, s 164(2)	General decommissioning expenditure	2 years
	Ships	
CAA 2001, s 130(4)	(a) Postponement, disclaimer or reduction of first year allowances or writing down allowances	1 year after 31 January following tax year in which chargeable period ends (IT); 2 years after chargeable period (CT)
CAA 2001, s 129(2)	(b) 'Single ship pool' provisions not to apply	1 year after 31 January following tax year in which chargeable period ends (IT); 2 years after chargeable period (CT)
	Short life assets	
CAA 2001, s 85(2)	(a) Plant or machinery to be treated as short life assets	1 year after 31 January following tax year in which chargeable period ends (IT); 2 years after chargeable period (CT)
CAA 2001, s 89(6)	(b) Transfer of short life asset to connected person at tax wdv	2 years after chargeable period
Chargeable gains		(CT limits in parentheses)
	Assets held on 6 April 1965	
TCGA 1992, Sch 2 para 4	(a) All disposals of quoted securities to be treated as acquired at market value on that date	1 year after 31 January following (2 years after end of) chargeable period in which first relevant disposal after 5 April 1985. After 5 April 2008, CT only
TCGA 1992, Sch 2 para 17	(b) Disposals of other assets computed by reference to market value on that date	1 year after 31 January following (2 years after end of) chargeable period of disposal. After 5 April 2008, CT only
	Assets held on 31 March 1982	
TCGA 1992, s 35(5)(6)	(a) Universal re-basing	1 year after 31 January following (2 years after end of) chargeable period in which first relevant disposal after 5 April 1988. After 5 April 2008, CT only
TCGA 1992, Sch 4 para 9	(b) 50% reduction in taxing deferred gains arising from assets acquired before 31 March 1982	1 year after 31 January following (2 years after end of) chargeable period of disposal or in which gain treated as accruing. After 5 April 2008, CT only
TCGA 1992, s 187(1)	**Companies ceasing to be UK resident**—postponement of charge on deemed disposal where 75% subsidiary	2 years after ceasing to be UK resident
		1 year after 31 January following tax year of loss
TGCA 1992, ss 169H–169S	**Entrepreneurs' relief**	1 year after 31 January following tax year of qualifying business disposal
TCGA 1992, s 162A	**Incorporation relief**—election to disapply incorporation relief under *TCGA 1992, s 162* on a transfer of a business	2 years after 31 January following tax year in which transfer takes place (reduced by 1 year where transferor disposes of all shares received in exchange by end of the tax year following that in which transfer takes place
TCGA 1992, s 253(3)(3A)	**Loans to traders** becoming irrecoverable	2 years
TCGA 1992, s 24(2)	**Negligible value securities**	2 years after end of chargeable period of deemed sale and reacquisition
TCGA 1992, s 222	**Private residences**—determination of main residence	2 years after acquisition of second residence
TCGA 1992, s 261B	**Trading losses** to be relieved against gains	1 year after 31 January following tax year of loss
TCGA 1992, s 62(7)	**Variations and disclaimers** of dispositions made within two years of death	6 months after making the instrument

Time limits claims and elections

	Provision	Time limit
Inheritance tax		
	Death	
IHTA 1984, s 142	(a) Variations and disclaimer of dispositions made within two years of death	6 months after making the instrument
IHTA 1984, s 125	(b) Valuation of woodlands	2 years after death
IHTA 1984, ss 8A, 8B	(c) Transfer of unused nil-rate band to spouse or civil partner	2 years after end of month of survivor's death or, if later, 3 months after personal representatives first act
IHTA 1984, s 57	**Termination of interest in possession**—notice to trustees of available exemptions on termination	6 months after termination
IHTA 1984, ss 30, 78	**National Heritage property**—property transferred to be designated as such, and thus exempt	2 years after transfer or other chargeable event after 16 March 1998

Annual accounting scheme

A business may, subject to conditions, complete one VAT return each year. It can join the scheme if taxable supplies in the next tax year are not expected to exceed

1.4.06 onwards	£1,350,000
1.4.04–31.3.06	£660,000
1.4.01–31.3.04	£600,000

but must leave at the end of any accounting year in which taxable supplies in that year have exceeded

1.4.06 onwards	£1,600,000
1.4.04–31.3.06	£825,000
1.4.01–31.3.04	£750,000

Before 1 April 2006, only businesses with taxable turnover up to £150,000 could join the scheme immediately; other qualifying businesses had to have been registered for 12 months. Quarterly or monthly payments on account may be required.

Capital goods scheme *[SI No 2518, Regs 112-116]*

The scheme applies to capital items within the list below which the owner (or person who holds an interest) uses in the course of, and for the purpose of, a business carried on by him. Input tax adjustments are required where, during the adjustment period, there is a change in the extent of the taxable use of the item.

Item	Minimum value	Adjustment period
Land	£250,000*	10 years
Building (or part)	£250,000	10 years
Civil engineering work (or part of such a work)	£250,000	10 years
Computer or computer equipment	£50,000	5 years
Aircraft	£50,000	5 years
Ship, boat or other vessel	£50,000	5 years

Aircraft, ships, boats and other vessels are within the scheme only where the item is acquired on or after 1 January 2011. The adjustment period is shortened in certain cases where, at the time of the owner's first use of the item, the number of yearly intervals in the adjustment period exceeds the number of complete years that his interest in the item has to run or where the owner already owned the item prior to VAT registration. For land, buildings and civil engineering work where the adjustment period started before 1 January 2011, the adjustment period is reduced to five years where the owner's interest had less than ten years to run on acquisition.

The adjustment formula is:

$$\frac{\text{Total VAT on item}}{\text{Length of adjustment period}} \times \text{adjustment percentage}$$

where the 'adjustment percentage' is the percentage change in the extent to which the item is used (or treated as used) in making taxable supplies between the time at which the original entitlement to deduction of the input tax was determined and the adjustment period interval in question. For goods acquired on or after 1 January 2011 total input tax includes any non-business VAT.

* Figure reduced to £1 where owner ('O') of item or a person to whom O has granted an interest in that item:

(a) uses that item to make a grant falling within VATA 1994 Sch 9 Group1 Item 1(ka) (self-storage facilities excluded from exemption);
(b) decides, no later than 31 March 2013, to treat the item as a capital item; and
(c) makes a written record to that effect, specifying the date of the decision

Cash accounting scheme

A business may, subject to conditions, account for and pay VAT on the basis of cash paid and received. It can join the scheme if taxable supplies in the next year are not expected to exceed

1.4.07 onwards	£1,350,000
1.4.04–31.3.07	£660,000
1.4.01–31.3.04	£600,000

but must leave if taxable supplies in the previous year have exceeded

1.4.07 onwards	£1,600,000
1.4.04–31.3.07	£825,000
1.4.01–31.3.04	£750,000

Deregistration

(i) UK taxable supplies

A registered taxable person ceases to be liable to be registered if, at any time, HMRC are satisfied that the value of his taxable supplies in the year then beginning will not exceed the following limits

Effective date	£	Effective date	£
1.4.13	77,000	1.5.10	68,000
1.4.12	75,000	1.4.09	66,000
1.4.11	71,000	1.4.08	65,000

unless the reason the value of taxable supplies will not exceed the limit is that in the period in question the person will cease making taxable supplies or will suspend making them for a period of 30 days or more

(ii) Supplies from other EC countries ('distance selling')

A person registered under these provisions ceases to be liable to be registered if, at any time

(a) his relevant supplies in the year ended 31 December last before that time did not exceed the following limits; and

(b) HMRC are satisfied that the value of his relevant supplies in the year immediately following that year will not exceed the following limits

Effective date	£
1.1.93	70,000

(iii) Acquisitions from other EC countries

A person registered under these provisions ceases to be liable to be registered if, at any time

(a) his relevant acquisitions in the year ended 31 December last before that time did not exceed the following limits; and

(b) HMRC are satisfied that the value of his relevant acquisitions in the year immediately following that year will not exceed the following limits

Effective date	£	Effective date	£
1.4.13	79,000	1.5.10	70,000
1.4.12	77,000	1.4.09	68,000
1.4.11	73,000	1.4.08	67,000

EU country codes

Any registration number contained in a VAT invoice provided to a registered person in another EU country must include the appropriate country code as listed below. Country codes are also needed for the completion of EU sales lists.

Country	Code	Country	Code
Austria	AT	Italy	IT
Belgium	BE	Latvia	LV
Bulgaria	BG	Lithuania	LT
Croatia	HR	Luxembourg	LU
Cyprus	CY	Malta	MT
Czech Republic	CZ	Netherlands	NL
Denmark	DK	Poland	PL
Estonia	EE	Portugal	PT
Finland	FI	Romania	RO
France	FR	Slovak Republic	SK
Germany	DE	Slovenia	SI
Greece	EL	Spain	ES
Hungary	HU	Sweden	SE
Ireland	IE	United Kingdom	GB

EU sales lists [*SI 1995 No 2518, Regs 21-23*]

A business registered for VAT in the UK which:

(a) makes supplies of goods to traders registered for VAT in other EU countries;
(b) transfers its own goods from the UK to another EU country;
(c) is the intermediary in triangular transactions between VAT-registered traders in other EU countries; or
(d) (with effect from 1 January 2010) makes supplies of services to a person in another EU country which subject to the reverse charge in the customer's country,

must submit to HMRC statements ('EU sales lists') containing particulars of the transactions involved. Such lists may be submitted electronically or using Form VAT 101 as follows.

Type of supply		Frequency
Goods only	Where the value of supplies to registered traders in other EU countries exceeds £35,000 (£70,000 before 1 January 2012) in the current or four previous quarters	Calendar monthly
	Where the value of supplies to registered traders in other EU countries exceeds £35,000 (£70,000 before 1 January 2012) in the current or four previous quarters	Quarterly (i.e. for each calendar quarter ending 31 March, 30 June, 30 September and 31 December)

Type of supply	Frequency
Services subject to reverse charge	Quarterly (as above), but business may choose to submit lists monthly
Goods and services (where monthly lists required for goods)	Monthly for all supplies, or monthly for goods and quarterly for services

A business which makes annual VAT returns can apply to HMRC for approval to submit an ESL once a year only if total annual taxable turnover does not exceed £145,000; the annual value of supplies to other EU countries does not exceed £11,000 and sales do not include new means of transport (boats, aircraft and motorised land vehicles). A business can apply to HMRC for approval to submit a simplified annual ESL if total taxable annual turnover does not exceed the VAT registration threshold plus £25,500; supplies to customers in other EU countries do not exceed £11,000 per year and sales do not include new means of transport.

If an ESL is completed online it must be submitted within 21 days after the end of the reporting period. In other cases the list must be submitted within 14 days after the end of the reporting period.

Exempt supplies [*VATA 1994, Sch 9*]

A supply of goods or services is an exempt supply if falling within one of the Groups listed below. Where a supply falls within one of the Groups but is also covered by the zero-rating provisions, the latter takes priority.

Group 1	Land
Group 2	Insurance
Group 3	Postal services
Group 4	Betting, gaming and lotteries
Group 5	Finance
Group 6	Education
Group 7	Health and welfare
Group 8	Burial and cremation
Group 9	Subscriptions to trade unions, professional and other public interest bodies
Group 10	Sport, sports competitions and physical education
Group 11	Works of art, etc.
Group 12	Fund-raising events by charities and other qualifying bodies
Group 13	Cultural services, etc.
Group 14	Supplies of goods where input tax cannot be recovered
Group 15	Investment gold
Group 16	Supplies of services by groups involving cost sharing (from 17 July 2012)

Flat-rate scheme for small businesses

A business which expects its taxable supplies (excluding VAT) in the next year to be no more than £150,000 and, before 1 April 2009, its total business income to be no more than £187,500 can opt to join a flat-rate scheme. It can then calculate net VAT due by applying the appropriate flat-rate percentage from the list below to total turnover generated, including exempt income.

Category of business	*Appropriate %*		
	1.12.08–31.12.09	*1.1.10–3.1.11*	*4.1.11 onwards*
Accountancy or book-keeping	11.5	13	14.5
Advertising	8.5	10	11
Agricultural services	7	10	11
Any other activity not listed elsewhere	9	10.5	12
Architects	11	13	14.5
Boarding or care of animals	9.5	10.5	12
Business services that are not listed elsewhere	9.5	10.5	12
Catering services, including restaurants and take-aways	10.5	11	12.5
Civil and structural engineers and surveyors	11	13	14.5
Computer and IT consultancy or data processing	11.5	13	14.5
Computer repair services	10	9.5	10.5
Dealing in waste or scrap	8.5	9.5	10.5
Entertainment (excluding film, radio, television or video production, see below) or journalism	9.5	11	12.5
Estate agency or property management services	9.5	10.5	12
Farming or agriculture that is not listed elsewhere	5.5	6	6.5
Film, radio, television or video production	9.5	11.5	13
Financial services	10.5	12	13.5
Forestry or fishing	8	9.5	10.5
General building or construction services (note (a))	7.5	8.5	9.5
Hairdressing or other beauty treatment services	10.5	11.5	13
Hiring or renting goods	7.5	8.5	9.5
Hotel or accommodation	8.5	9.5	10.5
Investigation or security	9	10.5	12
Labour-only building or construction services (note (a))	11.5	13	14.5
Laundry or dry-cleaning services	9.5	10.5	12
Lawyers or legal services	12	13	14.5
Library, archive, museum or other cultural activities	7.5	8.5	9.5
Management consultancy	11	12.5	14
Manufacturing fabricated metal products	8.5	9.5	10.5
Manufacturing food	7	8	9
Manufacturing that is not listed elsewhere	7.5	8.5	9.5
Manufacturing yarn, textiles or clothing	7.5	8	9
Membership organizations	5.5	7	8
Mining or quarrying	8	9	10
Packaging	7.5	8	9
Photography	8.5	10	11
Post offices	2	4.5	5
Printing	6.5	7.5	8.5
Publishing	8.5	10	11
Pubs	5.5	6	6.5
Real estate activities not listed elsewhere	11	12.5	14
Repairing personal or household goods	7.5	9	10
Repairing vehicles	6.5	7.5	8.5
Retailing food, confectionery, tobacco, newspapers or children's clothing	2	3.5	4
Retailing pharmaceuticals, medical goods, cosmetics or toiletries	6	7	8
Retailing that is not listed elsewhere	5.5	6.5	7.5
Retailing vehicles or fuel	5.5	6	6.5
Secretarial services	9.5	11.5	13
Social work	8	10	11
Sport or recreation	6	7.5	8.5
Transport or storage, including couriers, freight, removals and taxis (note (b))	8	9	10
Travel agency	8	9.5	10.5
Veterinary medicine	8	10	11
Wholesaling agricultural products	5.5	7	8
Wholesaling food	5	6.5	7.5
Wholesaling that is not listed elsewhere	6	7.5	8.5

Note

(a) 'Labour-only building or construction services' means building or construction services where the value of materials supplied is less than 10% of relevant turnover from such services; any other building or construction services are 'general building or construction services'.

(b) Once in the scheme a business may continue to use it until its total business income exceeds £230,000, and if income does exceed this limit, the business can still remain in the scheme if the income in the following year is estimated not to exceed £191,500. The £230,000 threshold is normally compared to total income (including VAT but excluding sales of capital assets) in the year to the anniversary of the start date (of using the flat rate scheme). However it is also necessary to leave the scheme when there are reasonable grounds to believe the total value of income in the next 30 days will exceed £230,000.

Interest

Default Interest [*VATA 1994, s 74*]

Interest runs on the amount of any VAT assessed (or the amount of any VAT paid late by voluntary disclosure) from the reckonable date (normally the latest date on which a return is required for the period in question) until the date of payment (although in practice it runs to the date shown on the notice of assessment or notice of voluntary disclosure if paid within 30 days of that date). The period of interest cannot commence more than three years before the date of assessment or payment. The rates of interest are as follows

6.9.05–5.9.06	6.5%
6.9.06–5.8.07	7.5%
6.8.07–5.1.08	8.5%
6.1.08–5.11.08	7.5%
6.11.08–5.12.08	6.5%
6.12.08–5.1.09	5.5%
6.1.09–26.1.09	4.5%
27.1.09–23.3.09	3.5%
24.3.09–28.9.09	2.5%
29.9.09–	3%

Interest in cases of official error [*VATA 1994, s 78*]

Where VAT has been overpaid or underclaimed due to an error by HMRC, then on a claim HMRC must pay interest from the date they receive payment (or authorise a repayment) for the return period in question until the date on which they authorise payment of the amount on which interest is due. This provision does not require HMRC to pay interest on an amount on which repayment supplement is due. The rates of interest are as follows

6.9.05–5.9.06	3%
6.9.06–5.8.07	4%
6.8.07–5.1.08	5%
6.1.08 5.11.08	4%
6.11.08–5.12.08	3%
6.12.09–5.1.09	2%
6.1.09–26.1.09	1%
27.1.09–28.9.09	0%
29.9.09–	0.5%

Note

(a) *FA 2009, ss 101–104A, Schs 53–54A* create a harmonised interest regime for all taxes and duties administered by HMRC. The regime is being phased in over a number of years for different taxes.

Repayment supplement — VAT [*VATA 1994, s 79*]

Where a person is entitled to a repayment of VAT, the payment due is increased by a supplement of the greater of (i) 5% of that amount; or (ii) £50 provided

(a) the return or claim is received by HMRC not later than the last day on which it is required to be made;
(b) HMRC do not issue a written instruction making the refund within the relevant period; and
(c) the amount shown on the return or claim does not exceed the amount due by more than 5% of that amount or £250 whichever is the greater.

The '*relevant period*' is 30 days beginning with the receipt of the return or claim or, if later, the day after the last day of the VAT period to which the return or claim relates.

Partial exemption

A registered person who makes taxable and exempt supplies is partly exempt and may not be able to deduct (or reclaim) all his input tax. Where, however, the input tax attributable to exempt supplies in a prescribed accounting period or tax year is within certain de minimis limits, all such input tax is treated as attributable to taxable supplies and recoverable (subject to the normal rules). The de minimis limits are

Exempt input tax not exceeding	£625 per month on average: and 50% of all input tax for the period concerned

Rates

Standard rate	4.1.11 onwards	20%	VAT fraction 1/6
	1.1.10–3.1.11	17½%	7/47
	1.12.08–31.12.09	15%	3/23
	before 1.12.08	17½%	7/47
Reduced rate		5%	1/21
Flat-rate scheme for farmers		4% flat-rate addition to sale price	

Reduced rate supplies [*VATA 1994, Sch 7A*]

A supply of goods or services is charged at the reduced rate if falling within one of the following Groups.

Group 1	Domestic fuel and power
Group 2	Installation of energy-saving materials
Group 3	Grant-funded installation of heating equipment or security goods or connection of a gas supply
Group 4	Women's sanitary products
Group 5	Children's car seats (and, from 1 July 2009, car seat bases)
Group 6	Residential conversions
Group 7	Residential renovations and alterations
Group 8	Contraceptive products (from 1 July 2006)
Group 9	Welfare advice or information (from 1 July 2006)
Group 10	Installation of mobility aids for the elderly (from 1 July 2007)
Group 11	Smoking cessation products (from 1 July 2007)
Group 12	Caravans (from 6 April 2013)
Group 13	Cable-suspended transport systems (from 1 April 2013)

Value added tax registration, returns and payment of VAT, and zero-rated supplies

Registration

(i) UK taxable supplies

A person who makes taxable supplies is liable to be registered

(a) at the end of any month if the value of taxable supplies in the year then ending has exceeded the limit in column A below; or

(b) at any time, if there are reasonable grounds for believing that the value of taxable supplies in the next 30 days will exceed the limit in column A below

except that a person does not become liable to be registered under (a) above if HMRC are satisfied that the value of taxable supplies in the year beginning at the time he would be liable to be registered will not exceed the limit in column B below. With effect from 1 December 2012 a non-UK established business is required to register for VAT regardless of the value of taxable supplies in the UK.

Effective date	*A (£)*	*B (£)*
1.4.13	79,000	77,000
1.4.12	77,000	75,000
1.4.11	73,000	71,000
1.4.10	70,000	68,000
1.5.09	68,000	66,000
1.4.08	67,000	65,000

(ii) Supplies from other EC countries ('distance selling')

A business person in another EC country not registered or liable to be registered in the UK under (i) above is liable to be registered on any day if, in the period beginning with 1 January in that year, he has made, and is responsible for the delivery of, supplies to non-taxable persons in the UK exceeding the following limits

Effective date	£
1.1.93	70,000

(iii) Acquisitions from EC countries

A person not registered or liable to be registered under (i) or (ii) above is liable to be registered

(a) at the end of any month if, in the period beginning with 1 January in that year, he has made acquisitions of taxable goods for business purposes (or for non-business purposes if a public body, charity, club, etc.) from suppliers in other EC countries whose value exceeds the following limits; or

(b) at any time, if there are reasonable grounds for believing that the value of such acquisitions in the next 30 days will exceed the following limits

Effective date	£	Effective date	£
1.4.13	79,000	1.5.10	70,000
1.4.12	77,000	1.4.09	68,000
1.4.11	73,000	1.4.08	67,000

Returns and payment of VAT

Subject to below, a completed VAT return must be sent to HMRC, and any VAT due paid, not later than one month after the end of the return period. The prescribed VAT returns are

Form VAT 100	All purposes except where Form VAT 193 applies
Form VAT 193	Final VAT return (unless registration allocated to the purchaser on the transfer of a business as a going concern)

From 1 April 2012 all businesses (subject to limited exceptions in the case of insolvency or religious objection) must submit returns online using the eVAT service. Previously, from 1 April 2010, businesses with VAT-exclusive turnover of £100,000 or more had to submit returns online using the service as did businesses registering for VAT on or after that date. In other cases, returns could be submitted by post or online.

Where returns are sent electronically via the eVAT service, any VAT due must also be paid electronically. Otherwise, payment can be made by post to VAT Central Unit at Southend-on-Sea, by debit card or, subject to a fee, by credit card, or electronically by Bank Giro Credit transfer, BACS or CHAPS.

Where payment is made electronically, a business automatically receives a 7-day extension for the submission of the return and payment of VAT. The concession cannot be used (i) by businesses required to make payments on account unless it makes monthly returns; (ii) by businesses using the annual accounting scheme; or (iii) to make VAT payments other than VAT return payments (e.g. assessments).

Businesses with an annual VAT liability of £2.3m or more (£2m or more before 1 June 2011 (1 December 2011 for annual reviews)) must make interim payments on account (POAs) at the end of the second and third months of each VAT quarter with a balancing payment for the quarter with the VAT return. All POAs and balancing payments must be made by electronic transfer.

Zero-rated supplies [*VATA 1994, Sch 8*]

A supply of goods or services is a zero-rated supply if falling within one of the following Groups. Such a supply is a taxable supply with a nil rate of tax

Group 1	Food
Group 2	Sewerage services and water
Group 3	Books, etc.
Group 4	Talking books for the blind and handicapped and wireless sets for the blind
Group 5	Construction of buildings, etc.
Group 6	Protected buildings
Group 7	International services
Group 8	Transport
Group 9	Caravans and houseboats
Group 10	Gold
Group 11	Bank notes
Group 12	Drugs, medicines, aids for handicapped, etc.
Group 13	Imports, exports, etc.
Group 15	Charities, etc.
Group 16	Clothing and footwear
Group 18	European Research Infrastructure Consortia (from 1 January 2013)

Value added tax car fuel scale rates

CO_2 emissions g/km	Scale charge Yearly returns £	Quarterly returns £	Monthly returns £
Return periods beginning 1.5.11–30.4.12			
120 or below	630	157	52
125	945	236	78
130	1,010	252	84
135	1,070	268	89
140	1,135	283	94
145	1,200	299	99
150	1,260	315	105
155	1,325	331	110
160	1,385	346	115
165	1,450	362	120
170	1,515	378	126
175	1,575	394	131
180	1,640	409	136
185	1,705	425	141
190	1,765	441	147
195	1,830	457	152
200	1,890	472	157
205	1,955	488	162
210	2,020	504	168
215	2,080	520	173
220	2,145	536	178
225 or more	2,205	551	183

CO_2 emissions g/km	Scale charge Yearly returns £	Quarterly returns £	Monthly returns £
Return periods beginning 1.5.12–30.4.13			
120 or below	665	166	55
125	1,000	250	83
130	1,065	266	88
135	1,135	283	94
140	1,200	300	100
145	1,270	316	105
150	1,335	333	111
155	1,400	350	116
160	1,470	366	122
165	1,535	383	127
170	1,600	400	133
175	1,670	416	138
180	1,735	433	144
185	1,800	450	150
190	1,870	467	155
195	1,935	483	161
200	2,000	500	166
205	2,070	517	172
210	2,135	533	177
215	2,200	550	183
220	2,270	567	189
225 or more	2,335	583	194

CO_2 emissions g/km	Scale charge Yearly returns £	Quarterly returns £	Monthly returns £
Return periods beginning after 30.4.13			
120 or below	675	168	56
125	1,010	253	84
130	1,080	269	89
135	1,145	286	95
140	1,215	303	101
145	1,280	320	106
150	1,350	337	112
155	1,415	354	118
160	1,485	371	123
165	1,550	388	129
170	1,620	404	134
175	1,685	421	140
180	1,755	438	146
185	1,820	455	151
190	1,890	472	157
195	1,955	489	163
200	2,025	506	168
205	2,090	523	174
210	2,160	539	179
215	2,225	556	185
220	2,295	573	191
225 or more	2,360	590	196

Notes

(a) Subject to (d) below, a taxable person is required to account for output tax where fuel is supplied for private motoring to either himself or his employees. [*VATA 1994, ss 56, 57*]. The scale charges set out above represent the tax-inclusive value of the fuel supplied and apply separately to supplies to each individual in any prescribed accounting period in respect of any one vehicle.

(b) The rules apply to all cars but not to other vehicles such as vans, motorcycles and invalid cars. They do not apply to pooled cars or cars used exclusively for business purposes. Travel between home and work is regarded as a private rather than business journey.

(c) Where the above scale rates are used, a taxable person can reclaim input tax on all fuel purchased, even if used for private motoring.

(d) A taxable person need not use the above scale charges where there is an element of private motoring provided he does not reclaim input tax on *any* fuel purchased, whether used for business or private purposes and whether in cars or commercial vehicles.

(e) For return periods beginning after 30 April 2007, where the CO_2 emissions figure of a vehicle is not a multiple of five, the figure is rounded down to the next multiple of five to determine the level of charge. For bi-fuel vehicles, the lower CO_2 emissions figure is used. Vehicles which are too old to have a CO_2 emissions figure are treated as having an emissions figure of 140 g/km for vehicles with an engine capacity of 1,400 cc or less, 175 g/km for vehicles with an engine capacity between 1,401 cc and 2,000 cc and 225 or more g/km for vehicles with an engine capacity of more than 2,000 cc (230 or more g/km before 1.5.11; 235 or more g/km before 1.5.10; 240 or more before 1.5.08).

(f) Employers can use HMRC's advisory fuel rates to reclaim VAT on fuel costs reimbursed for business travel by employees in company cars. The employer must obtain and keep a valid VAT invoice. See page 76.

(g) From 1 February 2014, FA 2013, Sch 38 introduces a new flat rate similar to the existing car fuel scale rates above.

	Nature of offence	Penalty
Default surcharge [*VATA 1994, s 59*]	Failure to furnish a return in time or pay the VAT shown on it as due. Where no VAT is due or the VAT due is paid on time but the return is submitted late, although HMRC record the default there is no *liability* to a surcharge The provisions also apply to the Payments on Account Scheme	The greater of £30 or the following percentages of outstanding VAT 1st default in surcharge period 2% 2nd default in surcharge period 5% 3rd default in surcharge period 10% 4th default in surcharge period 15% 5th default in surcharge period 15% Further defaults 15%
VAT evasion (note (a)) [*VATA 1994, s 60*]	Any act or omission for the purpose of evading VAT where conduct involves dishonesty	The amount of the VAT evaded (or sought to be evaded)
Incorrect zero-rating [*VATA 1994, s 62*]	Issuing an incorrect certificate stating that certain supplies fall to be zero-rated or taxed at the reduced rate	Difference between the VAT which should have been charged and the VAT actually charged
Misdeclaration or neglect (note (a)) [*VATA 1994, s 63*]	(a) submission of a return understating liability to VAT or overstating entitlement to a repayment; or (b) failing, within 30 days of the issue of an assessment, to draw any understatement to the attention of HMRC where the VAT which would have otherwise been lost exceeds specified limits	15% of the VAT which would have been lost
Repeated misdeclarations (note (a)) [*VATA 1994, s 64*]	Submission of a return understating liability to VAT or overstating entitlement to a repayment where the VAT which would otherwise have been lost equals or exceeds specified limits	15% of the VAT which would have been lost on the second and subsequent material inaccuracies within a penalty period
EC sales lists (ESL)	(a) Submission of an ESL containing a material inaccuracy. [*VATA 1994, s 65*] (b) Failure to submit an ESL. [*VATA 1994, s 66*]	£100 for each ESL submitted within two years following a penalty notice from HMRC identifying an earlier material inaccuracy Greater of £50 or a daily penalty (maximum 100 days) of £5, £10 or £15 depending upon whether the ESL is the first, second, or third or subsequent ESL in a default period specified by HMRC
Import VAT [*FA 2003, ss 24–41*]	(a) Non-compliance in cases of 'occasional serious error' involving at least £10,000 duty and/or VAT; persistent failure to comply with regulatory obligations; and failure to correct deficiencies in systems, etc. (b) Evasion penalty (as an alternative to criminal prosecution)	£2,500 maximum Up to the amount of duty and/or VAT sought to be evaded
Failure to notify [*VATA 1994, s 67*]	Failure to notify (a) liability for registration; or (b) Changes in the nature of supplies, etc. by a person exempt from registration (c) Acquisition of excise duty goods or new means of transport (Replaced, from 1 April 2010 by penalty under *FA 2008, Sch 41* – see page 91)	Greater of £50 and the following percentages of the VAT for which the person would have been liable *Period of failure* (a) and (b) / (c) 9 months or less / 3 months or less 5% 10–18 months / 4–6 months 10% Over 18 months / Over 6 months 15%

Value added tax civil penalties

	Nature of offence	Penalty
Unauthorised issue of invoices [*VATA 1994, s 67*]	Issue of invoice by any person not authorised to do so (Replaced, from 1 April 2010 by penalty under *FA 2008, Sch 41* – see page 91)	15% of the amount shown as or representing VAT or, if greater, £50
Electronic returns [*SI 1995 No 2518, Reg 25A*]	Failure to make return electronically by person required to do so	*Annual VAT exclusive turnover* — *Penalty* £100,000 or less — £100 £100,001–£5,600,000 — £200 £5,600,001–£22,800,000 — £300 £22,800,001 or more — £400
Breach of walking possession agreement [*VATA 1994, s 68*]	Breach of agreement under which property distrained remains in possession of a person who has failed to pay VAT	One half of the VAT due or amount recoverable
Records [*VATA 1994, ss 69, 69B*]	Failure to preserve for six years or such lesser period as HMRC allow Failure to preserve records specified in HMRC direction	£500 £200 for each day of failure (maximum 30 days)
Breaches of regulatory provisions [*VATA 1994, s 69*]	Failure to notify end of liability or entitlement to be registered, failure to keep records or failure to comply with any regulations, order or rules made under *VATA 1994*	Greater of £50 or a daily penalty (maximum 100 days) of No of failures in previous two years — Daily rate 0 — £5* 1 — £10* 2 — £15* * or, where the failure consists of not paying VAT or not making a return in the required time, 1/6, 1/3 and 1/2 of 1% of the VAT due respectively, if greater
Tribunals [*VATA 1994, Sch 12 para 10*]	Failure to comply with directions of a tribunal Repealed with effect from 1 April 2009	Up to £1,000
Investment gold [*VATA 1994, s 69A*]	Failure to comply with key requirements of the investment gold scheme	17½% of the value of the transaction concerned
Use of avoidance schemes [*VATA 1994, Sch 11A paras 10, 11*]	Businesses with supplies over £600,000 — failure to disclose the use of an avoidance scheme included in a statutory list published by HMRC Businesses with supplies over £10 million — failure to disclose use of certain schemes within 30 days of the due date for the first VAT return affected (unless the promoter of the scheme has already registered it with HMRC)	15% of the VAT avoided £5,000

Note

(a) Penalties under *VATA 1994, ss 63* and *64* are replaced, and that under *VATA 1994, s 60* partially replaced, by the general penalty for careless or deliberate errors in a taxpayer's document under *FA 2007, Sch 24* with effect for return periods beginning on or after 1 April 2008 for which the return is required to be made on or after 1 April 2009. See page 91. Penalties under *VATA 1994, s 60* continue to be charged for acts or omissions not relating to an inaccuracy in a document or failure to notify HMRC of an under-assessment and not within *FA 2008, Sch 41*.

Index

Entries printed in bold type are main subject headings

Index

Index

Index